Praise for *Updat*

"A moving, humorous, and beautifully written memoir about being a CNN foreign correspondent in the Middle East. Melding memoir with history, Young has created a unique and timely work."

CARYLE MURPHY   Pulitzer Prize-winning
reporter, *The Washington Post*

"A wild ride, spanning both millennia and some of the most important stories of our time. This book is exceptional not just for its story, but its energy and clarity. Rarely do we get such a wise, inside perspective on the machinations of history."

MICHAEL J. HENRY   Executive Director and
Co-founder of Lighthouse Writers Workshop

"Witty, wise, and brimming with insight, Young's memoir is a story of war, womanhood, ambition, and identity—and the surprising ways history can reach across time to illuminate our present. Perfect for readers who love bold women and the messy, meaningful work of making your mark."

CARRIE KLEWIN LAWRENCE   Author of *Origin Story*

UPDATE

UPDATE

REPORTING FROM
AN ANCIENT LAND

GAYLE YOUNG

BOLD
STORY
PRESS

CHEVY CHASE, MARYLAND

Bold Story Press, Chevy Chase, MD 20815
www.boldstorypress.com

First edition: June 2025

Library of Congress Control Number: 2025910587
ISBN: 978-1-954805-82-8 (paperback)
ISBN: 978-1-954805-83-5 (e-book)

Cover and interior design by KP Books

Printed in the United States of America
10 9 8 7 6 5 4 3 2 1

Well hello Steve Cassidy, this book is for you

CONTENTS

PROLOGUE

My grandmother was a somewhat humorless and man-crazy woman from Kentucky whose maiden name was—fittingly for a southerner—Bell. After I had launched a fairly successful career as a newspaper reporter in my twenties, she asked me if I would ever consider becoming a television correspondent or a news anchor.

"Oh, grandmother," I said, shyly ducking my head. "I'm not pretty enough to be on TV."

She scoffed.

"Don't be silly," she admonished emphatically. "There are *plenty* of unattractive people on television!"

She drifted out of the room while I stood dumbfounded.

To be fair, I have always tended toward messy hair, light makeup, and clothes too baggy for my slender frame. I didn't quite fit the image of a telegenic girl reporter of the 1980s, but I had decided in my early teens that I definitely wanted to be a journalist. It was a profession that involved everything I ever wanted: getting paid to travel around the world, the opportunity to learn new things, and endless banter with snarky coworkers.

Then, in the early 1990s, only a few years after my grandmother's encouraging yet humbling suggestion, I was unexpectedly catapulted into the position of CNN Cairo Bureau Chief. At the same time, I became fascinated with an ancient Syrian queen named Zenobia who was about my age when she unexpectedly seized Egypt from the Roman Empire in the 270s AD. We were both in the same place, at the right time—seventeen centuries apart.

Zenobia *made* history; I *reported* on people who made history. Yet, our paths kept overlapping throughout my television career. She started a war; I was in wars. Her city was under siege; I'd been in a siege. She ruled Egypt; I lived in Egypt. She ended her career in Rome, and so did I. As younger women in the Middle East, we grappled with similar issues: how to be a female boss in a patriarchal society, how to navigate sexual politics, what to wear when meeting a world leader.

Zenobia had all of the qualities I aspired to: She was bold and ambitious, seemingly fearless. Through the lens of our shared experiences, I discovered how warfare, ambition, and the perceptions of women in antiquity compare with the world today. Over time, I also learned truths about myself.

This is the story of us both.

ONE

PALMYRA

The first time I visited the ruins of Palmyra, I took a car and driver from the Sheraton Hotel in Damascus, Syria, where I was on assignment for CNN during the summer and fall of 1991. Mohammad, the driver, looked to be about sixty but was probably younger, with a stubbly unshaved face and rotted teeth. He peered at me in the rearview mirror.

"How old are you?"

Since I'd moved to the Middle East a year earlier, I'd come to realize that age, marital status, and income were favored conversation starters. I could roll with that.

"Thirty-one."

"Ahh, you are old!"

"True."

"You are married? Husband?"

"No."

"No husband?"

"No."

"No?"

"No."

He tapped a laminated photo of an unsmiling woman attached to the dashboard of the car and proudly announced she was his wife. "She is nineteen! Very beautiful!"

"*Miskeena*," I murmured. This is one of the first words I learned in Arabic. It means hopeless or pitiful, an Arabic version of "bless her heart" or "poor little thing."

Mohammad was surprised and confused. "No. She is happy! She loves me!"

"But you are old, and your teeth are bad."

I could be blunt, too. The rest of the ride was quiet, but not hostile or awkward. Bluntness has its benefits when mutually deployed and taken in the spirit intended.

The drive from Damascus to Palmyra takes about three hours. We slipped through the new part of the city center and headed northeast, leaving behind the stained cement apartment blocks, towering palms, and swarms of yellow taxis. The car sped along a ribbon of road through a tan landscape, only broken by a few treeless hills and ridges on the horizon. I was thirty-one years old and unmarried, wearing a brightly printed cotton skirt and a plain T-shirt from my favorite mall outlet, Casual Corner, stuck with brooding Mohammad in the middle of the Syrian desert.

It was a long way from where I grew up, in a family so typical it checked every box of the American dream. Mom and dad, son and daughter, dog and cat, living in a four-bedroom, two-and-a-half-bath suburban home with a two-car garage and a quarter acre of grass that needed to be mowed weekly during the summer.

But I came of age in a time before the internet, the gig economy, or tight budgets that maximize shareholder profits. Finding an enjoyable way to get paid was possible if you just showed up and looked eager. During my junior year in college, I wandered into the offices of *The Village Voice* and asked at the front desk about the possibility of an internship. They shuffled me over to the guy who managed the interns, who was sarcastic and unpleasant as he explained that many, many young people wanted to work long hours doing grunt work for free at New York's famed alternative newspaper. The phone on his desk jangled and he interrupted our little chat to pick up the receiver. He seemed delighted by the caller and said loudly into the phone for my benefit: "So, you're calling about a possible internship. Well, well, well! What can I tell you?" He smirked at me.

I mouthed at him: "Tell them it's already filled."

He blinked. Then said slowly to the caller, "It's already filled."

I had used the same "just show up" technique in the winter of 1990 when I moved to Cairo and inserted myself into the CNN bureau as a freelancer when they were desperate for help during Desert Storm, the UN mission to oust Iraq from Kuwait.

After freelancing for months in the CNN Cairo bureau, I was sent to Syria for an extended assignment. The Muslim Shiite militia group Hezbollah in neighboring Lebanon was freeing Western hostages in Beirut one by one, sending them in cars across the border into Syria to drop them off at the Canadian embassy in Damascus. Once we learned that a hostage was en route, a mob of international journalists would pour out of the Damascus Sheraton to cover the story. The hostage, dazed and exhausted, would emerge from the embassy for a brief photo-op before being whisked off under heavy escort to the Damascus airport, bound for a US military flight to Rhein-Main Air Base in Western Germany for medical and dental treatment, a thorough debrief, reunion with their ecstatic loved ones, and, more often than not, a hamburger and milkshake.

Then the waiting game began again for journalists who were on standby at the hotel for the release of the next hostage. It was a slow trickle of men, mostly Americans, who had been held captive for years.

My assignment at the Sheraton was extended for days then weeks then months. Our CNN office was an empty hotel room on the ground floor. We laid tables end to end as a platform for broadcast production equipment. In the early 1990s, our gear consisted of heavy video decks the size of ancient Samsonite suitcases. And since all the networks and agencies used different formats of videotapes, we needed multiple decks to convert tapes into a compatible format so that CNN editors could piece together images on massive editing machines. Our computers were not quite as bulky but still required valuable table real estate. On the walls, we taped sheets of paper listing phone numbers, staffing schedules, cartoons, *New York Times* articles about Hezbollah, and, to be honest, tennis scores.

Nestled within the L-shape of the hotel was a large swimming pool and multiple tennis courts ringed by a fragrant garden populated by friendly stray cats. During the long days waiting for Hezbollah to make its next move, most journalists channeled their competitive spirit in games. I don't play tennis, so my time was spent in the pool. The water was cool as heavy silk and the sky seemed the same shade of blue you'd find in the American Midwest: not too bright, but deep and calming with wisps of pure white clouds. Arab women would sit fully clothed on chairs along the pool deck, watching their sons splash and yelp as fathers lifted them high in the air and gently tossed them back into the depths. The daughters were sometimes allowed to swim, too. If not, they ran along the tiled edge, giggling and shouting, or sat on the steps so they could put their feet in the cool water and sop the hems of their dresses.

On slow days I would head into the historic center of Damascus, where streets were narrow, buildings were squat rectangles, and cars rarely seen. My favorite time to visit was in the evening, when the interior courtyards were lit up like theater stages with strings of electric lights or even candles and lanterns. I'd peek through a building's massive arched entryway to see women gathered by a blue-tiled courtyard fountain, finishing up chores: sweeping, rinsing rags, brushing their daughters' hair. Arabic music played on a tinny radio. The children would be giggly, and tired, and playful. Sometimes it felt like I was walking a hundred years back in history.

I'd heard about Palmyra, the remains of an ancient city more than 150 miles northeast of Damascus. Some said it was better preserved than the ruins of Pompeii. I knew nothing then of Palmyra's unique history, but I was an amateur historian who could never pass up an opportunity to investigate an archaeological site. So, on a rare day off, I climbed into the back seat of one of the CNN cars at the crack of dawn, behind the driver Mohammad with the stubbly beard and stubbly teeth, and set off on the three-hour drive east into the desert.

The parking lot next to Palmyra was empty; there were not many tourists in Syria at the time. But an older gentleman neatly dressed in pressed trousers and a button-down shirt greeted me at the gate. I believe he may have been Khaled al-Asaad, the chief archeologist who had looked after the Syrian heritage site for decades. He was happy to have a visitor and first led me to a series of towers and cone-shaped tombs outside the city walls. Shrouded from the intense sun, he showed me the carved and painted funerary portraits of Palmyra's inhabitants wearing their rich clothes and jewelry, dining, listening to music, sipping wine, gazing at each other with knowing smiles. They were of all shapes and ages, some looking happy, some serious, some distracted. It was the Palmyrene welcoming committee.

The older archeologist was clearly disappointed that I knew nothing about Palmyra, which the Syrians call Tadmor. I felt guilty about my ignorance, but this was before the advent of Google, let alone Wikipedia, and I hadn't yet tracked down a guidebook. The only thing I knew about Palmyra was that colleagues at the hotel said it was interesting, and it was old. An assistant came to tell my guide he had a phone call in his office, so we parted ways and I went on to explore on my own.

The ancient city covers 200 acres and is situated in an arid valley of rock, nestled under a steep hill topped with a massive temple dedicated to the ancient Syrian god Baal. The city was abandoned seventeen centuries ago and never rebuilt, so it was still possible to walk along the original streets. Most of the buildings had decayed into rubble, but other edifices were still standing and there was a wide, kilometer-long avenue that cut through the center of the city, flanked on either side by the remains of 1,500 Corinthian columns.

Ruins only give a glimpse of the past; imagination fills in the rest. The great caravans traversing the Silk Road once headed down this grand thoroughfare. Camels have padded feet that splay out like snowshoes, so they would have been surprisingly quiet as they plodded along, but bells on their harnesses would have jingled as they swayed under the weight of precious metals and bolts of silk wrapped in canvas, the scent of packed spices masking that of unwashed beasts. I'd seen camel caravans in Egypt; their handlers use long sticks to keep recalcitrant animals in line, alternately berating and praising them. The word 'camel' is derived from the Arabic word for beautiful. They have surprisingly long lashes to keep the sand out of their eyes, which they bat flirtatiously. But, when they're irritated, they make unearthly noises and spit out a vile-smelling substance. I tend to keep my distance from camels.

In Palmyra that day, it was hot and the water in my bottle was the temperature of a tepid bath. I headed back to the car to wake Mohammad from his nap, and the older archeologist came out to bid me goodbye. He mentioned that Palmyra had been ruled by a young queen. Channeling Mohammad, I asked how old she had been, and he told me she was in her early thirties. Just like me. I asked if she had been married. Husband? No, he explained, a widow.

Her name was Zenobia. I'd never heard of her, but my interest was piqued. A young woman my age without a husband in the Middle East.

When I returned to my home base in Cairo months later, I visited a small English-language library in the expat community of Maadi. The books were housed in an old apartment, its rooms lined with wooden bookcases stretching higher than anyone could possibly reach.

This was a repository of paperback spy novels, children's illustrated stories, coffee table gifts, bodice-rippers, and a decent collection of history and political science books donated by English-speakers working and living in Cairo. I spent many hours there, not because it was particularly welcoming, but because nothing was cataloged so I had to go through the shelves book by book to find what I wanted.

It was there that I stumbled on an English translation of the *Historia Nova*, a history of the Roman Empire by the Greek scholar Zosimus who lived in the early 500s AD. Flipping to the index, my heart skipped with excitement when I saw many entries for Zenobia. I carted it home along with a copy of *Little House on the Prairie* and *A Brief History of Time*. I could write a treatise on the entire canon of the *Little House* book series by Laura Ingalls Wilder, which I reread in its entirety in Cairo. I admit I never read past the first few pages of Stephen Hawking's renowned history of time. As for Zosimus's book, it traveled with me for years and helped me piece together Zenobia's life, with details filled in later when the internet was expanded and I could more easily access obscure sources.

The more I learned about Zenobia, the more I felt a sort of kinship across the centuries. She was the type of woman I aspired to become; brave and daring, but private and low-key. We were both in many of the same places at around the same age. However, her childhood was vastly different from my own insulated years growing up in American suburbia.

Zenobia was born sometime around 240 AD, some two hundred years after the death of Cleopatra and two hundred years before the fall of Rome. She was the daughter of a nomadic chieftain whose given name, Julius Aurelius, suggests the family had been Roman citizens for a long time.

In 240 AD, Syrians did not speak Arabic and were not Muslim. The religion of Islam wouldn't be established until 610, so Syrians in Zenobia's time were Pagan and spoke Aramaic, the same language as Jesus. It was a decidedly paternalistic society, yet when she was a young teen Zenobia took over her father's tribe upon his death and led them on their nomadic wanderings between seasonal pastures. Her remarkable childhood would explain traits that later astounded the Romans, such as her expertise in riding horses, hunting, and ordering troops into combat. It was unusual, even shocking, for a young female in that era, in that place, to have been so bold and accomplished.

I encountered many nomadic communities when I lived in the Middle East. Most had permanent homes, cinder-block rectangles built seemingly in the middle of nowhere. But they often moved outside seasonally and pitched tents, tending flocks of sheep along with horses and camels. I rarely was able to speak with young nomadic girls. They would peek out of the tents, quiet and shy.

But, years later, I had a different experience when I spent time with the Samburu tribe in Kenya while working for the World Bank. A cameraman and I followed a herder named Joseph who wrapped himself in a vivid red toga of traditional cloth, with a fedora on his head and a smartphone in his hand. Their community lived inside a massive national safari park filled with elephants, giraffes, ostriches, and zebras.

Every morning, Samburu children walked to a local school in groups, a herd of small humans banding together for safety in case they encountered wild animals along the way. Joseph preferred his traditional lifestyle, but he wanted his children to be educated and ultimately pursue careers outside of the reserve. Except for one. Joseph's adolescent daughter Caroline was determined to become a traditional herder even though it was a male occupation. Unlike her siblings, she refused to wear a school uniform and instead wore only traditional Samburu clothing. Joseph chuckled as he recounted how he had ordered her to walk to school with the other children, but she would run away at the first opportunity. She'd scramble across rocky outcrops covered with acacia trees until she located her father's herd of goats. Joseph finally relented. Even though she was only thirteen years old, she was a force to be reckoned with.

That evening, the cameraman and I joined the family in Joseph's boma and waited for Caroline to return home with the herd. The family lived in a collection of huts that were encircled by a wide ring of thorny acacia bushes, woven together to create an impenetrable fence against predators. As the sun grew low on the horizon, there were murmurings of concern. Caroline was late. Her older brothers were preparing to hike out to see if she needed help. But then, there she was, striding over the rise of a low hill with hundreds of goats in her wake. She was tall for her age and slender, holding a staff twice her height. Like her father, she was wrapped in red, but around her neck was a shimmering bib of multi-colored beads that covered her shoulders and chest.

Caroline calmly led the herd into the boma, leaving her brothers to secure the gap with more acacia bushes, locking up the homestead for the night. When we interviewed her on camera, she gave the universal adolescent eyeroll, along with one-word answers to my questions, then slipped into one of the huts for some food. Darkness fell quickly and the cold set in. I sat on a log, warmed by the radiating heat from hundreds of goats that bleated softly and shuffled as they prepared for a safe night's rest. Next to me, some of Joseph's younger children giggled as they took turns trying to balance on a plank of wood placed on top of a rock. The sky grew velvet black and stars appeared as if someone had flipped a switch overhead. The only light from within the acacia ring came from a few lanterns in the huts, where I could hear Joseph's three wives rattling pots and soothing babies. I inhaled deeply the scent of smoke and goat and thought of Zenobia's childhood, wondering if she had been lithe and beautiful like Caroline. She was a young girl who could hold her own in a harsh and dangerous environment and could slide into a man's domain with such grace that she was admired, not admonished.

I later learned that Caroline's elaborate beaded necklace was a sign that she had been betrothed. She was an anomaly in a man's world but, like Zenobia, she was still destined to be married within her tribal community.

It's not known exactly when Zenobia wed the great Palmyrene king Septimus Odaenathus, who was a distant member of her tribe. Perhaps there was a "meet-cute" like in romance movies, when he glimpsed her galloping across the desert on a spirited horse and instantly knew that he must win her over. More likely, it was a decision made by men in a tent, or within the king's palace, drinking tea while reclining on cushions and discussing alliances, gold, and territories. Some stories suggest Zenobia was only fourteen when she married and became a queen.

Zenobia was not the king's first wife; Odaenathus was in his thirties, and he already had a grown son, Herodes,

11

who had been designated his heir. We don't know if she was feeling excitement or dread when she left her remote desert home and moved to Palmyra, a city of 200,000 people and an epicenter of Middle Eastern politics.

By the time of the marriage, Palmyra was experiencing serious financial setbacks. The Persians had seized control of the Euphrates River and were intermittently blocking passage along the Silk Road, Palmyra's lifeline. The city state was part of the Roman Empire, but no Roman legions appeared to beat back the Persians on Palmyra's behalf.

It was bad timing. Rome was in the middle of a tumultuous era known to historians as the Crisis of the Third Century. Within a span of fifty years, more than two dozen Roman emperors would seize power, but almost all of them were either quickly assassinated or defeated in battle by their successors. Rome slipped into chaos and Palmyra's problems on the far eastern edge of the Empire were not particularly high on the priority list.

Soon after their marriage, however, Zenobia's husband, King Odaenathus, took matters in his own hands and marshalled the Palmyrene army, defeating the Persians himself. Zenobia was apparently in the thick of the action, accompanying her husband on marches into battle and perhaps venturing with him into Persia, where she could gain valuable insight and experience in foreign relations.

Rome was exceedingly grateful for the help. Odaenathus was first made the Roman governor of Syria and then, a few years later, governor of the eastern part of the Roman Empire. Everything was going splendidly for the royal couple. They had several children. They were successful and celebrated and, with the Silk Road routes safe again, they quickly became very rich, building palaces in multiple cities.

Yet, Odaenathus did not have long to savor his remarkable victories. He and his heir Herodes were killed sometime around the year 266 in the Syrian city of Antioch.

Like any murder mystery, the details around the death of Zenobia's husband are murky and there is a slew of potential suspects with plausible motives. Some ancient historians speculate that the Roman emperor Gallienus, fearful of Palmyra's growing military might, conspired to have Odaenathus secretly assassinated. Others blamed the king's demise on vengeful Persians. Still others suggested it was a conspiracy orchestrated by Zenobia to ensure that her own son inherited the throne. The most likely story is that Odaenathus and Herodes were killed by the king's disgruntled nephew, who had been punished for misbehaving during a family hunting expedition.

The loss of the king at the peak of his power was a shock. We don't know if Zenobia witnessed the killing of her husband and stepson, but she was likely in Antioch at the time. The death of both men left a power vacuum that would be filled by her son Vaballathus, but he was only about seven years old and would need a regent until he was older. There were likely men in the family who could have stepped into the position of regent, but ultimately Zenobia emerged as the best candidate.

By her late twenties, Zenobia had gone from being a nomadic princess to trophy wife to mother of the 'spare heir' to ruler of a fast-expanding and powerful domain that stretched across the Middle East. She could have laid low in her spectacularly beautiful city of Palmyra while she waited for her son to come of age. Instead, she seized the reins of power as she had seized the reins of horses she galloped across the desert.

As a journalist and amateur historian, I've always marveled that the passage from obscurity to fame is largely dictated by chance and circumstances; Being in the right place at the right time; Stepping up when opportunities fall into laps; Playing the cards you've been dealt.

By the early 1990s, some seventeen centuries after Zenobia assumed power, I was on that same Middle Eastern stage. My catapult into an unexpected position was not as dramatic as hers, but chance and circumstance propelled my own personal trajectory.

TWO

CNN

As a young boomer from an upper middle-class family, I was never too concerned about my future, nor did I have solid plans for a career. I studied Marxian economics and ancient history at the University of Massachusetts without thinking about how that would translate into viable employment. However, I was determined to be a journalist of some sort. I had my semester-long internship at *The Village Voice* and worked summers for my hometown's twice-weekly newspaper in Connecticut.

I spent many hours on campus writing and editing our school newspaper in a windowless basement newsroom. In one corner we had the old teletype machines from the big news agencies, known as "the wires." The teletypes were roughly the size and shape of the dodgy ATMs found today in gas stations, but devoid of touchscreens, which weren't a thing yet. We would put a thick roll of twelve-inch-wide newsprint onto a roller and thread an inked ribbon into a cartridge, then electrical pulses sent from the Associated Press would trigger the keys to type out news from all over the world. If the news was really important, the wire machine bell would ring loudly. If it was a really, really important story it would ring several times. This was how we got our breaking news before twenty-four-hour news channels created ominous musical cues and phones received text alerts.

After graduation, my friend Fran and I purchased a joint copy of Frommer's travel guide, *Europe on $15 a Day*, and spent the summer traveling with backpacks full of sundresses. We started in Europe but also went to Greece and then Israel, staying in bug-infested youth hostels or sleeping on trains. It was my first trip outside of the Americas and I especially loved old Jerusalem, the thick gold walls encompassing streets so narrow you had to walk single file. I was enchanted by the scent of spices, grilled meat, pine trees, and olive wood, and even the shopkeepers who blocked my exit while trying to sell me a pungent sheepskin. Somehow, I knew this part of the world would be my future.

I don't remember worrying much about rent, retirement benefits, marriage, ticking clocks, debts, or insurance during my twenties. The cost of living comparative to income in the United States was low, so I always made enough money for a room in a shared house and a plane ticket to somewhere. I freelanced for newspapers and worked for a few years as a science reporter in New York for the failing news agency United Press International, which was teetering on bankruptcy.

Despite the financial uncertainty, UPI made me an official member of the press corps, which allowed me to cover major news stories and attend significant events. I sailed on tall ships in New York harbor, flew to the arctic to cover the start of Will Steger's dogsled expedition to the North Pole, interviewed sex experts William Masters and Virginia Johnson, watched a veterinarian operate on a walrus at the Bronx Zoo, drove into Charleston in advance of Hurricane Hugo while everyone else was fleeing in the opposite direction. I attended many parties and press events at the best hotels, complete with flowing champagne and cold shrimp, where celebrities looked somewhat bored, and Donald Trump was usually lurking about seeking validation. Once, I was standing near CNN founder Ted Turner when he introduced Yoko Ono and Jimmy Carter. "Jimmy, this is Yoko, she was married to one of The Beatles. Yoko, this is Jimmy. Jimmy Carter. He used to be president."

I had discovered something called the Foundation Center, which had offices in New York and Washington, DC. You could go in during office hours and root through hundreds of file folders to research awards and short-term programs for young journalists. I'd photocopy applications, fill them out by hand, add a typed bio or mission statement as required, then mail the package to the host organization with an enclosed SASE.

Without internet, the pool of candidates was limited. Not everyone knew about the Foundation Center, so I was often the only person in the research room. By default, I was often successful. I was the youngest semi-finalist for NASA's Journalist in Space Project; volunteered for a month on an archeology site in Jerusalem; spent a summer studying squid brains for a science writer's fellowship at the Marine Biological Laboratory in Woods Hole; and, studied Arabic in Tunisia at the Institut Bourguiba des

Langues Vivantes. Between jobs, I lived for months in my Toyota Corolla as I drove across America and wrote for *The Washington Post* travel section. I had purchased a small pup tent for the trip, but knew nothing about camping except how to instinctively attract unwanted wild animals to my campsites.

In my late twenties, I was awarded an Organization of American States fellowship and lived in Kingston, Jamaica, for a year and a half, where I reported for the *Daily Gleaner* newspaper and studied sociology at the University of the West Indies. Jamaica was my starter country. Everyone spoke English and it was near the United States, but rich in its own unique culture and traditions. It prepared me for the years ahead as an expat.

Travel at that time was also cheaper, and employers' budgets were more generous. For a while, I worked freelance for a travel magazine, staying in gorgeous hotels and treated to sumptuous dinners because the hospitality industry was eager for press—any press—to draw in tourists. Advertising was mostly print-based, so to get coverage in the travel section of a magazine or newspaper was golden. Americans traveled all over the world, but fewer of them than today. Planes were rarely full, and hotels sent representatives to airports to rustle up guests at the arrival gate.

In August of 1990 I was thirty and in Mexico, working on a travel story about Oaxaca. I didn't have a wire machine bell to alert me to breaking news, but one evening I turned on the hotel TV and could decipher enough of the Spanish-language newscast to understand that Iraq had invaded the oil-rich emirate of Kuwait.

I was desperate to move to the Middle East and had been studying Arabic off and on for years. The Iraqi invasion of Kuwait was a major story as the United States prepared to enter the fray, so I made a deal with UPI to quit my salaried staff job to work as a full-time freelancer in their Cairo bureau. I gave my cat to my long-suffering parents in Connecticut. Poor Samantha; I'd brought her back as a kitten from Jamaica and she always hated snow. Then I packed a bag and bought a one-way ticket to Egypt—a country I had never visited. I tried to research what it was like to live there, but I couldn't find any useful information in my local library. I had no idea what apartments were like or transportation or telecommunications or the costs of goods and services. UPI was putting me up at The Cosmopolitan Hotel for a week near the UPI bureau in downtown Cairo, but I would have to find an apartment on my own afterwards. I packed light.

Before I left the US, I had managed to sign up for Arabic lessons at The American University in Cairo and subsequently received a phone call from another incoming AU student named Jenny who was hoping to find a roommate. I was in a rush when she called, but I mentioned where I'd be staying and gave a vague suggestion that we should meet up once I was settled. Days after my arrival in Egypt, I returned to the hotel from a long day of work to find her sleeping on the floor by my bed. Somehow, she had convinced the hotel staff to let her into my room. At first, I was taken aback and accused her of using my toothbrush, which she vehemently denied. But it was clear we had the same sense of humor and affinity for the Middle East. We ended up finding a fully furnished apartment downtown that came with a young Saudi guy sleeping on the couch and a weasel living in a nest of purloined chicken bones under the TV cabinet.

In our efforts to get rid of both the Saudi guy and the weasel, we bonded.

That first month in Egypt I went to a stakeout for UPI at the Marriott hotel where Middle Eastern defense ministers were meeting to discuss a proposed UN intervention to kick Iraqi troops out of Kuwait. A stakeout is when journalists gather—often in a hotel lobby or in front of a building—and wait for someone important to exit, hoping they will say a few words on the record. This stakeout lasted for hours and I made a new friend with the only other American woman journalist waiting in the Marriott lobby. Pat Neal was a CNN correspondent based in Miami, but she was temporarily assigned to head the CNN Cairo bureau while the Cairo correspondent was sent to the perimeter of Iraq. She was engaged to Charles Jaco, CNN's on-the-ground war correspondent, dubbed the Scud Stud by the tabloids for his smooth reporting on Iraq's ballistic missiles.

Over the next months, I helped Pat out a few times and she was convinced that my rudimentary Arabic equaled fluency. In January, the UN forces stormed into occupied Kuwait in an offense known as Operation Desert Storm, sending Iraqi troops scrambling. Pat was overwhelmed with work, and offered me a freelance gig as her assistant at CNN. It was temporary, part-time, and held no expectation of lasting more than a few weeks. But that was enough for me to ditch UPI. Over the next months, she extended my employment and graciously gave me tutorials on writing and reporting for television. She also helped me with hair and makeup.

Through Pat, I connected with Steve Cassidy, head of the international desk at CNN's Atlanta headquarters. He was the guy who doled out assignments, made sure every story was covered, kept everyone safe, and settled squabbles. Somehow, I managed to impress him enough that he took me under his wing and kept giving me assignments, even after Desert Storm wrapped up and Pat returned home to Miami.

The CNN Cairo bureau chief was often away from Egypt covering more important stories. I was left to pick up the slack even though I had zero experience reporting for television. Steve told me that he was willing to give me a chance because "it's easier to teach television production to a journalist than it is to teach journalism to someone who only knows television production."

The CNN office was a second-floor apartment in a run-down building in the shadow of Egypt's towering Ministry of Information building. The floors were scuffed wood and the plaster walls were once painted white. Our front windows looked out on the Corniche el Nil, the stately avenue that runs along the banks of the Nile. If the glass had not been coated with black grime from vehicle exhaust, we could have seen the flowing river.

I claimed one of the bedrooms as my office space, working off a dining room table that came with the apartment. We had an accountant named Hosam in the living room, and our crew Amr and Ali in a shared office that used to be the smallest bedroom in the back. The last bedroom housed our editing equipment and shelves lined floor to ceiling with videotapes in book-sized gray plastic cases. A teenager named Salah ruled over the kitchen. There were men in most Egyptian offices whose primary function was to serve tea to workers and their guests. These men, young and old, also kept the work area tidy and ran errands.

My inexperience in television was augmented by Amr, the cameraman, who suffered from recurrent eye infections so he often couldn't see well enough to shoot. Ali, the soundman, was partially deaf. Our driver had zero sense of direction and could not read road signs. He refused to stop and ask for directions because it was embarrassing for him.

Fortunately, the building next door housed Video Cairo, a large video services provider where I could rent cameras and crew members who were able to see and hear. It was owned by Mohammed Gohar, who helped me transmit our CNN stories to Atlanta via an industrial satellite dish on his roof. I wore a path down the stairway from the CNN office, along the sidewalk for a few yards, then up the stairs to Video Cairo. Gohar taught me everything about video production, including patience. Once, we had a breaking story but our video feed to Atlanta was a complete mess. The images were marred by static and Atlanta techs complained to me over the phone. Gohar looked at my tear-stained face and said, "It's only television." I adopted this mantra whenever things went awry and tensions were high.

My stint in Syria covering the release of the Hezbollah hostages from Beirut was my first assignment for CNN outside of Egypt. By then, I was working for the network full-time, but still not on staff, nor was I reporting on air. But, like Zenobia, I was in the right place, at the right time, with the right set of skills.

And luck was on my side. I had a string of incredible scoops starting in Damascus.

As the summer slipped into fall, it was too costly to keep a horde of journalists swimming and playing tennis at the Damascus Sheraton, so the US formed a press pool comprised of a single news-gathering crew that would represent all of the major networks—NBC, CBS, ABC, and CNN. The four networks would jointly make decisions on coverage and share any video taken by the video pool crew. Steve Cassidy, my supportive boss in Atlanta, left me in Damascus to represent CNN's interests while all of my more seasoned CNN colleagues left for their home bureaus.

I rattled around the Damascus Sheraton in search of food and books. My life took on a rhythm of long walks around the old city, long calls from the CNN office landline to family and friends, and enjoying the lavish Friday night weddings in the Sheraton courtyard that usually involved deafening Arabic music and fabulous beaded silk dresses.

One morning, I settled into an armchair in the empty CNN office with a large bag of peanut M&Ms and the latest bestselling novel *Scarlett*, an 832-page authorized sequel to *Gone with the Wind*. Other international networks and newspapers had makeshift offices in rooms along the same hotel corridor, so journalists and officials were always coming and going. Deeply immersed in my turgid romance, I didn't notice a figure in the doorway until he rapped loudly on the doorframe.

"Are you CNN?"

I looked up from my book, swallowed an M&M, and affirmed that I was, indeed, CNN.

"Do you want to interview Terry Anderson?"

This was unexpected. Terry Anderson was the Associated Press bureau chief in Beirut who had been abducted off a street and bundled into the trunk of a car by Hezbollah kidnappers in 1985. Of all the US hostages held by Hezbollah, Terry had been in captivity the longest—more than six and a half years. He was also arguably the most well-known of the hostages, with his family and AP colleagues working tirelessly to publicize his plight and gain his freedom. Over the first few years, Hezbollah would periodically release photos and videos of Terry in captivity. But in recent years, communication from him or about him had gone dark. Some speculated that he had died but that Hezbollah was reluctant to confirm the loss of their most valuable bargaining chip. No one seemed to have any idea where he was, how he was doing, whether he was sick or well or hopeful or despondent.

I did not know this man standing in the doorway or whether he had any access to Terry, but my heart skipped a beat. He explained he wanted me to give him a list of questions that he would take back to Beirut, read to Terry, record his responses, and then return that evening to give me a videotape of the interview. The mystery guy refused to tell me his name or whom he represented or to give me a contact number. I mentally shrugged and typed up questions about the conditions Terry faced in captivity and whether he sensed any movement toward his release. The visitor took a printout of my list and disappeared as quickly as he had arrived.

Was Mystery Guy legit? I walked up and down the hallway poking my head into other offices. Most were unoccupied and the few people who were around hadn't noted any Hezbollah agents roaming the corridor. Curious but skeptical, I curled back up with my book and M&Ms, occasionally checking the clock and the hallway.

Much later that afternoon, a Syrian journalist burst through the door and asked if I had been in contact with Terry Anderson because he'd just been informed that a car from Beirut had crossed the Lebanon-Syria border and was headed to Damascus with a taped interview for CNN.

"Is that your tape?" he demanded.

"Why, yes," I replied. "Yes, it is."

The VHS cassette landed in my lap an hour later, delivered by a breathless courier driver. I popped it into the deck and there was Terry looking fairly healthy and optimistic. International journalists raced to report on the interview but, because it was a CNN exclusive, they had to attribute the video and Terry's comments to CNN. Atlanta directed me to answer questions from news organizations about how CNN acquired the interview, and I was widely quoted, including a front page story in *The New York Times*.

US and Syrian intelligence agents called on me early the next morning in an attempt to confiscate the VHS tape, which I had tucked into the back waistband of my skirt under a flowing blouse so they couldn't see it. To hand it over would jeopardize CNN's status as an independent news source.

My senior boss from Atlanta, Eason Jordan, arrived in Damascus a few days later and asked me how I'd managed to get the interview.

"Ah, well," I said confidently. "A Hezbollah contact of mine arranged everything. I can't really say more than that."

He nodded solemnly.

The scoop certainly raised my profile in Atlanta. And since good things happen in threes, there were two other incidents that occurred around the same time that helped assure my future as a CNN correspondent. That same autumn, when I had returned from Syria to my home in Cairo for a few weeks, I read in *The New York Times* that one of the finalists for the position of Secretary General of the United Nations was a Coptic Christian Egyptian named Boutros Boutros-Ghali, which happened to be the same name as my new doctor. It turned out they were first cousins.

Up until I started working for CNN in Cairo, my career had been in magazines, newspapers, and wire services. The standard practice in print journalism was to write bios and stories in advance about anyone in line for important positions, or who were close to death, so that the story could be published immediately when the news broke. I assumed the same was true in broadcast journalism.

Without asking anyone in CNN headquarters for permission, I got the number of Boutros-Ghali from my doctor and set up an interview with the CNN bureau chief, who was back in Cairo at that time. I asked the UN candidate for copies of personal photos dating back to his childhood and even took the crew to shoot video of his family home and church, along with shots of him working at his desk. During his interview with the CNN bureau chief, Boutros-Ghali shared his opinions of the United Nations and his thoughts concerning some of the major conflicts facing the world. All good. We edited a 'package'—what CNN called a recorded and edited story—and sent it off to Atlanta.

The editor on the international news desk who called me the next day did not offer the positive reinforcement I was expecting. "What are we supposed to do with this?" The editor explained with some irritation that it was an egregious waste of money and resources to shoot and edit an entire video package that might never be used.

He was right, and I felt terrible. But twenty-four hours later I felt less terrible, because it was announced that Boutros-Ghali had indeed been chosen as the new United Nations Secretary General. He declined all interview requests in those first days after the announcement, so every news organization had to quote our interview and once again credit CNN. Boutros-Ghali's statements about world conflicts made huge news across the globe. I had delivered CNN another major scoop.

My third scoop came early the following spring, just after the CNN Cairo bureau chief moved to London, leaving the position vacant and me alone in the bureau with the crew. Late one evening, a prop plane carrying Palestinian leader Yasser Arafat disappeared somewhere over the Libyan desert. My phone rang in the middle of the night, jolting me from a deep sleep. I grabbed the receiver without turning on the light. It was the news desk in Atlanta telling me that the plane had been reported missing for several hours and could I confirm that Arafat was on board? It would significantly impact the ongoing Middle East peace process if Arafat was on that plane and had died. He headed the Palestine Liberation Organization (or PLO), a complex organization comprised of both extreme militants and pragmatic statesmen. The 1978 Camp David Accords brokered by then-President Jimmy Carter between Arafat and then-Israeli Prime Minister Menachem Begin had created a framework for Palestinian self-governance that was slowly moving to fruition, and the sixty-two-year-old militant-turned-statesman Arafat was a key player.

I had one PLO contact in Cairo who was pretty much the contact for every Western journalist in the city. No one had mobile phones at that time, so I pulled out my Filofax and looked up his home number. I was somewhat surprised he answered my call, but then Egyptian phones were not equipped with caller ID, so he had no way of knowing who would be on the line. Graciously, he confirmed Arafat was on the plane and that it had crashed. He said a search and rescue mission had been dispatched to the site and he was waiting for word of survivors.

I called Atlanta back to tell the editors what I had learned and that I was confident my contact was senior enough to be well informed. Before I could say much else, I was patched through to the news anchor so I could report live on air. The interview was over a landline—just my voice and an embarrassingly awful thumbnail photo of me in the corner of the screen. I was still sitting in bed in a T-shirt and still a little groggy. Before it started, I looked out my bedroom window at the shimmering lights on the Nile below my rooftop apartment, listening to the breaking news music cue through the phone receiver. Deep breath.

The anchor came on the line and started firing off questions. I quoted my PLO source and reported what I knew.

"Gayle, what will happen within the PLO if Arafat *has* died?" It was a perfectly legitimate question from the anchor. Frankly, the odds didn't look like they were in Arafat's favor, but I was not yet an expert on the PLO; I didn't know exactly how his death might change the organization or who else was waiting in the wings to take over the top spot, and I had no way of finding out more information at that moment.

I was terrified of saying the wrong thing. My only choice was to become ever-so-slightly insistent that we didn't know yet if Arafat was dead. No one within the PLO would want to speak about the ramifications of his death until they were sure he was actually no longer around to hear about it.

The anchor seemed a little pouty, but, once again, I was vindicated.

In the morning we learned Arafat *had* survived. The Antonov 26 twin-prop aircraft was forced to make an emergency landing in a sandstorm while headed to a Palestinian training camp in southern Libya. I heard later that as the plane started its rapid descent, Arafat's aides bundled him in coats and blankets and shoved him to the back of the plane to cushion the impact. The pilots reportedly angled the plane so that the front section would take the brunt of the crash. Three crew members at the front died, but Arafat was pulled from the tail section at dawn, almost nine hours after the plane went down, with only bruises and a black eye.

The international desk editors told me my refusal to speculate that Arafat was dead had been the right call.

CNN flew me to Atlanta for a screen test. I purchased a coral T-shirt because someone suggested that would be a great color on me. One of the news readers loaned me her jacket and clipped a clothespin in the back of my shirt to make it fit smoothly. The hair and makeup people did their thing. They sat me down at the main anchor desk at CNN Center and turned on an arc of blinding lights, fired up the massive studio cameras, loaded the teleprompter, and had me read a few headlines and narrate the major story of the day. I was more bemused than nervous. It felt so surreal.

That same afternoon, I was hired as CNN's Cairo bureau chief. I had just turned thirty-two years old. Steve Cassidy told me I would make $35,000 a year and was amused that I was perfectly happy with that offer. The editors took me to a bar to celebrate and the hostess said she would have to see my ID—in an era when the only people carded were those who looked like teenagers. All told, it was the best day of my life.

Unlike Zenobia, I was not a famous world figure but, by fortune and chance, I was catapulted onto the sidelines of the same world stage with an express pass to witness history. I had been at the right place at the right time.

As one of CNN's most venerated correspondents, the devastatingly witty Jim Clancy, once told me, "It's better to be lucky than good."

THREE

CLEOPATRA

Raised by her mother to speak the Egyptian language, Zenobia claimed to be a direct descendant of Cleopatra through the Egyptian queen's only daughter. Zenobia's claim can't be proven, but it's not implausible. Cleopatra had given birth to twins with Marc Antony in 40 BC: a girl named Selene, the ancient Greek word for moon, and a boy named Alexander Helios, meaning sun. The couple had another son, Ptolemy Philadelphus, the following year. These three younger children had an older half-brother, Caesarion, who was the child of Cleopatra and Julius Caesar. Caesarion was heir to the throne of Egypt, but the younger children also sat on pint-sized thrones during royal events. Selene was a cosseted princess expected to someday marry her oldest half-brother as queen consort of Egypt.

After Antony and Cleopatra were defeated in the Battle of Actium and died in 30 BC, Rome took control of

Egypt and stripped the royal family of its power. The older heir, seventeen-year-old Caesarion, was executed by order of Augustus so that he wouldn't become a rallying point for Egyptian unrest. The younger children were brought to Rome and raised by Antony's former wife, Octavia.

This is why women in history are so interesting. Here is Octavia, a wife publicly humiliated when her husband left for another woman in a scandal for the ages. Octavia was so loyal that she raised troops for her wayward husband and marched to the East to deliver them personally. Antony took the troops, sent Octavia packing, and scuttled back to Cleopatra, who I imagine was drumming her fingers in irritation. Octavia's brother, Octavian, expressed outrage over the betrayal of his dear sister and vanquished both Antony and Cleopatra in a protracted and vicious civil war, eventually assuming the mantel of sole emperor of the Roman Empire under the name Augustus. Yet despite everything, Octavia opted to take in her late husband's children and raised them along with her biological children in, by all accounts, a stable and supportive household.

It's not clear what happened to Cleopatra's youngest sons, Helios and Ptolemy. They disappeared from historical records, which suggests they may have died young, perhaps by illness or perhaps by execution. But Selene survived and married the king of Numidia in North Africa in 25 BC when she was around fifteen. They ruled their kingdom, in what is now Libya, for two decades before Selene died when she was thirty-five.

Some Arab historians have speculated that Zenobia's mother was a descendent of Selene's granddaughter, Drusilla of Mauretania, who settled in Syria. Drusilla married the king of Emesa—an ancient city state located in what is now the Syrian city of Homs—about 150 years before Zenobia's birth. Zenobia grew up speaking the Egyptian language, which was not widely used in Syria, suggesting she learned it within her family, perhaps from her mother or a grandparent who kept track of the family tree. True or not, Zenobia believed she was descended from Cleopatra and exhibited great admiration for her ancestor.

In Zenobia's time, two centuries after Cleopatra's death by asp, Egypt was still a secure Roman possession and its capital, Alexandria, remained the most important city of the imperial province. It had been built hundreds of years earlier by Alexander the Great in 331 BC on the shores of the Mediterranean where the Nile Delta empties into the sea. Further south, Egypt was populated by millions of peasants who grew wheat along both banks of the river. Mounds and mounds of wheat in rich fertile soil, which was replenished every year when the Nile flooded and then receded.

It is estimated Egypt's villagers produced enough wheat to export 26 million metric tons to Rome each year. If they weren't growing wheat, the villagers were growing premium cotton for Rome's finest households. Egypt also exported paper that was made from the pith of the papyrus plant, an aquatic flowering reed that chokes the Nile. And they exported glass that was manufactured from the abundance of desert sand. In short, Egypt fueled the Roman Empire with goods it badly needed to function.

Like their founder Alexander, most residents of Alexandria spoke Greek throughout antiquity while the peasants toiling in the countryside spoke Egyptian. The same held true even when I was living in Egypt in the 1990s. Many of the oldest and wealthiest Alexandrians still spoke Greek, or more often French, while Egyptians outside of Alexandria spoke almost exclusively Arabic. I remember one elderly doyen from Alexandria who was aghast that I was not fluent in French. She claimed she did not speak Arabic despite coming from a family that had been Egyptian citizens for centuries, if not millennia. But I didn't quite believe her. Surely, she watched the endless Arabic soap operas on Egyptian television.

To this day, Alexandria remains Egypt's main port and the country still exports wheat and cotton but nowhere near the amounts they did in Zenobia's time. In the 270s AD, hundreds of merchant galleys would have pulled in and out of the great harbor fully loaded with grain. Powered by canvas sails and supplemented by banks of oars, the largest of these ships could carry up to 600 tons of wheat and thousands of amphorae, the ceramic two-handled vessels for storing wine and olive oil.

It would take about three weeks to traverse 1,600 miles over the Mediterranean to Ostia, the harbor of Rome. The grain would be decanted into large public granaries then doled out every month to hundreds of thousands of poorer and middle-class Roman citizens in an efficient, albeit complicated, system involving registration, master lists, and a grain goddess named Ceres. The Romans had been doing this for centuries. Grain was a commodity, bought and sold, and the grain dole was an unalienable right of Roman citizens. Any interference with the grain supply from Alexandria to Rome would create massive political and social upheaval.

All this to say Egypt was vital to the Roman Empire. The mere thought of losing control of Egypt would leave the ancients more aghast than the present-day Alexandrians who scoffed at my French. Egypt was an imperial province run by a Roman military governor armed with legions of Roman soldiers. Most of the troops were stationed in Alexandria, but they also manned Roman fortresses up and down the Nile. Yet, just as Zenobia was elevated to Syria's regent queen, the Romans let down their guard. The ongoing Crisis of the Third Century, with Roman emperors dying one after the other in a constant state of civil war, was taking its toll. The number of Roman troops stationed in Egypt had dwindled and, in 270 AD, Zenobia saw her chance.

The Roman-appointed governor, Tenagino Probus, and his army vacated Alexandria to pursue pirates that were harassing the grain supply chain. With the city unguarded, Timagenes, an Egyptian military leader, mounted a nationalist rebellion in support of Palmyra. His rallying cry was that Egypt should be ruled by a leader from the East, rather than Roman bureaucrats. There are conflicting versions among historians about whether Zenobia seized an unexpected opportunity or if the fortuitous rebellion was part of a vast plan hatched earlier by her late husband. Either way, Zenobia rose to the occasion and dispatched her best general, Zabdas, and 70,000 Palmyrene soldiers to Egypt. With the Roman governor away chasing pirates, the Palmyrene forces were able to seize control of Alexandria against a small cadre of Roman loyalists. Zabdas secured the city with a garrison of 5,000 Syrian troops and started his victory march home.

Poor Governor Probus was likely shocked when he got word that Palmyra had seized Alexandria in his absence. He abandoned his pirate project posthaste and headed back to Alexandria with his troops. Initially, he was able to drive out the Palmyrene garrison left by Zabdas and then started to chase the rebel leader, Timagenes, who fled up the Nile toward a fortress situated across the river from the great pyramids of Giza.

There, in what is now a middle-class suburb of Cairo, Timagenes laid a trap. He turned his fleeing troops around, took the high ground, and launched a counterattack with 2,000 men. They defeated the Romans and captured Probus, who committed suicide to escape his fate at the hands of the enemy. With no Roman backup troops on the horizon to challenge her victory, Zenobia was now ruler of Egypt and all of its riches. Cleopatra's descendant had retaken the kingdom. According to inscriptions dating from this period, Zenobia's young son, Vaballathus, was officially declared King of Egypt, a title that had been dormant since the death of Cleopatra's father. But Zenobia gave herself equal billing. She was styled the Queen of Egypt or sometimes Mother of the King of Egypt. She had done the seemingly impossible, wrestling away from Rome the most important source of grain in the empire.

It's not known if Zenobia ever visited Alexandria, but it seems plausible that she would want to spend time in the city of her revered ancestress. Historians noted repeatedly that she spoke the Egyptian language, which suggests she was speaking it with Egyptians—in Egypt. Gushed one: "She herself was not wholly conversant with the Latin tongue, but nevertheless, mastering her timidity she would speak it; Egyptian, on the other hand, she spoke very well." Historians say she also was "so well versed in the history of Alexandria and the Orient" that she wrote a short summation of the sweeping topic, an ancient version of cliff notes. I'd like to think, as a good reporter, that she visited Alexandria to conduct her research.

The coastal city must have still been impressive circa 270 AD with extensive palaces, statues, and gardens. For centuries, the lighthouse that towered over the harbor was the world's tallest manmade edifice and considered one of the Seven Wonders of the ancient world. If she visited Alexandria, Zenobia could have camped out in Cleopatra's old palace, which would have still been standing then, the massive halls painted with colorful lotus blossoms and stiff Egyptian figures wearing the tall crowns that looked like bowling pins. The paint would have faded, the red and green columns chipped, but the sheer grandeur would be inspiring as young Zenobia contemplated her achievements and her destiny.

Perhaps she took a shallow barge up the Nile. Egypt is ninety-eight percent desert, but Zenobia would have seen ribbons of green on either side of the great river, fields of wheat swaying in the breeze, dotted with small mud-baked houses. Water buffalo would be in the shallows, and hippos and crocodiles cruising alongside her. It still looked like that when I took a boat down the Nile in the 1990s, except for the hippos and crocs that had migrated farther south over the centuries.

If she had continued further south, Zenobia would definitely have stopped before the three great pyramids of Giza guarded by the Sphinx, which would have been 2,700 years old at that point. Impossibly old, even then. The city of Cairo, located next to Giza, did not yet exist in Zenobia's time, but there would be the remains of the ancient city of Memphis nearby where great Egyptian kings like Ramses had ruled upper and lower Egypt from this strategic spot near the middle of the kingdom.

Zenobia had seized power but she was shrewd enough to at least attempt to appease the vastly larger and more powerful Romans. The coins she minted proclaimed her son Vaballathus as joint ruler with Aurelian, a conciliatory gesture to Rome's latest emperor who was busy fighting enemies on the opposite end of the empire. Perhaps she hoped that Aurelian would be satisfied with her unilateral decision to co-rule Egypt. Or perhaps she assumed he would shortly be overthrown like his predecessors. Some historians, though, have suggested a theory I find the most plausible. Proclaiming Aurelian co-ruler was a strategy to appease Roman bureaucrats so they would remain in their jobs shipping grain and collecting taxes. The bureaucrats could always shrug and argue later that they were under the impression they were still working for Rome. The supply lines kept moving.

To cement loyalty with the locals, the Syrian queen flaunted her Egyptian roots, her link to Cleopatra, and her fluency in Egyptian. According to the Roman's collective historical documents, Zenobia "boasting herself of the family of Cleopatra . . . proceeded to cast about her shoulders the imperial mantle." An inscription now housed in Cairo refers to Zenobia as a Ptolemy, a member of Cleopatra's family dating back to Alexander the Great.

There were coins from Zenobia's reign that were minted and widely circulated to her new subjects. On the obverse of the coin is a portrait of the new queen with the initials "AVG" after her name that denotes "Augusta," the feminine form of the title given to Roman emperors. On the reverse side is a depiction of Juno, the most powerful of Roman goddesses, holding a ritual dish as a symbol of piety and a peacock, the symbol of longevity, at her feet. In the background is a star, which may have been an Egyptian symbol of the afterlife or a reference to Zenobia's reputed ancestor, Selene.

But what's striking is Zenobia's portrait stamped into the metal. Her hair is braided, or perhaps in dreadlocks, looped closely to her head in an arrangement that appears melon-shaped with wide ridges. This was the same hairstyle worn by Cleopatra for her portraits on her coins. It was thought that the late Egyptian queen had adopted this unusual hairstyle to emulate wigs worn by the original Egyptians who ruled for thousands of years before her family, the Ptolemies, took over. Copying Cleopatra was a bid by Zenobia to legitimize her takeover. Who better to rule the ancient kingdom than the heir of its last pharaoh?

It was a slippery slope. Emphasizing her connections to Cleopatra would help gain the loyalty of the Egyptians, but it would leave a bad taste for Romans. They hated the ancient Egyptian queen—and her hair.

Here's a stanza from a poem by the Roman poet Martial:

You lie around in an Egyptian wig like Cleopatra,
flashing false teeth and winking phony eyelashes.

His revulsion was echoed in Roman literature from the days of Cleopatra to the time of Zenobia. For Romans, Cleopatra and her ilk were objects of derision—ugly, ambitious women who used sex and manipulation to ruin men.

Zenobia, however, was undaunted by Roman opinion. She was busy consolidating her power in Alexandria, the third largest city in the Roman world. It's not known if the new queen built her own palace or a temple to a Syrian god or expanded the library, because that city no longer exists. Earthquakes, combined with periodic fires and the general rise of sea levels, obliterated the ancient city.

I was terribly disappointed when I first visited Alexandria. There were no fluted columns, or colorful friezes of festivals, no ruins of any sort from antiquity. A multi-lane highway arcs along the edge of the harbor, lined with dull hotels, fish restaurants, and a multitude of gray and brown cement apartment blocks. Traffic and honking horns drown out the sound of waves lapping a sliver of rocky beach below the pylons. At the end of a jetty jutting into the harbor is a small lighthouse, marking the approximate spot where the Lighthouse of Alexandria once towered. The original edifice, and the spectacular city that was briefly Zenobia's, now lays in rubble under a choppy Mediterranean Sea.

In 1994, marine archeologists announced they had discovered the remains of Cleopatra's palace at the bottom of the harbor. Egypt wisely decided to keep the ruins where they had fallen, eventually creating an underwater archeological park. But authorities agreed to haul up a segment of a colossal statue to show the world a glimpse of the treasures that lay beneath the dark gray surface. A CNN crew and I made the three-hour drive from Cairo to Alexandria with lofty expectations. Photographers and journalists from around the world lined up along the harbor in a spot the archeologists said would be prime viewing of the statue emerging from the waves.

The wind was strong and fresh sea air blasted into my lungs and whipped my hair behind me. The Mediterranean stretched into a gray-blue horizon and the noisy city behind us seemed to momentarily fade away. Slowly, a crane on a barge maneuvered into place while divers popped to the surface and submerged again like playful seals, their black Neoprene-clad heads glistening. It took hours, which gave me time to daydream of an ancient city. A skyscraper of a lighthouse towering thirty-five stories high with a massive mirror facing out to sea, lit by a roaring fire at night that must have hissed and danced in the relentless wind. Along the shore, palaces would be terraced down to the water's edge, dull Egyptian marble painted vivid red and blue and green. Sandals clacking gently on stone. Palms bending in the breeze. No car horns. Possibly fish restaurants.

The chains on the crane tightened as they began to pull on something heavy beneath the surface. Slowly, guided by the seal-head divers, a large white object broke through the waves, cradled in a web of chains, lifted into the air. There were gasps. It was the torso of a woman, from neck to lower ribcage—basically a massive pair of breasts draped by a hint of gauzy cloth.

Excited shouts of "Cleopatra!" sounded all around. I wondered if maybe, just maybe, it was not a statue of Cleopatra, but of her great, great, great granddaughter Zenobia being resurrected from the ruins on this beautiful day.

FOUR

CAIRO

Some mornings in Cairo I would wake up an hour before dawn and wander out on my terrace. My apartment was like a small ranch house perched on the rooftop of an innocuous seven-story apartment building on Zamalek, a fairly large island in the Nile, surrounded by other apartment houses, embassies, and a major hotel—the Marriott Gezira—that had been built a decade earlier within the gardens of a former palace.

To reach my apartment, you would step off a bustling dusty street through a door built wide enough to once accommodate horse-drawn carriages. The lobby was cavernous and dimly lit, the white marble stained gray and brown from time and use. Like all lobbies in Cairo, it was guarded by doormen known as *bowabs*, if I may butcher Arabic grammar by using an 's' to denote plural. Anyone who came to visit had to pay the *bowab* a small fee, known as *baksheesh*, to gain access to a decrepit phone-booth-sized elevator that jerked and wheezed its way to the top floor. Most of my friends took the elevator just once, then preferred to skip the *baksheesh* and trudge up the drafty central spiral staircase.

Once you reached the top floor, you had to duck through a small door at the end of a corridor that led to a crumbling exterior staircase to the roof. My apartment was a small building set on one end of the rooftop facing the Nile and my neighbor, Dr. Mahmood, had a similar structure set on the back end. He was a gaunt, friendly older physician who allegedly treated prostitutes for venereal disease. Never proven, but he did seem to have a lot of tearful women visitors who no doubt had to pay the *bowabs* extra *baksheesh* to get access to whatever treatment they desperately needed. Between our two edifices was a small expanse of open rooftop with painted green trellises and Dr. Mahmood's collection of plants in large terracotta pots. It almost never rains in Cairo, so the plants were coated in a thick layer of dust and looked . . . sad. However, it was still a little slice of Cairo heaven.

My furnished apartment had two bedrooms, a bath, and—a rarity in Egyptian apartments—an open-concept room with a kitchen in the corner, a small dining area, and a raised platform with a large yet uncomfortable U-shaped couch. It was built-in, essentially a wooden bench with hard cushions covered in scratchy dark blue fabric. There was a wagon wheel hammered at one end to serve as an arm rest, but I pried it off and rolled it out of the apartment my first month there. My landlord was shocked I didn't want it.

The real beauty of that apartment was the terrace. It faced east, with an unobstructed view of the Nile that stretched from one horizon to the other. On the far bank there were a few high-rise hotels and the towering Ministry of Information, but there were not enough tall buildings to block the expanse of city that stretched out behind them like a worn brown carpet. Minarets spiked upwards and the rooftops of apartment buildings were crowded with other little dwellings like mine, strung with ropes of laundry, and edged with potted plants. In the evenings, Egyptians would head to the rooftops to fly kites handmade from newspapers that would bob and weave in the warm breezes blowing from the Nile Delta, creating a floating squadron of paper craft hovering over the city.

As night fell, a massive neon Coca-Cola sign flickered to life almost directly opposite my terrace, its reflection shimmering bright red on the black water below. The sign was never lit on a set schedule, which suggested it was operated manually. Sometimes it came on early, sometimes embarrassingly late. Once, it was dark for several nights in a row and I worried that the person tasked with turning it on was seriously ill. He either recovered or died and someone else got the job because on the fourth night the Coca-Cola sign blazed forth.

When the sun set behind my house, it cast a golden halo of light across the city on the far bank, while small bats squeezed out of the roof tiles and dive bombed for an evening meal of gnats and other insects, then disappeared as quickly as they had arrived. The breeze would pick up, rippling the darkened river and filling the flat square sails of little river boats, known as feluccas.

But it was in the very early mornings that I loved my terrace best. The red neon Coca-Cola sign had been doused. The city was dark and still and uncharacteristically quiet.

Pots of jasmine at my feet would exude the most achingly sweet scent that almost overpowered the smell of dust and exhaust. Two kittens rescued from the souk curled up by my side. And then there was the cackle of loudspeakers as the muezzin began the first call to prayer of the day from a thousand minarets across the city. Each recording was slightly out of synch with the others, making a beautiful cacophony to wake up the faithful before dawn. *Allahu Akbar! Allahu Akbar! As-salatu Khayrun Minan-nawm*, "God is great. God is great. Prayer is better than sleeping." Soon the sun would rise and I would face another hot, chaotic day of honking horns, crappy phone lines, translation mishaps, rancid cooking oil, and catcalls.

It was a universal truth that people from Westernized countries either loved Egypt or hated it.

My college roommate, Carol Rosenberg, who was the Jerusalem bureau chief for *The Miami Herald* at the time, was sometimes in the latter camp. Once on a work trip to Cairo, she slipped on a street and fell into a gutter. Scratched and covered in filth, she struggled to her feet as a man raced to her side. Instead of offering help, he thrust a sheaf of garish Egyptian hieroglyphics in her face and asked eagerly: "Pretty lady, buy papyrus from me?" She told me the story as she examined her scratches for infection. "Gah, I hate this city," she snapped in frustration.

I, however, loved Cairo. Every minute of it.

In the mornings I would walk from my island apartment building to the CNN bureau on the opposite bank, crossing the Nile on an ornate steel pedestrian bridge. Legend was that Gustave Eiffel built it then threw himself into the river because the mechanism to swing it open for ships failed to work properly. That's not true. Eiffel did not build the bridge, and he died in his bed in Paris while listening to Beethoven. However, the swing mechanism did fail, and the bridge was a crumbling wreck by the 1990s. I could look through holes in the pavement beneath my feet and see water swirling below.

Once I officially became CNN bureau chief, I made some changes to our office. Amr, our cameraman, was on strike most of the time and had to go. Once, we were shooting a story in front of the Egyptian Museum in nearby Tahrir Square. I was in the middle of a "standup," facing the camera while recording a segment about terrorism against tourists, when we were startled by a massive bang. I could see a plume of smoke rising in the air over a parking lot behind Amr's back, where someone had placed a bomb on a tour bus. I shouted to Amr urgently, "Turn the camera! Turn the camera!" so he could record the aftermath of the attack. He glared, folded his arms, and said: "If you're going to yell, film it yourself."

As other camera crews descended on the scene, Amr took our car and returned to the bureau, leaving me behind to walk back to Video Cairo and use footage taken by their crews for my report. The bus was empty so there were no injuries, but the Ministry of Information was understandably convinced that I knew about the bombing beforehand, went to the site to watch the bus blown up, and didn't warn them. Not true, of course; it was just an incredible coincidence.

Amr was replaced by CNN legend Mary Rogers, a chain-smoking badass with a passion for videography and no fear. With her came a long-overdue Betacam camera and edit bay to accommodate smaller videocassettes. Before Mary, we'd traveled around with ancient U-Matic gear that required tapes the size of a dictionary and had a heavy sound recording deck that was cabled to the camera. Amr with the camera on his shoulder and Ali with the deck slung around his neck were like conjoined twins who often headed in opposite directions, snapping back together again when the cable reached its limit.

The CNN bureau also gained new freelance producer and translator James Martone, whom I met through *The Washington Post* bureau chief. James had come to Egypt to teach English to Coptic holy men in an isolated monastery in the desert, emerging months later perfectly fluent in Arabic. He could charm anyone into granting us an interview in half a dozen languages, because they knew he genuinely cared about what they had to say. My friend Jenny, who had crashed on my hotel floor and possibly used my toothbrush, also worked with us on CNN stories from time to time. Her Arabic improved markedly when she acquired an Egyptian husband after we left our weasel-infested apartment. Jenny also worked for an English-language magazine where she wrote a column about interesting shops and exhibits under the nom-de-plume "Sammy the Squirrel." There are no squirrels in Egypt.

We were young and excited to live in Cairo. James and I set up a badminton net in the garden of *The Washington Post* reporter's house and used it exactly once. We started a Shakespeare reading group with an enthusiastic collection of expats, but our first meeting turned into a party and we forgot about the bard. Jenny and I would go to the souk together, drink tea, rescue cats off the streets, and bargain for perfumed oil and gold earrings. For the majority of my time in Egypt, I was out of the country on assignment, usually with our camerawoman Mary. But, when we worked out of the Cairo bureau, we often brought along James to translate and help gather information. I can remember a long drive to upper Egypt while James and I sang Broadway show tunes for hours, and Mary curled up in the corner of the back seat, smoking out the window and sighing deeply.

I covered the floors of our dingy office with colorful kilim rugs and set out ornate copper coffee pots filled with fresh flowers. A florist in Zamalek would hand over massive bouquets of fragrant pink Egyptian roses for a few Egyptian pounds. I got a desk to replace the dining room table, but replacing the chair was a process. Our accountant Hosam had purchased an executive office chair that was bestowed on me after the former bureau chief moved to London. It was made of faux leather the color of vomit and had a high back and a sloping broken seat. I had to squeeze my thighs together to prevent myself from sliding to the floor. Whenever I shifted my weight, it let out a massive squeak and the high back would tilt forward and bang into my head. Every morning, I would drag this abomination of a chair into the reception area and place a dining room chair at my desk. Every evening, our helper Salah would drag it back. Hosam patiently explained it was the executive chair, and I had to sit in it because I was the bureau chief.

Salah also took issue with my choice of beverage. I drink my coffee black.

"No sugar?"

"No. No sugar."

"No sugar?"

"No. Please do not put sugar in my coffee."

We had this discussion daily and when the coffee landed on my desk it always had sugar. I'm sure he thought if I just tasted it, I would have an epiphany. *Wow! Coffee tastes great with sugar!* Instead, I'd march into the kitchen and pour myself a cup of black coffee and return to my desk. I also insisted that Salah stop cleaning the kitchen counters with a gasoline-soaked rag. That took some time to work out, as well, and was never completely resolved even after seven years. I'd walk into the bureau after being absent for weeks and the place would reek like a broken gas station hose.

With Mary shooting and editing, James working as a producer, Jenny popping by, and reporters coming round to chat, the Cairo bureau became a lovely haven in a chaotic city. An American veterinarian gave me her pet cockatiel when she moved back to the States. I placed his cage in the reception area where he could squawk like a doorbell when anyone entered the bureau. Cockatiels are great mimics, and he had picked up an unusual repertoire from his former home in the vet's office. When he was upset, he made noises like a frightened puppy getting vaccinated. I named him Cassidy after my boss Steve. Once a month, our local bird guy came to the office to deliver seeds.

Originally, we had communicated with Atlanta through a bulky telex machine in the dining room area. It clattered as it typed messages and memos onto long rolls of paper, just like the old wire machines from college. The CNN International Desk would also fax us stories from the major newspapers and news agencies. In turn, I would write my scripts on a word processor, print them, and fax them to Atlanta. Eventually, the telex and fax were replaced by an internal computer network so we could message other CNN staff and share documents. The World Wide Web was launched in 1991, but it was still in its infancy.

For much of the time I lived in Egypt we didn't have mobile phones, only dodgy landlines. These lines were serviced by an equally dodgy technician known as a *muhandis*, or engineer, a title bestowed on anyone who did anything remotely technical. Once, my home phone service failed and the engineer climbed out on the roof and chose a telephone line that serviced another apartment somewhere in the bowels of my apartment building. He snipped that cable and wired it to the line leading into my apartment. I could make outgoing calls, but incoming calls were solely from the friends and family of the unknown, and furious, neighbor below me. We eventually got a phone for our CNN car that was installed in the center console and attached to an antenna arcing over the car roof, but we didn't get cellphones until later in the decade.

Unlike James and Jenny, I struggled with Arabic because I spoke almost exclusively English at work and with my expat friends. I had picked up a tutor named Hanaan who taught me a dialect of Egyptian Arabic from a poorer neighborhood in Cairo. What little Arabic I spoke was choppy and comprised of urban slang and idioms, but people in other Arabic-speaking countries could understand me because they heard the same dialect in popular Egyptian movies.

Although I often reported from the Middle East, my boss Steve would dispatch me to do stories in Africa and Europe, as well. CNN had a limited number of bureaus and international correspondents, so when there was a major breaking news story, we would all meet up to work as a team. Sometimes we moved as a pack from one crisis to the next. I had a small, articulated clay puppet on my desk from Mexico—a cow with its head and legs attached by string—and whenever Steve called me, I would jangle it until its little legs were flailing in all directions. "Hey babe, I need you in Somalia." "Get Libyan visas for you and Mary, and James, too." "How fast can you get to Sarajevo?" I had a monthly subscription to a thick book with small print that listed all scheduled international flights. I'd thumb through it to determine the best route then call the Atlanta travel desk to help me book. Since the Cairo airport is a major hub for the Middle East and Africa, I could usually fly out that day, grabbing a suitcase I had already packed in anticipation of last-minute assignments. The one time I ever planned an evening dinner party at my apartment, I was called away to Kinshasa that afternoon. I left my apartment door unlocked with directions so my guests could heat the food I'd left in the refrigerator and drink the wine I'd left on the counter.

My boss Steve was the most important person in my life. He was the one who was ready to medevac me out of Amman when I fainted at the airport because I'd skipped breakfast. The one who routed me through Paris and London for layovers after particularly brutal assignments. The one who guided me through my new career in television and gave me opportunities to gain skills and confidence. I would jump through hoops for Steve. He once called me in Tripoli and told me to get to Baghdad ASAP. Libya and Iraq were the two countries in the world under international flight bans. I had to take a ten-hour car ride from Tripoli to Tunis, fly to Amman, Jordan, then take another twelve-hour car ride to Baghdad.

In an average year, I traveled so much that I only spent a few months in Egypt cumulatively. But I loved coming home to my little apartment on the Nile, my cats, my crazy office with the smell of gasoline wafting from the kitchen, and fat pink roses on my desk. My friends, almost all journalists, were funny, kind, supportive, and with shared experiences. My friend Kim surmised that if she unexpectedly died in her apartment, the delivery guy from the only American fast-food outlet in Egypt, Pizza Hut, would be the first to report her missing because she ordered a small personal pan pizza pretty much every night. The Balmoral Chinese restaurant would be the first to miss me. My usual order was "everything fried rice" and chicken dumplings. As soon as they heard my voice on the phone, they'd say *mashi*, meaning "got it," and hang up. Twenty minutes later, the breathless delivery guy was at my door, having successfully dodged the *bowabs* in the lobby by trudging up the stairs rather than taking the elevator.

James and I came up with endless ideas for stories about Egyptian life at a time when CNN was still open to running features as well as hard news. We went to people's homes, their workshops, their places of worship, and their schools. Sipping hundreds of glasses of sweet tea, always offered as a sign of hospitality. There were still families in Cairo that lived on small fishing boats in the Nile, docking along busy streets to sell their catch to businessmen on their way home from work. Men who bred Arabian horses that had perfect triangular faces and massive dark eyes fringed with lashes. Traditional *musaharati*, who during Ramadan walked the streets before dawn with a drum and a lantern, waking neighbors so they could eat before the religious fast began at sunrise. On slow days in Cairo, we would track down Zahi Hawass, the director of antiquities, for news about discoveries at the pyramids. We could put him in front of a camera, ask a single question, and walk away with enough soundbites for three stories.

Mary and I once arranged to sail along the upper Nile in a felucca to record imagery of rural Egyptians. We set out from Luxor at five in the morning to catch the sunrise, and I immediately curled up on deck under the sail and fell back asleep. When I awoke hours later, I saw that our wooden sailboat had only progressed a few hundred yards from the dock. Apparently, the wind had died. So, we ditched the felucca for a barge-like power boat designed to take tourists on cocktail cruises.

Many villages at that time were comprised of a dozen dirt brown adobe houses set along a single unpaved street parallel to the Nile. The women wore long colorful dresses and headscarves, and the men white ankle-length tunics called *galabeya* with white turbans. The children wore modern Western clothes, a mishmash of dresses, shorts, and school uniforms. Everyone wore *shibshib* on their feet, what we call flip-flops.

As in the old city of Damascus, I could imagine how Egypt looked in antiquity because not much had changed. There were hardly any vehicles or televisions, so it was quiet. You could hear the wind in the palms and the lowering of animals. Men drew water from canals with a *shaduf*, a small fulcrum of long sticks with a leather bucket attached to one end. Water buffalo, called *gamoos*, would wander on the banks of the river until evening, when they headed to their respective homes along well-worn paths. Watching from the boat, it looked like a bovine rush hour of commuters.

The doorways of almost every home were marked with a collage of dull red handprints. After a sheep or cow was slaughtered for the major Islamic holiday known as the

Eid al-Kabir, the homeowner would dip his hand in the blood and slap it against the entrance as a blessing. Inside these village homes were beds with colorful blankets and walls decorated with magazine pages or ornately framed photos of older family members, looking somber and faded. There were often cushions on the floor or low couches where people could gather and drink tea, heavy with sugar. It was served in small, narrow glasses etched in gold and the amber liquid was whipped to a froth.

It was not a story book, however. Egypt was as deeply flawed as any other country.

Many visitors, especially women, couldn't tolerate the rampant harassment or they hated the constant bartering and requests for *baksheesh*. Living there, I learned to ignore catcalls or to sometimes chide men for being rude, which garnered the support of bystanders. Once, Jenny and I were harassed by a very young boy on a narrow pedestrian walkway within the souk. She admonished him and a nearby shopkeeper jumped in to give the kid a whack that sent him reeling to the doorway of the next shop where that shopkeeper gave him another whack that sent him stumbling further up the street where yet another shopkeeper was waiting to whack him again. It was like watching a pinball as the poor youngster ricocheted from one side of the lane to the other. Jenny could be merciless. When a guy in a parked car exposed himself to her on a busy street, she pulled open the door and started shouting in Arabic, "A pervert! Everyone come look at the pervert!" He tried to straighten his pants and start the engine as a crowd quickly gathered, craning their necks to see what he was doing.

Harassment was mostly an inconvenience, like dodgy telephone lines, clouds of DDT sprayed in the streets to combat mosquitos or the wind-born desert sand that crept into my kitchen cabinets and coated my dishes. But the inability of Egypt to protect many of its poor and vulnerable citizens was a tragedy.

Durunka was a small village at the base of a hill, on the top of which were three massive fuel tanks. It rarely rained in Egypt, but one night, when villagers were tucked into their collection of little houses, it started to rain and rain hard. The hill looming over Durunka was mostly made of sand and it gave way under a flood of water, pulling down electrical lines that sparked and ignited the fuel tanks. It was a catastrophe of biblical proportions. The oily water became a sheet of fire that raced down the slope and through the village, incinerating everything in its path—houses, cars, livestock, and more than 450 people. By morning, there was nothing left but scorched earth and rubble. It was impossible to identify human remains.

Most of those who survived were men who had hiked up the hill before the disaster to inspect the water drainage. We interviewed one man who had lost his wife, parents, all seven of his children, livestock, home, and all his worldly possessions. As we spoke, a government car pulled up to distribute blankets to the few survivors. Even though it was three days after the tragedy, they were still sleeping on bare ground and wandering about without direction, unsure where to go or what to do. When the officials suspected that people from a second, nearby village were trying to also obtain the free blankets, they angrily snatched the blankets back from everyone and drove off. The man we were interviewing wandered away, without a blanket, in a daze.

Human rights violations were rampant as the military-backed government tried to annihilate Islamic Extremists.

A string of terrorist attacks on tourists had given the impression that Egypt was dangerous to visit, devastating the tourism industry that provided livelihoods for millions of people. Trials of accused terrorists, placed in large cages inside the courtroom, were held in heavily guarded military compounds. I was conflicted because, while I despise terrorism, these trials were very short and almost always resulted in a guilty verdict. During a break in one proceeding, I saw a young woman with a black *niqab*—a veil that covered not only her hair but the lower part of her face—approach her husband who was in the cage with a dozen other accused men. She raised a black gloved hand, and they touched their fingertips together, gazing into each other's eyes through the bars. It was only a moment, and then she had to move away while he was sentenced to be executed.

For the most part, expats living in Egypt in the 1990s were safe. There was hardly any crime; I could walk home at night from a belly dancing club without fear. But the police would sometimes try to stop us from filming or take us into temporary custody for a perceived offense. We kept photos in the CNN car of us posing with President Hosni Mubarak and various ministers, which usually worked to get us off the hook.

Journalists were closely monitored. Security services didn't even try to hide that they were tapping my home phone; I could hear agents on the line groaning and sighing audibly when I babbled for too long with my mother. Once, I made a call and became distracted when my party didn't answer and I let the phone ring and ring without hanging up. An irritated voice snapped in my ear, "He's not home! Hang up already!"

The longer I lived in Cairo, the more I felt like I belonged. I figured out how to navigate the city, how to minimize harassment, and where to procure whatever I needed for a comfortable life. When I'd first moved into my rooftop apartment, I was irritated by the lightbulb situation. And it became a thing. The bulbs were locally produced and would burn out with a pop after only a few months of moderate use, sometimes after only a few weeks, or even days. But I didn't know where to buy new ones. There were no department stores in Cairo, nothing close to resembling a Target or a hardware store. Almost all goods were sold in specialty shops. If you wanted a desk, you went to a specific street in downtown Cairo where there were five shops in a row that sold nothing but desks. If you needed a basket, you went to a store that sold nothing but baskets. I didn't know where the lightbulb store was, and no one would tell me how to find it.

Every week I had to pay one of the *bowabs*, the doorman in my building, to go buy me a lightbulb. I'd beg him to pick up a dozen, but he'd return always with a single bulb in a plastic bag. I realized that by bringing me one bulb at a time he could maximize his *baksheesh*. A cumulative tip of twelve Egyptian lira for twelve individual lightbulbs was a better deal than a single tip of one lira for a dozen bulbs. But it was a major hassle to get the *bowab* to bring me even one bulb, and I spent too many nights bumping around my apartment in the dark.

Then, one fateful evening, I was walking on an unfamiliar street in my island neighborhood of Zamalek and turned a corner. There, tucked between two little shops, was an open storefront with a counter behind which were shelves upon shelves of lightbulbs. It was lit up in the night like a stage, with three bored young men sitting with their heads in their hands at the counter, staring back at me as I stared at them in amazement. I bought two dozen bulbs. When I sashayed into the lobby of my building, swinging my plastic bags of treasure, I saw the *bowab's* face fall. The jig was up. I compensated with an increase in his monthly tip, but it felt like he never forgave me.

I did a story once about a Cairo tour company that specialized in clients who believed in reincarnation and could remember their past lives in ancient Egypt. I was on the tour bus when it picked up a considerable number of excited Americans who had apparently been born in Egypt thousands of years earlier.

"I was Seti the First!" I heard one passenger say, followed by his companion's confusion. "That's impossible—*I* was Seti the First!"

As we rolled toward the Giza plateau, the guide grabbed the bus microphone. "Welcome home, everyone," he intoned gravely over the loudspeaker. "Welcome home."

I don't believe I was reincarnated, but I was home.

FIVE

AMBITION

Once, while driving along the eastern coast of Italy, I stopped in an unremarkable industrial town to see the famed Rubicon. The river was noted in antiquity for being shallow, and by the time I visited it looked more like a drainage ditch. But I got a little bit of a thrill walking across a short bridge, thus "crossing the Rubicon," because I am a history geek.

In the days of Julius Caesar, the Rubicon was the boundary 200 miles from Rome that armed Roman legions were forbidden to cross. The capital of the empire was a military-free zone where leading Roman men vied for power in the Senate and not on a battlefield. Because many senators were also generals, there were fears that they would bring their loyal troops home with them and intimidate the populace. It just wasn't done.

But, on the morning of January 10, 49 BC, Julius Caesar faced a difficult choice. He was returning to Rome after spending almost a decade conquering Gaul, a vast territory that included what is today France, Belgium, and parts of Germany and the Netherlands. He had expanded the Roman Empire to a staggering extent and filled the Roman treasury with confiscated wealth and increased tax revenue. But, while he was battling Celtic tribes, Caesar's opponents in the Senate feared he had become too powerful.

Caesar knew that when he returned home the Senate planned to strip him of his command and put him on trial for exceeding his authority. He could obey the law and order his troops to set up camp on the far side of the Rubicon. Or he could say the Latin equivalent of "to hell with this," order them to wade through the shallow river, continue toward Rome, and initiate a civil war. He chose to cross. To this day, "crossing the Rubicon" means making an irrevocable decision, a point of no return.

Zenobia crossed her own Rubicon more than two centuries after Caesar's bold move. She could have mourned the death of her husband and settled in her beautiful city of Palmyra with her children, ruling nominally through her young son with a cadre of trusted advisors. Palmyra was secure and she had control of a considerable fortune— her late husband Odaenathus had plundered much of the wealth of the Persian Empire before his death.

But Zenobia was not the type of woman to settle down in her early thirties. Along with her significant fortune, she had at her disposal a considerable army of professional soldiers led by seasoned generals who were ready and willing to follow her orders. The historian Zosimus says the Palmyrene troops admired their new ruler because she was just as capable of command as the recently deceased king.

So, instead of adopting a low-key regency and flying under Rome's radar, Zenobia chose to fly in its face. Seizing Egypt was a bold step over a line drawn in the sand, the Middle East's Rubicon. After 300 years of Roman rule, a young, previously unknown, Syrian queen now controlled the vital supply of wheat that not only fed the citizens of Rome but was a foundation of the Roman economy.

Flushed with success, Zenobia spent the early years of her reign expanding her own empire stretching from Egypt up through modern day Turkey and east to the Asian side of Bosphorus. Historic sources would suggest she largely accomplished this feat with persuasion, rather than military might. City-states in the region were becoming increasingly uncomfortable under the yoke of Roman domination. The ongoing Roman Crisis of the Third Century had triggered an economic downturn and weakened security, with the Middle East beset by local bandits and encroaching armies from the far east. Aligning with the wealthy and well-armed Palmyra would have offered kingdoms and city-states a measure of protection and stability.

But Zenobia was comfortable using force to get what she wanted when diplomacy failed. Her troops not only vanquished the Roman governor of Egypt, they also killed the Roman governor of Arabia. She secured all of Syria and Egypt by conquering a massive confederation of Arab tribes and she established military outposts throughout what is now Turkey. Within a few years, she had effectively seized one third of the Roman Empire.

Zenobia pushed other boundaries, as well. She adopted the title of Augusta for herself and Augustus for her son, Vaballathus, and minted coins in their likeness and carved their names into stone edifices across her domain. Officials back in Rome would have been horrified. Augustus was considered a sacred name reserved solely for the Roman imperial family. Zenobia's appropriation of the August title was an outrage, a bold and deliberate provocation.

In those early years of her rule, Zenobia was safe to do as she wished. But, unfortunately for her, the Crisis of the Third Century was starting to wrap up, and a considerable challenge was on the horizon.

The emperor Aurelian is an integral part of Zenobia's history. He was born to obscure parents in the Roman outpost of Dacia, in what is now Serbia, sometime around 210 AD. His father was likely a former Roman soldier who had taken up farming, while his mother was described in some histories as a priestess of Sol, an ancient god of the sun. Aurelian was born a Roman citizen but, like Zenobia, he was not of Roman heritage. He was an Illyrian—part of a tribal group that spoke their own language and were known to the ancients for their extensive expertise in sailing, piracy, and warfare.

Rome had extended citizenship throughout the empire since the days of Augustus as an incentive for conquered nations to be loyal subjects and pay taxes. Early in Rome's history, just a few elite families had dominated Roman politics—they were of noble birth and largely called all the shots. But as the empire expanded over the centuries, newly minted Roman citizens born of humble families outside of Rome managed to work their way into positions of power. By the 270s AD, three former Roman emperors had been, like Zenobia, of Syrian birth.

This included Emperor Elagabalus, whose flamboyant disregard for Roman religion and social norms had sparked the Crisis of the Third Century in the first place. Elagabalus had married a Vestal Virgin, prostituted himself in brothels, and was possibly one of history's first known transgender rulers. He dressed in women's clothing and there is speculation he may have pursued an early form of reassignment surgery. After four tumultuous years as emperor, Elagabalus was still a teenager when he was assassinated in 222 AD. His death led to a power vacuum and Roman generals fought each other for the position of emperor throughout the fifty years that followed.

The last emperor standing was Aurelian. A typical Illyrian, he distinguished himself as a master of warfare, a capable soldier, and a leader within the Roman army. He had ample opportunity to hone his military skills during the crisis as he maneuvered to fight on whichever side was winning. He was instrumental in helping Emperor Gallienus, the same Roman Emperor who had expressed gratitude to Zenobia's husband Odaenathus for defeating the Persians. When Gallienus was murdered in 268 by his guards, he was succeeded by Claudius Gothicus, who ruled for two years before dying of the plague in 270 AD. He, in turn, was succeeded by his brother Quintillus, who only managed to survive as emperor for a few weeks before he was killed under murky circumstances. At this point, Aurelian made his move. Backed by his seasoned troops and impressive reputation, he seized power in a move that would ultimately end the five decades of constant turmoil and largely restore Rome to normalcy.

By the time Aurelian took control of the empire in the summer of 270 AD, Zenobia had been a widow for three years and was busy minting coins and having accounts of her accomplishments chiseled in stone. It seems likely she was banking that Aurelian would quickly be assassinated or die of mysterious illnesses like the Roman rulers before him.

It was true that the new emperor was not in a position to immediately march on Palmyra. As soon as Aurelian assumed power, the tribes in what is now northern Europe mounted a series of invasions. But Rome's clever new ruler managed to thwart their ambitions by snatching away all of the crops and domesticated animals in their path, leaving them starved and weakened. As soon as he drove those invaders out of the empire, he was beset by a wave of invading Germanic Goths and Vandals who were in the mood to fight. They stormed into Italy and headed toward Rome. Aurelian managed to defeat them, as well, but civilians in the capital were understandably rattled. To assuage Roman fears of further foreign invasions, Aurelian ordered the construction of a massive wall around the city, now known as the Aurelian Wall that still partially stands today.

Aurelian not only had to contend with this plethora of invading hordes, he also was beset by Romans within the city who challenged his rule. A man named Felicissimus, who was in charge of minting imperial coins, raised a rebellion of engravers that ended in a battle involving 7,000 troops in one of Rome's poshest neighborhoods. The rebels were massacred and several senators executed.

While Aurelian was preoccupied, Zenobia had two years of grace to consolidate her power within her newly expanded domain. She would have to persuade the entire region that she was capable of leading the opposition against this new Roman ruler. It would not have been easy. She was a relative newcomer—a young woman in a deeply patriarchal society within a harsh, largely desert environment.

A female leader in the ancient Middle East was not a complete outlier. There is evidence that Palmyra was full of capable and admired women; inscriptions show they were active participants in Palmyrene society and titans of commerce. Still, the powerful men of the East would have been skeptical of Zenobia at best or hostile at worst. Her control of a large and well-equipped army was her most persuasive quality, to be sure, but Zenobia was also able to win male leaders over with her personality. She was a woman who could speak their languages and shared their passions for horses, hunting, and warfare.

Multiple historians gush over Zenobia's excellent horsemanship, which would have won her points in antiquity, just as it would in the Middle East today. Many Arabs love their distinctively beautiful horses, which are fast, strong, and have considerable endurance. I'd visited stables in Egypt where the Arabians had stalls nicer than my apartment, and Bedouins still kept their horses in their tents at night lest they be injured by wild animals or stolen by thieves.

Once, I went horseback riding at the pyramids with a young American expat renowned for her waist-length curly brown hair. Sue was the daughter of an American oil executive and had grown up with horses in Saudi Arabia. I remember the men from the stables watching her and her mount streaking across the desert, tinged red in the late afternoon sun. Then, mid-stride, her horse slid on a rock and stumbled as it tried to recover its footing. Sue flew out of the saddle and clung to the side of the falling horse. There was a collective gasp from the men, but she artfully recovered her seat and righted the horse without slowing down for a moment, her hair still flying. The men grunted in appreciation and exchanged looks of disbelief and collective respect. Zenobia would have elicited the same reaction, I'm sure.

The queen's ability to ride was handy because she was frequently on the move. She was said to eschew the luxurious carts and curtained litters typically used by women travelers in the ancient world. Instead, she rode a horse or walked alongside her troops or rode in chariots, as most men did.

Zenobia also liked to hunt—a male pursuit often associated with kings. Most hunting involved shooting prey with bow and arrow, a tricky business that required the strength to draw the arrow and keep it steady while jostling on the back of a horse. Although much of the Middle East is comprised of desert, there were plenty of targets roaming about in antiquity, including Asiatic lions. One of the surviving treasures of Palmyra is a sculpture of a ferocious lion guarding the temple of al-Lat, an Arabian goddess. There's no evidence Zenobia ever bagged a lion, but she would have been able to slay gazelles in the desert, along with red deer, mountain goats, and wild boars.

Syrians also hunted wild asses by lassoing them with ropes. It wasn't as easy as it sounds. The ancients complained that the asses would fake out the hunters by running and stopping, then quickly switch directions. Zenobia would perhaps have had more success hunting a lion than an ass. Whatever her prey, histories praise her prowess, relating she was like Artemis, the Greek goddess of the hunt who helped her devotees navigate the wilderness. Zenobia "hunted with the eagerness of a Spaniard," effused one historian—presumably a compliment.

"She drank, too, with the Persians and the Armenians," confided another. Wine in antiquity was abundant and sweet. Even though mixed with water, it must have been potent given the numerous accounts of men getting stupidly drunk. Another popular choice of beverage was beer, which was possibly brewed using wild wheat. There's a somewhat famous inscription depicting an Assyrian mercenary chugging beer with an Egyptian comrade.

Conservative Romans avowed that a respectable woman would never drink alcohol, but there's considerable evidence to the contrary. Zenobia's drinking was notable but not shocking. Historians stress that she didn't drink to excess, and in fact only drank to get the better of her allies and enemies, nursing a beer perhaps while the men raised their cups for another round. But she also might have just enjoyed having a drink now and then. It's intriguing to imagine the new queen sharing an amphora of fine Italian wine with her allies after a successful hunt, perhaps accompanied by the braying of an indignant ass in the background.

She must have possessed considerable charm. Since she was educated in the history of the region and noted for her fluency in languages, she was able to chat with her subjects from all corners of her newly minted empire. She garnered respect by walking the line between being a strong leader and a kind person. As one historian noted: "Her sternness, when necessity demanded, was that of a tyrant, her clemency, when her sense of right called for it, that of a good emperor."

Five years after the death of her husband, Zenobia was entrenched as ruler of a third of the original Roman Empire. She was minting coins, collecting taxes, issuing edicts, dispensing justice, and controlling vital trade routes. She was bold, unconventional, confident, and seemingly fearless.

I wanted to be a bold and confident woman in the Middle East, as well. I certainly had some incredible role models, like Christiane Amanpour at CNN. The first time I worked with her was in Algeria, which quickly became my least favorite country in the world. As a female member of the Western press in the 1990s, I was welcomed, or at least respected, in most of the Middle East. But when Christiane and I arrived in Algiers, people spat on us and called us *koos*, the vilest insult in Arabic, starting from the moment we exited the airport with our CNN crew. Our only refuge was our gorgeous hotel, a haven of beautiful blue Moroccan tiles and gently swaying date trees. Amr, the Cairo bureau cameraman at the time, refused to step foot out of the hotel grounds. He said it was too dangerous, and to be fair, he wasn't wrong. Christiane was understandably exasperated, but I managed to get hold of another freelance crew to accompany us into the streets.

We wandered around an older part of the city, the casbah, and took video known as b-roll, random shots of places and people that we would edit into Christiane's stories to set the scene. The secret police, or *mukhabarat*, were dogging our steps. *Mukhabarat* operated almost everywhere in the Arab world, and it was usually easy to spot them. Depending on the country, they would adopt certain articles of clothing or expose the bulge of a gun in their waistband, sport identical haircuts and facial hair, or wear distinctive types of shoes. They wanted to be noticed so that law-abiding citizens were intimidated and dissenters scared. In Algiers, the *mukhabarat* uniform consisted of brightly colored athletic tracksuits with matching jackets and sweatpants.

As we made our way down one street, a young man in a tracksuit sidled up to us and hissed in English, "I want to kill you!" I prepared to skitter back to the hotel, but not Christiane. She grabbed the cameraman and spun around to face the guy, stuck a microphone in his face, and started interviewing him. "Why do you want to kill us?" she asked eagerly. The secret agent, like me, was momentarily frozen. He stuttered. It was clear Christiane wasn't challenging him, she just really wanted to know the answer. "Tell us why you want to kill us," she urged politely. The two of them ended up having a whole conversation that went from broken English to a deeper discussion in French and Arabic. The young man let his guard down and revealed the festering frustration that Algerians had with the West, especially America, as they grappled with rampant poverty, a fierce civil war, and the threat of Islamic extremism. I wouldn't say we parted friends, but the tension between the crowd and the CNN team had eased considerably. It was a bold move. Just a few years later, two ABC News journalists were shot in the same casbah.

Like Zenobia, Christiane was seemingly fearless. Once, we were in a car headed up an extremely precarious switchback mountain road outside of Sarajevo. The road was becoming narrower and narrower, and it was clear the driver had no idea where we were headed. He stopped short, unsure of what to do next. On one side of us was a wall of rock and on the other was a sheer drop to the valley below. The hapless driver was unable to either back up or turn around. Christiane sighed deeply and ordered him to swap seats. *She* would turn the SUV around so we could head back down the mountain. I was crowded in the back seat with the crew as Christiane took the wheel. I opened the door and crawled out, telling Christiane if the car plummeted, I would survive to report the incident. Of course, she managed to turn the car around.

Another of my role models was Marie Colvin, with whom I worked briefly at UPI. Marie's goodbye party in Washington, DC, before being sent overseas, was so epic that she was bundled onto the plane and reportedly arrived at the London bureau with only one shoe. She was quickly recruited by *The Sunday Times* of London and left UPI for an esteemed career. We later crossed paths in the Middle East, mostly in Iraq. Because of the no-fly order, we occasionally shared the long rides from Amman, Jordan, to the Iraqi capital Baghdad, giving me time to marvel at her confidence and poise.

The last time I saw her, we were hanging out at an Amman hotel for a few days, waiting for a summit with Arab leaders and the US secretary of state. She was a fixture at the hotel bar, drinking with her Bolivian husband, who was a correspondent for the Spanish newspaper *El País*. It was years before his suicide and before the eye injury in Sri Lanka that left her with an eye patch. They did shots of whisky with other members of the press corps and traded stories of near-death experiences. I stood on the sideline sipping a Stella beer, feeling like I didn't quite belong.

And then there was Ilaria Alpi, who worked for the Italian news network RAI-3. She was a good friend of my friend James. When he brought her to my Cairo apartment for Christmas one year, I opened my only bottle of decent wine—which was hard to come by in Egypt—and pulled out some goat cheese and crackers. We talked at length about Somalia, where I had been on assignment for the past two months. Ilaria had been there frequently and was headed back after her holiday break. I admitted to her that the violence between warlords in Somalia terrified me, and I hoped I would never have to return there. She was the opposite. She loved it. The guns, the chaos, the factions, the unpredictability. I was envious of her confidence and irritated with myself that I was so timid.

These were just a few of the many bold and accomplished women I encountered in the Middle East, including Arab women who defied social norms and were excellent reporters. They were brave, took risks, and were fueled with ambition and daring. I'm sure if they had lived in ancient Syria, they would have been drinking beer with potentates and hunting gazelle with ease.

In the earliest days of CNN, I thought it would be exciting to cover conflict, to face danger. I aspired to be a star, like Christiane and Marie, fearless like Ilaria. But, as much as I wanted to be a hard-drinking, cigarette-smoking veteran war correspondent, I just couldn't quite pull it off. I discovered that I did not have driving ambition nor fearlessness—and I was a sloppy drunk. I was not a danger junkie like other war correspondents. This epiphany would come in an assignment at the end of 1992.

SIX

MOGADISHU

H ere is what a real-life dystopian landscape looks like.

Mogadishu is the capital of Somalia, located just a hair north of the equator in Africa, on the shoreline of the Indian Ocean. There are massive cement and brick buildings on either side of the road leading into the city, with gaping black holes where there had been windows and doors. Everything has been stripped: doorknobs and light fixtures and handrails. Walls busted open and electrical wiring removed and sold as scrap metal. Plumbing pipes dug up, torn out, and carted off. Tiles, wood, tar, metal frames, roofing—all gone.

In the city, the streets are so full of potholes and mortar craters that the few vehicles with gasoline creep along at the same pace as pedestrians. Most people walk, rarely speaking because they are conserving their energy. Some are pulling carts laden with children. They have no possessions to put into the carts, and even if they did, they would be stolen by men with guns. The chassis of a Ford sedan perches on the top of one cart, pulled by donkeys because the owner doesn't have the money, or the gun-power, to obtain gasoline.

The few operational vehicles on the road are known as "Technicals." They are aged pickup trucks or jeeps with machine guns mounted on swivel platforms, with gun-men spinning the barrels 360 degrees in search of possible targets. The passengers in the back seats are flanked by at least two other gunmen facing outward, and there are more armed guards on the hood or clinging to the back. Technicals are the province of the powerful warlords, the wealthy, the aid workers, and journalists. Some desperate entrepreneurs try to earn a little money by filling in potholes, then flagging down the Technicals for a small donation, completely voluntary. The guns signify that the owners can do what they want.

There are no gas stations. Gasoline is procured from neighboring countries and carried in plastic jugs, often by donkeys. There are no government offices, schools, hospitals, fire trucks, restaurants, hotels, or stores. There is no mail service, police protection, trash pickup, public services, electricity, or running water. Everything has been destroyed.

The women wear loose dresses with their heads wrapped in scarves against the scorching sun, cloth pulled over nose and mouth against the dust. Men wear old T-shirts with faded logos and bright printed sarongs knotted at their waists. They have automatic weapons slung over their slender shoulders and ammunition strapped across their chests. There are guns everywhere. Chinese Kalashnikovs, old M-16 assault rifles, and Russian-made

AK-47s, plus revolvers, flame throwers, and an astonishing variety of incendiary devices, from hand grenades to missiles. The sounds of guns clicking, loading, unloading, and clattering is louder than the plodding footsteps of the silent pedestrians.

Everyone is reed thin. There has been a horrible famine, followed by a host of infectious diseases. Some of the sick and starving are lying outside on the ground, inert, eyes vacant, skin withered over skeletons. Others are laid side-by-side within the shells of buildings or under tarps, rasping their last breaths as flies walk on their eyeballs and burrow up their noses. The victims are too weak to brush them off. The dead are mostly buried where they fall, by the side of a road or in the backyards of dwellings. The only healthy people are the young men with the guns, and maybe some of the women who serve them.

Almost everyone who is ambulatory is chewing the leaves and stems of a shrub known as qat—a narcotic that provides a mild euphoria and, more importantly, a loss of appetite. Chewing qat can take the edge off the food shortage. It's shipped in huge quantities from neighboring Kenya and fought over by the warlords. People hopped up on qat have red eyes and a glassy stare, moving stiffly, not unlike zombies.

By the time I arrived in December 1992, the Somali famine was waning, but families were still struggling to survive in refugee camps or in barren hovels. An estimated 220,000 people had starved to death over the previous year and hundreds of thousands more were sick and weak from malnutrition. The country was still awash with dying children and old people, surrounded by healthy young men wearing faded T-shirts and sarongs, and carrying Kalashnikovs.

International aid workers had been struggling to provide food and healthcare to the victims but it was a dangerous and seemingly impossible task, in part because of the violent turf wars and in part because the country had been stripped of its infrastructure.

The International Red Cross had devoted half its annual budget to food for Somalia, but the men with the guns stole much of it along with anything else of value. Months earlier, an aid ship was looted in the harbor with the help of three rogue tanks armed by civilians. Procuring food was difficult; procuring arms was easier. In a dusty flat open space within the city was a gun bazaar where men could accumulate more weapons, most of them castoffs sold in bulk from the United States and China. Guns were thought to be cheaper than food, but ammunition had become scarcer and more expensive. By December, a single bullet cost one dollar. Random shots echoed continuously throughout the city, but not as much as they did when ammunition was cheaper.

Stories about Somalia had been popping up in the headlines throughout the summer, when an estimated 1,700 people a day were dying of starvation. The small country on the horn of Africa had been enmeshed in civil unrest for more than a decade, but it escalated in 1991 when President Siad Barre was ousted and competing warlords stepped up to fill the power vacuum. Militias and armed factions stole food from the fields. They would pull up in trucks and strip the crops while farmers stood by helplessly. The farmers had no money, or incentive, to start over, so food became scarcer still. A drought exacerbated the crop shortages. Society crumbled.

By the time the United Nations decided to dispatch a joint peace-keeping force in December, the country was still in absolute chaos. News organizations scrambled to get reporters into Mogadishu ahead of time so we could cover the US-led force marching in to save the day. I caught a night flight from Cairo to Nairobi with Carol, my old college roommate, who was based in Jerusalem for *The Miami Herald*. We often ran into each other on assignments and press stakeouts. People were always trying to introduce us. "Hey Gayle, do you know Carol from the *Herald*?" Why, yes, yes, I do!" By the time we arrived in Nairobi, the hotel favored by the press was packed, so I suggested Carol stay in my room booked earlier by CNN. At some point, she offered me Lariam, a relatively new drug for malaria that was touted as being superior to other approved medications. Most drugs to prevent malaria must be taken daily, but a big dose of Lariam was downed only once a week.

The airport in Nairobi was mobbed with journalists and some aid workers trying to catch chartered flights into Mogadishu before its airport was shut down completely. A skeleton crew of UN workers were managing the control tower to prevent collisions, but the situation in Somalia was becoming wildly unstable and they were planning to close the airport as soon as possible. I joined the queue as charters were cancelled by nervous operators. Christiane Amanpour pulled up at some point, strode into the terminal, and was the only journalist on the only flight out. She was magic. Finally, CNN managed to charter a plane for me and a few of my colleagues that would depart early the next morning. It was reportedly a plane that routinely flew qat into Somalia, but we offered more money than the drug dealers.

That night, I lay wide awake in my bed in the Nairobi hotel. I'd spent most of my career in faded hotels. The stale

recirculated air with a hint of insecticide, the stiff coverlet, the blinking pinpoint lights on the smoke detector, an
ancient TV, the almost imperceptible low-intensity buzz
from the inner-workings of building machinery. I lay on
my side, looking out the sliding glass door to a balcony, and
beyond that the sulfur yellow lights of Nairobi. I had an
overwhelming, almost overpowering urge to throw off the
coverlet, open the sliding door, and jump. I knew I would
die, of course, but that didn't seem like such a bad thing. It
seemed almost logical. The only thought that stopped me
was that I would disturb Carol sleeping in the other bed.
God damn that Lariam. How stupid was I to take a non-
prescribed medication from someone who drank Southern
Comfort and smoked Marlboros all through college? She
was a legend. I was made of less sterner stuff.

In the morning, another journalist asked if I was flying
out on the CNN charter plane. Bursting with uncontrol-
lable laughter, he told me that our pilot had been partying
all night at the hotel bar and was so wasted by dawn that
he could barely stand. Ten minutes later, another journalist
told me the same story with a few embellishments. I don't
remember the exact wording, but I believe the drunken
binge was an epic event for all those involved. All day long
people would exclaim, "Oh my God, that CNN pilot!"

Throughout my career, I've had a major, and frankly
embarrassing, impediment. I am terrified of flying. I think
it started when I was living in the Caribbean and taking
lots of BWIA West Indies Airways puddle jumpers. At
first, I thought it was charming because the pilot would
call back to the passengers in the tiny cabin every time he
passed over an island to ask if he should land.

"Taba? Anyone for Taba?"

If no one reacted, he would skip that island and head to the next airport on the itinerary. If someone raised their hand, or shouted they did want the island in question, we would go ahead and land on some weed-infested concrete runway, disembark the passenger, and take off again. But one night, my BWIA flight got caught in a major tropical storm. I looked out the window at a night black as ink, lit up by flashes of lightning that revealed towering ominous clouds surrounding our tiny aircraft. As we bucked and rattled, I could see the fixed black tire under the wing spinning, spinning in the gusts of rain. It was a scene from a horror movie and fodder for decades of nightmares.

I've never recovered. But I've also never let fear of flying stop me from living my life. I've been strapped to a soldier wearing a parachute on a military flight over Bosnia, so if we had to bail, he could kindly see me down to the ground. I was on a plane the size of a Toyota flying to Haiti with a pair of pilots who held up a road map of the island to compare it with the coastline below, trying to locate Port-au-Prince. I've landed on USS aircraft carriers with the gut-jerking assist of a tail hook—then been flung off again with a slingshot that left me momentarily weightless. I've flown in the bellies of cavernous Antenovs, the world's largest cargo planes, in seats that were hastily bolted to the floor to accommodate humans—no windows, no drinks cart. During a monsoon, our Pakistan International Airways flight was so violent that I clutched hands with a colleague I loathed while vowing before God that I would drive from Karachi to London and take the Queen Mary home. I didn't, of course. I spent the night curled up on a bench in the Karachi airport while a group of men arranged themselves in a semi-circle around me and stared at my body. In the morning, I boarded a prop plane with chipped paint for the connecting flight to Islamabad.

So, on the tarmac in Nairobi, I waited with grow-ing Larium-induced anxiety for our chartered plane and locally renowned alcoholic pilot to appear. There were only four of us from CNN in the commercial-sized jet, along with a mountain of gear. Back then, all of our videotapes had to be fed to Atlanta through a satellite uplink. Most countries had private or government-run telecommunica-tions centers, where we could pay to access commercial satellite dishes. But if we were going to a remote location, or if we were planning to stream live coverage for hours at a time, then we brought our own satellite uplink with us. Pieces of equipment would be shipped in heavy anvil cases then snapped together like Legos to create a dish the size of a hot tub.

By the time we loaded our gear and took off, we were the last plane headed to Mogadishu before the air control tower was to be shut down. When we reached sight of the city, we had to slowly circle the Indian Ocean and wait our turn to land. Too slowly. Suddenly, the plane sputtered, and we heard a calm yet ominous robotic voice rise from the open door of the cockpit.

"Danger. Stalled engine. Danger. Stalled engine."

Or something like that. My flying nightmares some-times merge with my memories of actual flights. I will give the epic alcoholic pilot credit: He restarted the engine and managed to be the last plane to land as Mogadishu's control tower was just shutting down. There was no gentle reminder to take care in opening the overhead bins. No orderly exit through the front cabin door. There was no jetway, and no stairs pulled up to the fuselage to assist our deplaning. Instead, the crew opened a trapdoor in the cabin floor, and I climbed down into the hold. From there, I wriggled through another trapdoor in the belly of the plane and hung like a confused sloth before dropping down to the tarmac below.

Night was falling fast and lots of men with guns were roaming around the runway. The outfitter CNN hired from Nairobi to provide additional supplies was pushing our things off the plane. He and the pilot wanted to take off as fast as possible and get the hell out of there. It was chaos and soon the only light available came from the plane's glaring headlights. My colleague Elisa Gambino was there on the tarmac to greet us, directing ad hoc workers to gather up our gear and cart it to the parking lot next to the terminal, where our Technicals were waiting to transport us to CNN's base inside the city. She was frustrated that the hired armed guards insisted on staying near their vehicles, rather than following her to the plane.

We had to cross a stretch of tarmac, now pitch black. It looked like an impenetrable abyss. There were no banks operating in Somalia, no credit card terminals or ATMs, so Elisa had cash in her bag—about $40,000, maybe more. We were stuck on an island of light under the plane, but it was preparing to take off, so we had no choice but to cross the dark abyss to the parking lot where hired guards would presumably protect us. The exhaust from aviation fuel burned my throat and the engines were so loud it was hard to hear what anyone was saying.

We'd barely made it ten paces away from the pool of light when a young boy with a knife sidled up to Elisa to grab her bag. She crumpled to the ground and I thought she was stabbed, so I went down with her. When I later worked at *National Geographic*, I saw a video that exactly represented that night in Somalia—a small fish, eaten by a bigger fish that was quickly snapped up by a mid-sized fish, that was then swallowed whole by a shark. That's what happened to the bag. Within seconds, it was grabbed by an older boy, who was then attacked by a young man, who was then felled by a massive guy with multiple guns. Somehow, Elisa got to her feet. She hadn't been stabbed, so we managed to stumble forward to the CNN guards and the Technicals. They shrugged. I realized they had probably sent the thieves to attack her because they knew she was carrying money. So much for employee loyalty.

CNN producers who arrived days earlier had rented a villa surrounded by high walls topped with barbed wire. Nairobi safari outfitters had been flying in everything we could possibly need—blankets, cots, mosquito netting, sunblock, OTC medicines, toilet paper, ChapStick, boxed pasta, bread, cookies, crackers, protein bars, jugs of petrol, and crates upon crates of bottled water. The CNN team had set up a little newsroom in the dining area next to some couches, and the living room had been cleared to create room for the banks of video decks and editing stations. Cameras and gear were everywhere. The armed guards had their own space in a multi-bay garage next to the house. There were also several Somali women living within the compound who prepared food and did the laundry.

I was to share a cot on the second floor with Christiane. I would sleep there at night when she was doing live shots for primetime audiences in the United States, then she would use it to catch up on sleep during the day. Under the careful guidance of Steve, I had only recently started to report on air. I'd done a few feature reports from Egypt and then some credible news packages from Iraq and Libya, but I was still a newbie. In Somalia, I would be both a behind-the-camera producer and on-air reporter. This was my moment to shine.

Around midnight, dozens of international journalists gathered on the beach on the outer perimeter of the darkened Mogadishu airport to wait for the UN troops to come ashore. The first to arrive were a handful of US Navy SEALs in amphibious assault vessels, wearing full combat gear, grease paint on their faces, and night vision goggles. The camera lights blinded them as journalists swarmed to get photos and video. The beach had fine white sand dunes that sank under boots like talcum powder. A brisk warm breeze blew in from the Indian Ocean and the moon was a bright crescent. Somewhere across the sea there were tourists on other tropical beaches, enjoying a romantic night on the Seychelles Islands.

The SEALs who landed in Mogadishu that night were the vanguard. Their arrival was followed within hours by more than a thousand Marines, mostly helicoptered ashore from US ships on the horizon. By dawn, they had secured the airport and over the course of the day they set up a camp in a field near the terminal, surrounded by layers of fencing and sturdy guard towers. It was like the boma encircled by acacia bushes I would later encounter in Kenya, but with barbed wire and guns instead of thorns. This was just the first wave. Troops from other countries would arrive in droves, part of an effort to restore order and ensure famine victims received aid under the UN program Restore Hope.

That first day of UN occupation was a madhouse in the CNN basecamp and throughout the city. Warlords had no idea how the UN troops would change their power structure. Elisa hired more and more gun-toting guards, acutely aware that they were more like blackmailers than hired hands. They promised not to shoot us—and to shoot others who might want to attack us—but in return we had to give them lots of money. As evening fell, we could hear an uptick of gunfire. I hadn't slept in days and the Lariam was still making my vision and brain fuzzy. It was December 9, my thirty-third birthday.

The head producer, who tried ineffectively to channel his hero Hunter S. Thompson by chomping on a cigarette holder, ordered me to go to the new UN encampment by the airport and ask one of the colonels to come back to the CNN base for a live interview. We had no means to call or contact the guy. So, the producer wanted me to hop in a Technical with our paid gunmen, park on the perimeter of the camp, and call to the colonel over the barbed wire. I explained that I was a little uncomfortable going out alone at night with no way to call CNN for help except for a limited range walkie talkie, in the company of the purported guards—or blackmailers—who had been harassing me earlier. The head producer got excited and asked if I fantasized about being raped by black men. I was like, "What? No!" But it got stuck in his head and he started announcing repeatedly to everyone, "Gayle has a fantasy about being raped by black guys! She's obsessed by it!"

Taking a Technical on unlit roads at night to the UN camp near the airport—a prime spot for conflict—was insane, much like jumping off my hotel balcony in Nairobi. But again, it sort of made sense. So, I did it. A lovely satellite technician from Atlanta volunteered to come with me, not unlike a guy walking me back from a frat party but with higher stakes. Sandwiched between gunmen, we rode to the camp, bullets hurtling somewhere out in the darkness.

I did manage to speak with the colonel, who confirmed I was insane and told me to get back to safety. Elisa greeted me at the CNN villa with an emergency candle stuck in a cellophane-wrapped snack cake. Happy birthday to me. Christiane was doing live shots, so I went up to our cot and finally slept for the first time in days.

Over the weeks, we settled into the CNN villa and learned the names of the guards, most of whom seemed to be related to each other. We hired fishermen to bring us lobsters every day because they were plentiful along the coast. So, that's what I ate in the midst of a famine: lobster, some mac and cheese, crackers, and lots of dry British biscuits that tasted like sawdust. Somalis were still starving to death, but under the protection of UN troops, aid workers quickly began outfitting healthcare facilities and distributing fortified, nutritious food to those who needed it most.

The intervention was too late for many famine victims. One day, I was covering the head of the International Red Cross, Elizabeth Dole, as she toured a newly opened hospital in Mogadishu, making a heroic effort to stop by every patient in a long line of beds to give them hope and comfort. As she made her way down the line, I saw one of the men gasp his last breath and die. I pointed it out to a nurse, and she went up to him and pulled his blanket over his head. When Dole reached the covered figure, she was told he was sleeping. She nodded knowingly and gently laid her fingers at the end of his bed and whispered what I imagine was a prayer.

At least the new hospital was cool and clean. When we traveled out of the city, we encountered people lying on the ground in hovels, completely still, not even blinking. Aid workers were flowing into the country, but some victims were too far gone, too weak and fragile to eat. They had no access yet to IVs. I felt so powerless, unable to help them. The crew took video, then we packed up and moved on.

Once on the way back into the city, our CNN Technical stopped for gas—that is, jugs of gasoline in the back of the truck were unpacked and poured into the gas tank. In the field alongside the road, I spotted a bristly warthog, a trapezoid-shaped beast with a beefy head and shoulders sloping to a tight little rear end. It was the first wild animal I'd seen in Africa, and I was excited. The guard next to me got excited too, and raised his Kalashnikov, taking aim. He wasn't going to kill the warthog for food, just for amusement. I was able to gently tug his arm and beg him not to fire, giving the warthog a chance to disappear into the bush. The guard laughed that I wanted to save it, and we resumed our slow torturous ride back to Mogadishu along the remains of what had once been a paved road. I was happy for a moment, then horrified that I could save a wild animal but not a human dying of hunger.

The armed guards gave us the illusion of safety, but camera gear was routinely stolen. The thieves would take a $20,000 camera and then try to sell it back to the victims for a few thousand cash. The press corps collectively agreed that we would take the loss and refuse to pay for any stolen goods. If we were amenable to paying to get items back, then the next logical step would be for the thieves to take our people and hold them for ransom. It was not worth the risk.

I started doing on-air reports. I wore a turquoise T-shirt Elisa lent to me because everyone agreed my own clothes were drab and too large for me. I was relegated to doing mostly features. At Christmas, I went with two crews to cover the troops' holiday celebration. The soldiers in the US camp had fashioned a little Christmas tree with ornaments made out of items from their MREs, the shelf-stable meals known as Meals Ready to Eat. They had little bottles of hot sauce, Hershey's kisses, and sugar packets with garlands crafted from aluminum cans. Dinner was turkey, mashed potatoes, and gravy, all eaten while standing with their plates balanced on a plank.

For our own Christmas, CNN gifted everyone sarongs and champagne—which was a big deal because per Ted Turner's order we were never allowed to use company money on booze. The CNN guys laughed at the gifted sarongs, at first. Within a week pretty much all the men were wearing them, cool and comfortable.

Much of my time was spent on the tarmac at the reopened airport, where blasting hot jet fuel seared my lungs. I stumbled upon a US network sound tech who had been in Damascus and we reminisced about those lovely days waiting for a hostage release, when everyone played tennis and lounged by the hotel pool ordering room service. His face covered in grime and sweat, he looked at my similar state and declared, "It's payback time, baby."

I was pulled from Somalia the week after New Year but was sent back for a second round exactly a year later in December 1993, spending yet another birthday in Mogadishu. By then, CNN staff had moved with the rest of the press corps to a newly functioning hotel that was pockmarked with bullet holes and chunks of missing concrete. The rooms were like cells with thin single beds, but at least it was an upgrade from the shared cot.

We had a large workspace in a room on the hotel's top floor. A long table was covered with walkie talkies, magazines, playing cards, sunscreen, and ashtrays. No mobile phones yet, but the walkie talkies were more reliable than they had been the previous year when I made the nighttime run to the military camp by the airport. We also had satellite phones that came in their own custom suitcases that held mini satellite dishes, which allowed us to stay in contact with Atlanta.

Troops from each country in the UN coalition had set up individual camps with their own food, music, and activities. The espresso in the Italian military camp was legendary. The New Zealand forces were unflappable and exuded seasoned warrior vibes. The Americans were rigid, with a million rules that must be followed regardless of the circumstances.

In many ways, Somalia at the end of 1993 was more orderly. People were getting food. Businesses were starting to open. Schools established. The potholes were semi-filled. But for journalists, it seemed worse, more threatening. When we bumped and rumbled down the street in our Technicals, I could hear a menacing hiss from the impoverished people trudging next to us. I went out with Mary, to get video in an area of the city where there had been a lot of unrest. Mary set up her tripod and camera on the roof of the jeep so she could get a better view, while I stood on the pavement below. Suddenly, bullets started to whiz over our heads and I instinctively dived into the vehicle. Mary was so intent on taking video that she snapped at me for rocking the car when I rolled onto the floor, which messed up her shot. Our translator told us, "Oh, they are just trying to scare you!" To which I replied, "It's working."

One evening, automatic gunfire erupted within the walled parking area of the hotel. It was a violent fight. I crouched on the cool linoleum floor of our workspace, unsure what to do next. When dangerous things happen, everything feels like chaos in slow motion. Some people run, others freeze, and still others shout questions that no one can answer. This time was no different. There was no clear indication of what was happening or what was the best course of action. Do you run, hide, or just stay very still?

Eventually, the gunfire stopped and we ventured out warily. There had been a fight between our guards who were from one Somali faction against another faction, but no one was clear what started it. One of the CNN drivers had been shot in the head and was loaded into the back of an SUV. I crowded in the back seat with another CNN producer. The plan was to drive him to the US medical camp and hope they would take care of him at our behest. The back area of the SUV was filled with blood, and there appeared to be white bone chips. The man's brother had crawled next to him, and other men were hanging onto the vehicle as we raced to the field hospital, where the wounded worker was loaded onto a stretcher. The medics tried to see what they could do, which wasn't much of anything. He was already gone. The victim's brother and the other guards and drivers were back at work the next morning, eyes red and lips pursed.

Fortunately, I didn't have to spend another Christmas in Mogadishu. I went back to Cairo and celebrated with my friend James and our Italian colleague Ilaria, who loved covering Somalia. In the new year, Atlanta sent me to KwaZulu-Natal outside of Durbin, South Africa, to cover factional violence ahead of Nelson Mandela's election. A cameraman and I wound up traveling with the

South African Defense Force in a large military vehicle that was configured like a party bus. It had benches down the sides, but with bulletproof glass, thick metal sides, and tank treads instead of wheels. We encountered a firefight in a semi-rural area, where a few small dwellings nestled between green hills.

The cameraman got out with the armed forces to shoot video of the conflict, while I stayed in the safety of the bulletproof vehicle. Then the heavy door was yanked open and an officer shoved a prisoner in with me, then shut and locked it. The prisoner was young and strong and insane with anger, pulling on his zip tied hands and ankles with so much force they were coming loose. He was writhing between me and the door. I tapped on the thick glass trying to get the attention of the officers outside who were attempting to quell the violence. Tap. Tap. Tap. "Hello! Hey! Excuse me!" It was pathetic. Finally, the door was yanked open again for more prisoners, and I was able to leap out into the firefight and cower next to the vehicle with the cameraman. I couldn't win.

At day's end, the tank-like bus dropped us off at our five-star hotel in Durbin, perfectly illustrating the insane extremes of my life. I remember waving at a soldier sticking out of the top hatch as the military vehicle lumbered away on its massive treads, along with the evening rush hour traffic. When I got to my room, I had a message from Atlanta. Ilaria, the lovely Italian journalist whom I'd just seen with James in Cairo, had been assassinated in the middle of a Mogadishu street in an area considered a no-go region for Westerners. Her body was lying under the hot sun because it was too dangerous for UN soldiers to move in and pick her up. I called James to tell him.

My epiphany wasn't that day. It was nothing in particular, nothing that sudden. I just realized over the years of similar scrapes and dangerous interludes that I did not have the makings of a successful war correspondent. I was a talented journalist—I would win multiple awards for my reporting over the years, including an Emmy for our coverage of Somalia. Yet I hated guns and chaos, imminent danger, and narrow escapes. I wouldn't jostle a colleague aside to get in front of a camera or nag Steve to send me to the heart of war zones. I'd still go to dangerous places if needed, but I would stay as safe as possible on the sidelines. I'm not bold like Zenobia. Had I been in her situation, I would have settled in Palmyra and been a small footnote in history. I wouldn't cross that Rubicon.

SEVEN

SEXUALITY

We know a staggering amount about Zenobia's love life. It was a popular topic for historians, although we don't know how much of it is true. Her history was written by men, centuries after her death, based on source material that is now lost. Gossip about her sexual proclivities during her lifetime would have been skewed to fit the agendas of the men spreading it around the empire.

The Persian historian al-Tabarī , who wrote more than a half-century after Zenobia's death, recounted some revealing stories about the Syrian queen. In his telling, she was known as al-Zabba, which in Aramaic meant a woman with long hair. One tale is about her interactions with a powerful king known as Jadhīma, a name that indicated he suffered from leprosy. It's not recorded if he was missing digits or facial features from the dreaded disease, but he did not let his medical condition deter him from rising from his position as an advisor to kings to becoming a king himself. In al-Tabarī's legend, Jadhīma ruled the west bank of the Euphrates River in what is now Iraq. While establishing his territory, he fought a significant battle with the Syrian tribal leader Amr ibn Tharab ibn Hassan, which the historian identified as the father of Zenobia. Amr was slain in the fight; Jadhīma's kingdom was secured.

In al-Tabarī's version of events, after her husband died, Zenobia sent Jadhīma a message suggesting a possible marriage between the two leaders, claiming that she was concerned that women were weak and inefficient rulers, whereas he was a competent and powerful king. She laid it on thick. "Come to me, join my kingdom to yours," she suggested coyly.

Jadhīma was "delighted with her invitation and excited by her offer." Zenobia was reputedly a beautiful young woman and Palmyra was a fabulously rich city-state. What was not to love? Despite being responsible for the death of her father, the Iraqi king made plans to head east and unite with his intended bride. His advisors suggested caution, but Jadhīma was renowned for being naïve and a drunkard.

Zenobia dispatched a welcoming party that met him on the outskirts of the city with flattering messages and expensive gifts. Somehow, in the midst of the festivities, Jadhīma was separated from his guards and his horse as he was merrily escorted into the palace and taken before the queen. She was likely wearing her famed jewels and perfumed silken robes, looking beautiful and very rich. But upon greeting him, Zenobia opened her robe and revealed that she had a shockingly excessive amount of pubic hair. It was so copious that she had it braided—giving a new meaning to the name al-Zabba, woman with long hair.

"Do you see the concern of a bride?" she asked.

Jadhīma, likely realizing the marriage negotiations were hitting a roadblock, replied dramatically, "The limit has been reached; the moist ground has dried up, and I see a case of treachery." To which Zenobia shot back, "By my deity, we do not suffer from a lack of razors, or scarcity of barbers, but it is a custom of men (to shave), not women."

Al-Tabarī's version of history suggests Zenobia was not fit for marriage because of her brazen display of sexuality. For the Romans, Zenobia's unshaven, excessively thick pubic hair would be a barrier to having sex. Either way, sharing a bed, let alone a kingdom, was off the table. Instead, Zenobia plied her would-be husband with strong wine. Jadhīma was either really in need of a drink or realized the gig was up. Either way, he reportedly drank himself into a stupor, after which Zenobia's attendants were able to neatly slit his wrists with a man's razor and drain his blood into a large golden bowl. It's not clear if she was acting to avenge the death of her father, or if she was humiliated by his reaction to her naked body.

The ancients also had a lot of stories about Zenobia's ancestress, Cleopatra. The Egyptian queen wed her brother, seduced Julius Caesar and bore him an illegitimate son, then took up with his comrade Marc Antony and had another son and a pair of twins. During the Augustan era, she was widely depicted as promiscuous—an independent and wealthy female who turned the most powerful men of Rome into her personal sex slaves. One historian stated that Cleopatra had "insatiable passion and insatiable avarice."

And another wrote, she was a "whore queen" who enjoyed "trysts with her slaves" while seducing Rome's most revered leaders. But Roman histories were uniformly written by wealthy and educated men, writing for an audience of other wealthy and educated men. They viewed powerful wealthy women as objects of particular contempt. Not just Cleopatra, but other women who dared to enter the political realm. Berenice of Judea, Boudica of Great Britain, Helen of Troy, Dido of Carthage were all disparaged as sexually licentious.

Yet, oddly, Zenobia—the warrior queen who seized a third of the empire—was considered as chaste as an old-fashioned Roman matron. As a wife and mother, she was of course not a virgin. But she was the next closest thing; a circumspect widow who abstained from sex after the death of her husband. There is no evidence that she had liaisons with powerful Romans or her generals or her rivals or her slaves. No whiff of scandal.

In fact, rumor had it that she abstained from sex even when she was married to Odaenathus. One history has a remarkable passage about Zenobia's marital relations, or lack thereof:

> *Such was her continence; it is said that she would not know even her own husband save for the purpose of conception. For when once she had lain with him, she would refrain until the time of menstruation to see if she were pregnant; if not, she would again grant him an opportunity of begetting children.*

Sex solely for procreation was not the norm in antiquity—historians thought Zenobia's bedroom rules were unusual enough to mention repeatedly over several centuries of

published works. Why was she so rigid? She may have dis-
liked having sex with men in general. Or maybe she just
wasn't attracted to her older husband in particular, although
they traveled together on his campaigns, which suggests
they got along outside of the bedroom.

It's been suggested by modern historians that Zenobia
was uncomfortable sharing Odaenathus with other women.
We don't know if the king's earlier wife, the mother of his
original heir, was still living when he married Zenobia. But
plural marriages were common among Eastern male leaders and Odaenathus was known for pursuing other women.
Historians say that shortly after he and Zenobia wed, the
king confiscated the entire harem of the conquered Persian leader Shapur II. One historian wrote Odaenathus
"captured the Persian king's treasures and he captured, too,
what the Persian monarchs hold dearer than treasures,
namely his concubines." Another passage reiterates breathlessly that Odaenathus "captured Shapur's concubines and
also a great amount of booty."

Modern scholars are skeptical about whether that really
happened, especially those who study history from the Persian point of view. But what would have Zenobia thought
about her husband bringing home an entire harem of the
most beautiful women of Persia? It would have made the
women's quarters in the palace in Palmyra quite crowded,
not to mention awkward. The problem with ancient history is that we know so little about women's lives, thoughts,
and beliefs. We don't know if Zenobia would be appalled
by the capture of a harem or if she was indifferent. And we
don't know how the women of the harem felt—terrified,
or resigned, or perhaps even relieved to be free of con-
straints in a new city where women were allowed to be out

and about in public. It's possible too, they were ransomed and returned home. Their fate was deemed insignificant by historians of the day.

For whatever her reasons, Zenobia's restricted sex life was likely her choice, because Roman historians regarded her as an attractive woman. We have only a few portraits of what she looked like, including the profile with the melon hairstyle on the coin she minted when she conquered Egypt, and some stylized stone carvings within the ruins of Palmyra. But according to ancient historical sources, she was renowned for her great beauty. "So white were her teeth that many thought that she had pearls in place of teeth. Her face was dark and of a swarthy hue, her eyes were black and powerful beyond the usual wont, her spirit divinely great, and her beauty incredible." Another passage reminds us, once again, that she rode horses, which made her "strong and graceful."

After her husband's death, Zenobia was likely courted by neighboring kings and rulers who, like the legendary Jadhīma, would desire her wealth as well as her beauty. The most powerful male citizens of Palmyra were probably also angling for a possible partnership. But Zenobia kept her distance.

It is said that the queen escaped the summer heat of Palmyra by traveling to a new palace she had built near the Euphrates River. There she lived with her sister Zabibah and their respective children. It must have been a sumptuous palace since Zenobia inherited some of her ancestress's taste for the good life. One historian reported: "At her banquets, Zenobia used vessels of gold and jewels, and she even used those that had been Cleopatra's." However, her parties were likely more circumspect than those of the famed

Egyptian queen, who seduced Caesar by dissolving a price-less pearl in a golden goblet of wine and then drinking it.

The same historian notes: "As servants she had eunuchs of advanced age." So not only were the servants castrated, but they were also elderly. Zenobia was taking no chances that even a breath of scandal would impugn her reputation as a chaste matron. She made it clear she was not inter-ested in sharing either her empire or her bed.

The public concern about women's chastity has continued through the centuries. When I lived in the Middle East, sex before marriage was still taboo and mar-ried women were expected to not only be monogamous, but circumspect around other men. Many, but not all, women in Cairo wore a headscarf known as a *higab* that covered their hair but not their faces, a symbol of their piety and propriety. In the rest of the Arab world the scarf is known as a *hijab*, but Egyptians turn the soft "j" letter into a hard "g." Women didn't wear the *higab* when they were at home with family, but if an unrelated male stopped by, even an old family friend, women grabbed their headscarves.

I almost never wore a *higab*, except occasionally in Saudi Arabia; it wasn't really expected of Western women. But one time in Syria, I attended a press conference called by Iranian officials. As we entered the room, an assistant was busy ripping a dirty velvet curtain into strips and handing them to the female reporters, ordering us to cover our hair. We were momentarily unsure what to do until a wonderful Western male reporter grabbed a strip of velvet and put it on his own head. Other male colleagues followed suit in solidarity with the women. The officials huffed in exaspera-tion, but we proceeded with the press conference.

The *higab*, and in some countries an accompanying face veil known as the *niqab*, have been a controversial political and social issue in the Middle East for many years, and each Islamic country has their own rules and expectations. In Egypt through the 1990s, I saw more and more women in Cairo adopting the *higab*, old and young, even though it was not required by law and modern Egyptian women had been going without it for decades. I knew some Egyptian women who surprised me by showing up in a *higab*, then a few years later returning to their previous decision to do without. It was a personal choice, especially in wealthier urban families. In the countryside, both men and women usually wore scarves and turbans. Women in antiquity also covered their hair with a veil or scarf when they were outside of their homes, probably more for practical than religious reasons. The region is sunny with patchy shade, so covering up makes sense.

There were other customs practiced by Egyptian women in the 1990s that may have been similar to those from ancient times. It was considered forbidden, or *haram*, for a woman of any age or marital status to be alone in a room with a man who was not her husband or a close family member. Some observe this rule even in America, such as former Vice President Mike Pence who would not have a meal alone with any woman other than his wife. Zenobia's castrated older servants were probably the only males whom she would encounter without a chaperone.

Ancient Romans were not as obsessed with female virginity as other civilizations in antiquity, but a bridegroom still expected to be his wife's first and only partner. Eastern cultures, such as Syria, placed more importance on the bride's chastity, tying it to religious significance and family honor. Centuries later, when I was in the Middle East, the virginity of girls was closely guarded by their families. It was a catastrophe for a young woman to lose it before marriage.

There was a story reported in the local Egyptian papers of a young woman who had rejected a potential suitor. Outraged, he followed her onto a public bus, wrestled her to the ground, and shoved his fingers under her dress to digitally penetrate her. It was a public outrage, and yet I was struck at the reaction of her family. It was shame. Her mother refused to cooperate with police and reportedly burned her daughter's bloodied underwear in an attempt to hide the evidence. The victim's family was terrified that their daughter would no longer be considered a virgin after the assault, limiting her ability to marry someone else. The scorned suitor knew exactly what he was doing.

I was sometimes asked if I was a virgin by the people I was interviewing, or sometimes by random shopkeepers. They weren't crude. They asked in a coded way; was I a *bint*, which means unmarried daughter, and therefore a virgin, or was I *niswan*, Egyptian dialect for a married woman or previously married woman, and therefore not a virgin.

In the first few months after I arrived in Cairo, I lived with Jenny in the apartment with the weasel near the American University of Cairo. I was new to the ways of Egypt, and especially new to the ways of our doormen, the *bowabs*. One night, I walked home with a guy I kind of liked. The breeze was warm and I was wearing a little necklace made of fragrant jasmine blooms that I'd purchased from a street vendor. The scent was intoxicating, and when we got to my apartment, we kissed on the front steps before parting. The next morning, the building's *bowab* appeared

at my apartment door. My Arabic was next to non-existent at that point, but I came to understand that he was
going to tell my landlady that he saw me kissing someone on the street. Confused, I shrugged and said "*mashi*,"
meaning, "Okay, cool." He looked at me dumbfounded.
"*Mashi?*" "Really?" His fury was palpable. Later, I realized
that he wanted *baksheesh* to withhold this incredibly damning information from my landlady. He was shocked that I
kissed a man in public, and more shocked that I didn't care
he saw me, and horrified that I didn't care if others knew.

All unmarried young Egyptians were expected to
abstain from sex, meaning it was technically *haram* for
boys as well as girls. Jenny met an Egyptian boy during
those first months in Egypt. She wanted to live with him,
so they got married and she moved into his family's tiny
apartment with his deaf mother and young sisters in one
of the poorer, more populated areas of the city. There was
no way she and Ahmed could have shared a bed without
a wedding. When I traveled with a boyfriend years later, I
wore a gold wedding ring so that we could get a hotel room
together. In fact, I wore a gold band pretty much all of
the time. It was easier than explaining I was an unmarried
thirty-something and juggling the question of whether I
was a *bint* or *niswan*.

The gender rules may seem rigid and confining, but in
many ways, they were there for the protection of women.
Just as Westerners pity women in the Middle East, many
Egyptians I met pitied American women who are left as
single mothers without financial support. It was incon-
ceivable to them that a man could have sex with a woman
and then skip town, leaving her to struggle on her own.
Yes, it is true a man in Islam can end his marriage by

turning toward Mecca and declaring three times that he is divorcing his wife. But he would have to bear the financial consequences. A divorced woman is legally entitled to a significant sum of money and jewelry given to her by the groom's family before the wedding. This is a dowry meant to safeguard her financial security if her husband leaves her or dies. In Egypt, the traditional gifts also include a furnished apartment so she has a place to live. In the 1990s, there were many single young men in Egypt desperately trying to come up with the money, and the apartment, so that they could get married, have sex, and have children.

Women can initiate divorce also but must go through the courts. The rationale is to protect a man from being fleeced by an unscrupulous woman, or her family, looking for a quick fortune. In contrast, a man can divorce quickly, but he must pay the price. A check and balance. It did not always work out equitably, but that was the intent.

Same for plural marriages. Men can marry up to four wives concurrently, but I met very few who did so, because it was expensive. All wives are entitled to equal housing and equal assets. In addition, some marriage contracts expressly prevent the groom from taking other wives in the future without the permission of the first wife. Ideally, the custom of plural marriage prevents women from being a castoff mistress who wasted the best years of her life on a married man, or the long-devoted wife ending up divorced and ashamed.

It's possible Zenobia may have approved of Odaenathus enjoying the Persian harem. In Jordan, I met a Bedouin with three wives and an economically advantageous flock of many sheep. Each wife had a cinderblock house, facing each other in a U-shaped compound. The two older wives assured me that they were very happy with the arrangement. I can't remember their precise words, but the gist was that they no longer wanted to sleep with their husband and were grateful that the youngest wife took a hit for the team. The youngest wife then jokingly suggested I could marry him and be the fourth wife, therefore relieving her of the burden. The small kitchen reverberated with laughter.

Not everyone was on board with plural marriages though—probably in antiquity as well as today. One of the older daughters of the Bedouin family was engaged to a nice young man, who was visiting the compound. He clearly adored her, and they were giddy with excitement, talking about their upcoming marriage. I asked her if she would be okay with her husband someday taking another wife, and you could see the cloud cross her lovely face. She forced a smile and nodded, saying it would be fine. Then looked anxiously at her intended. He met her gaze with a look of love and reassurance. Surrounded by her traditional polygamous family, they couldn't say it out loud, but in that exchange was a promise that they both would stay true to each other. I could see the relief wash across her face.

Despite the prohibitions against sex outside of marriage, the Egyptians I met seemed to be open about sexuality in a way that I found surprising, if not shocking. Sex within marriage was no-holds-barred and discussed publicly with gusto. Married women would sometimes interject during a casual conversation that they were achy from the pounding they got the night before. There were lingerie shops throughout downtown Cairo, with windows displaying brightly colored lace bras, corsets, and peek-a-boo nighties. Behind the glass you could see customers, most wearing *higab*, happily plowing through the hangers and laughing with friends and family. In some shops, a mannequin in the window would have a scarf covering her plastic head, while clad from the neck down in a double-D bra and silk tap pants.

I suspect, though, that for some women, sex was mainly for procreation, just as it was for Zenobia. One Friday morning, I was in an apartment filled with women in a provincial Egyptian town. Amr and Ali were filming in the mosque next door, where the men of the family were attending Friday prayers. As usual, the women quizzed me about my unmarried state as they bustled around the kitchen. They all agreed that being single was nicer than being married, but you had to be married to have children, and children were the most important thing in the world, so it was better to be married than single. But being a wealthy widow was best, because then you had children and money, but no husband. They pronounced this as the ideal scenario for a woman.

That's where Zenobia found herself after the death of Odaenathus. She had wealth, children, and no obligation to have sex at a proscribed time of the month. Perhaps like the Virgin Queen Elizabeth I of England, remaining single and sex-free helped her secure her power base. Factions wouldn't become anxious and antagonistic if she married a rival. Distant rulers couldn't upend the balance of regional power by uniting their kingdoms with hers. And after what happened to Jadhīma, who could blame them for staying in their lanes? Without a husband or lovers to take up her time, Zenobia could concentrate on attending to her subjects and expanding her domains. She'd also benefited from being lauded as an exemplary woman, not only by her own subjects but throughout the empire. As one Roman historian noted with approval, "Generous with prudence, she conserved her treasures beyond the wont of women."

Being a chaste widow may have been both a political as well as personal choice. Or, there may have been a more devastating reason she abstained from sex.

EIGHT

CIRCUMCISION

When my Arabic language tutor was born, her parents were disappointed that she was a girl. So they named her Mufeeda, which means "useful." When she became a teenager, she began to call herself Hanan, a beautiful and popular Egyptian name that means "kindness." When I wasn't traveling, Hanan came over to my apartment several times a week to teach me Arabic.

Hanan's aunt also came to help clean once a week, sometimes bringing her teenage daughter Saniya. Like most Egyptian parents, the aunt was called "mother of Saniya"—*Um Saniya*—after the name of her firstborn child. Saniya would pretend to study from a textbook as her mother bustled around my apartment making tea and flicking a rag at dust, causing it to float into the air and slowly settle elsewhere. I would later offer to pay for Saniya to continue her schooling, but she dropped out when she became a teenager.

Hanan, Saniya, and Um Saniya lived together with a dozen other family members in a small apartment in one of the poorest neighborhoods in the city. Hanan spoke no English and had no formal background as a teacher. She was just a gentle, sweet, open soul and it was a pleasure to sit with her a few times a week and try to communicate in a very specific Cairo-based dialect of Egyptian Arabic. I also studied classical Arabic with other teachers and could read Arabic script, but I was only ever semi-fluent in the urban slangy dialect taught to me by Hanan.

One day, several years after I had been in the country, Hanan mentioned that her younger, twelve-year-old sister was getting circumcised that weekend. It took me a while to understand what she was saying. With the help of a few pantomime gestures, I realized they were planning to cut off the child's clitoris. Trying to hide my horror, I asked if they could perhaps not do that. Hanan laughingly explained that all women in Egypt were circumcised.

"*Kullu*? All of them?" I asked in disbelief.

Yes, all of them, Hanan confirmed. All girls in Egypt were circumcised. Muslim and Christian. It was a necessity. It was for their own good.

I tried to counter her argument by saying it wasn't necessary—that *I* was not circumcised, and I was okay. But I realized that to Hanan, I was *not* okay. I was never married, living alone, and was not a *bint*, or virgin. She would be horrified if her sister ended up like me. My argument therefore did not sway Hanan against circumcision; rather, in her mind, it reinforced its necessity.

Over the next year or so, I tried to find out more about female circumcision in Egypt. There didn't seem to be any experts, any academic reports, or much available data at all.

A representative from the Ministry of Health looked at me askance when I asked about it and gave me a puzzled shrug. But, over time, I learned from friends, and friends of friends, that female circumcision was indeed pretty much universal in Egypt and likely had been for centuries.

Most Egyptian Muslim families thought, or assumed, it was a religious practice. But there is no tradition of circumcision in Islam, and only rarely practiced in a few other Arab countries. Coptic Christian families in Egypt were circumcising their daughters as well, and some historians I spoke with believed it was a holdover from ancient Pharaonic times. We know circumcision was practiced in ancient Egypt because circumcised female mummies have been found dating back to the fifth century BC. Ancient Romans were also reported to have cut the genitalia of female slaves to prevent pregnancies and it may even have been practiced in Syria at the time of Zenobia's birth, which could explain her reputed antipathy toward sex.

It seems astounding that circumcision could continue in Egypt for more than 2,000 years, but when I first arrived in Cairo in the early 1990s there were still older married couples who were said to be biologically brother and sister, holdovers from the practice of brother-sister marriages that had been established by Cleopatra's royal family as a strategy to consolidate wealth and power. Such marriages were extremely rare but apparently continued into the early twentieth century before completely dying out.

There are varying degrees of female circumcisions, also known as female genital mutilation, and Egyptians mostly practiced the least invasive. Basically, they snipped off the tip of the clitoris; rarely would they remove it entirely. Girls had the procedure done sometime after age six but before they turned fourteen and were usually feted with a little party after they recovered. It was a common rite of passage in wealthy families and nearly universal among the poor, yet it was rarely addressed. Decades earlier, the Egyptian Ministry of Health had banned public health workers from performing circumcisions, but few people seemed aware of this older decree. Sometimes the procedure was done in a private clinic or in a doctor's office, but more often it was performed at home by a local barber or midwife with clippers or a knife.

Egyptian families adore their children. Female circumcision was common because parents thought they were doing something good for their daughters, helping them overcome the stresses and pitfalls of adolescence. It was widely believed that without circumcision, girls would become troubled as they sexually matured. The clitoris would be stimulated by everyday activities, such as walking in nylon underwear or bending over as they did chores, and they would become wanton and out of control and therefore easy victims for unscrupulous men. The families knew nothing of the serious health consequences of the practice—the risks of infection, difficulty in giving birth, mental anguish, painful intercourse—or that someday their adult daughters would not fully enjoy sex with their partners. The idea that their daughters should be able to climax was not really on their radar.

There were several young producers cycling in and out of the CNN bureau over the years, mostly journalism students from the American University in Cairo. I'd asked one of these young Egyptian journalists if she could find a family that would be willing to let us shoot video of their daughter getting the procedure. It felt like a wild request, but she came back with several willing families over the months that followed. The circumstances or timing, though, were never quite right. Some parents demanded monetary compensation, which immediately ruled them out. CNN never paid for stories. Mary and I were also traveling a lot that year. We spent months in South Africa for the election of Nelson Mandela, then I went to Jerusalem to help out with coverage of Yassir Arafat, who became president of the Palestinian Authority following his return to Gaza. Our office assistant, Salah, had an engagement party that nixed one possible date, and another time we had to cancel when the CNN car we leased from Video Cairo randomly caught fire while I was out shopping.

Finally, in August, we all were in the Cairo bureau as we prepared for the major United Nations' International Conference on Population and Development that was scheduled to be held in Egypt in early September. The young producer had found a family that was planning to have their daughter circumcised on a Saturday afternoon, so we loaded up the new unscorched CNN car and headed to a populous neighborhood of Sayeda Zaynab—which coincidentally, is the Arabic version of the name Zenobia.

We arrived at a squat apartment building on a dusty street and made our way upstairs to a very small apartment. Walls were painted the ubiquitous dull green found in many Cairene homes, with the standard framed photos of late relatives hung next to calendars adorned with beautiful Arab women touting face creams. Negla was ten years old and a typical little Egyptian girl; thin limbed with large brown eyes. Her curly dark hair was pulled back and she wore her best dress for the occasion, a purple flowered skirt attached to a black bodice, topped with a fussy white ruffled collar. She was apprehensive but exceedingly polite as she was brought forward to greet us.

Her parents were older; I'd mistaken them for her grandparents. Her older siblings, a teenaged boy and a girl, were there, too. The room was crowded as Mary with her camera gear, the young producer, and I wedged between the brown couch and the dining area. The barber was at the table, making a show of cleaning his implements on a plastic tablecloth. He looked unshaven and grimy, wearing a dirty shirt, and he didn't bother to wash his hands. He introduced himself as Hagg Omar, with "Hagg" being an Egyptian title of respect given to men who had made the pilgrimage, or the *Hajj*, to Mecca. There was another man with him to help with the procedure but I was never sure if he was a family member or an assistant brought by the barber.

Things seemed to move at warp speed. The mother gave the barber an old lilac-patterned sheet that he ripped into strips. They lifted Negla's dress and tied the strips around her narrow waist, with a strip hanging down the back. At some point, her underwear came off and she was pulled into the lap of the assistant, facing the seated barber. The barber had the man hold the ankles of her thin little legs above her head, forming a V.

Mary jostled with her camera to find a position that wasn't graphically inappropriate, so we crowded behind her into the apartment's entryway. Negla's family assembled across the room, smiling and laughing and trying to keep the little girl's spirits up as she started to panic. The barber moved fast. It was hard to see exactly how he clipped her exposed genitals, but Negla's shrieks told the story. High-pitched and heartbreaking. Hagg Omar scoffed and punched her gently in the leg as he placed a cloth on the wound and pulled the strips of sheet up between her legs to form a sort of diaper. "Shame on you," he admonished her. "It's all over. You can go out and play now."

The two men got Negla to her feet, but she was shaking violently and crying and would have collapsed had they not held her up as Hagg Omar finished the bandaging process. Then this little girl did something I'd never seen an Egyptian child do, ever. She faced her family and screamed at them, "*Haram Alaikum!*"—one of the most damning phrases you can level at a Muslim. "Shame upon you." But it meant more than that; it meant you've sinned by doing something reprehensible and un-Islamic. She screamed again as her parents and siblings stood open-mouthed in shock. "*Haram Alaikum, kul wahid!*" meaning "Shame upon you, *every one of you!*" I knew that I was included in that curse. I was standing there with Mary filming this abomination.

We interviewed Hagg Omar while Negla was put to bed. He was confident he'd just done a good deed and was proud of his profession. He claimed he circumcised one thousand girls a year and he was a professional, just like his father before him. "It's a tradition, a cleansing," he insisted. "Some girls come to me with big clitorises, which creates friction. That girl gets hot and excited, she's boiling. But when you take away the sensitivity[,] that goes away and she becomes normal."

Negla moaned and cried, lying on her parents' big double bed under a light sheet. Her family tried to remain upbeat, but I could tell they were rattled by Negla's reaction. Her older sister, on camera, told us she, too, had been terrified when she was circumcised years earlier.

Her mother reached around and punched her in the arm, so she quickly added with a perky smile: "It's a tradition. We're used to it."

Mary shot a few more images of Negla, whose severed tissue was wrapped in gauze and tied to her wrist, another custom. Her best friend had been called in to help out. Having been circumcised herself a year earlier, the young friend sat by Negla's head and stroked her brow, sweetly murmuring words of sympathy and encouragement. Negla's parents and siblings were gathered at the end of the bed, trying hard to lighten the mood. They clapped and ululated, a distinct piercing sound of celebration Arab women make by vibrating their tongues while exhaling. "Don't be a brat," they tried to tease her playfully. "It's over. Be brave!" But Negla was having none of it. In front of us, she screamed again at her father: "I want you to know, Daddy, that I didn't want this! And you did it to me!" She closed her eyes and sobbed.

We clattered back down the stairs to the street and loaded up the car in a daze. I'm not sure what I had been expecting, but what we had just witnessed was not it. Mary lit up a cigarette and slumped in the back seat. Not for the first time, I wished I smoked, too. Hagg Omar was hanging out by the front doorway and approached us to ask for money for his cooperation. He'd asked before, and our producer explained again that we could not give him or the family any compensation. It was against CNN policy. He was handed a cigarette as an appeasement, and he skulked away.

We had talked before about doing a standup where I would narrate part of the story in front of the camera to show that I was present at the scene. But I nixed that. It seemed somehow jarring to have a Western woman with blonde hair and a blazer inserted in this incredibly intimate Egyptian story. So, we went back to the bureau to log the video and translate the soundbites. I wrote up a script, recorded the narration, and signed off with my usual, "Gayle Young, CNN Cairo." An editor who had come from Atlanta for the UN conference took Mary's incredibly shot video and turned it into an incredibly well-edited story.

We knew it was a powerful piece of reporting but were not prepared for the repercussions.

That week, I'd moved from my apartment into the Hilton Hotel on the Corniche el Nil to be with the rest of the CNN staff flying in from across the globe for the UN population conference. Heads of state were in town, with top academics, international health officials, sociologists, and lots of press. A teaser was running on CNN to hype that the conference was being covered by Christiane Amanpour, UN correspondent Richard Roth, and me. Seeing my name and face up there with CNN's top correspondents was like a banner that I was legit. I'd pre-recorded and edited a number of video packages on population and social issues that CNN would broadcast during the conference coverage, including the female circumcision story.

It aired September 7th. Christiane was anchoring from Cairo and introduced the story with a warning that it would be difficult for some viewers to watch. The master control technicians in Atlanta hit play and Negla's circumcision was beamed via satellites across the world. It replayed every hour for most of the day.

This was before the internet, so it is difficult to say that it went viral, but suddenly everyone was talking about that story. Christiane and I both spent the day fielding calls from other journalists and social activists, along with calls from Atlanta to discuss concerns raised by the multitude of viewers who were calling the network. The *Washington Post* reported that a congresswoman from Maryland, who was attending the UN conference, was so sickened by the video that she confronted President Hosni Mubarak about it during a high-level breakfast meeting. Christiane then followed through with an exclusive interview with Mubarak in which he stumbled while answering her questions, and claimed he was unaware of the practice. He was horrified and embarrassed.

The following morning, I was awakened before dawn by the phone ringing in my hotel room. Egyptian police had moved in overnight and arrested Negla's father, the barber Hagg Omar, his assistant, and my poor young female freelance producer. Every Egyptian on the CNN Cairo staff was visited, grilled by *mukhabarat* intelligence agents, and threatened with jail. One of our CNN producers, Khalid, who was Jenny's newest husband, left his home to hide from the police because he was a Lebanese citizen and feared deportation. No one approached me or Mary, the only Americans involved in the story, perhaps because we were staying in the Hilton and they didn't want to cause a scene.

The Egyptian government was mortified by the story. They were proud to host the UN conference and to spotlight the advances they had made in population control and social services, but Negla's heartbreaking screams of betrayal seemed to shatter their image overnight. I was told that in an extraordinary move, the Egyptian government made an official complaint to the State Department. Under the gun, my CNN Atlanta bosses called me out.

I tirelessly repeated how the story came about, how we found the family, how they voluntarily agreed to let us film. When we first arrived at Negla's apartment, we had videotaped ourselves speaking with the family, identifying that we were from CNN and asking her parents' permission to record. One CNN lawyer wanted to know if we had asked Negla herself if she was okay with our presence, and I choked. Like her parents, I was not trying to hurt her. Yet here we were.

My top boss, Eason, told me that CNN was hiring an investigator to uncover every facet of the story. He said something like, "If we discover that they were paid anything, even a small amount, even if you didn't know about it, you understand your employment with CNN is terminated." I gulped. I would never tolerate any compensation exchanged for a CNN story, but I worried that one of the Egyptians working for us might have doled out some customary *baksheesh* behind my back. However, the investigator would later conclude the family did not receive compensation. According to the Egyptian press, Negla's father confirmed that he had voluntarily invited us to his home for what he considered a family celebration. He told Egyptian reporters he was confused by the uproar because everyone circumcised their daughters, and he didn't believe he had done anything wrong.

Still, the Egyptian press condemned us for making Egypt look bad in the eyes of the world. The non-Egyptian press condemned us for videotaping a child in distress and doing nothing to stop the abuse. A headline in the Post read: *When Journalists Witness Atrocities* over a story about the ethics of filming Negla without intervening. But other opponents of female genital mutilation argued that exposing the painful reality of the process would ultimately spur efforts to end the practice.

Over time, the activists were proven correct. Within a little more than a week, the Grand Mufti Sheikh Mohammed Sayed Tantawi, Rector of Al-Azhar University in Cairo and a leading cleric in Sunni Islam worldwide, announced he would support a ban on female circumcision if doctors confirmed that it was harmful to Muslim women. Later, the Egyptian president's wife, Suzanne Mubarak, took up the cause and launched education campaigns and efforts to enforce an end to the practice. After the death of a young girl in 2007, the government officially banned female circumcision and started prosecuting those who broke the law.

Before our story aired in 1994, estimates suggested more than 90 percent of Egyptian girls were being circumcised. Today, that number is estimated to be less than 15 percent. The move against circumcision would have evolved in any event, but several academic works cite our CNN report as the catalyst for change.

I thought often of Negla and wished I could make it up to her, to fund her education or pay for therapy. But to do so would be regarded as compensating her for the story, so my hands were tied. Many years later, James showed me an interview with Negla in an Egyptian magazine. She was in high school by then. She stated she hated that we had filmed her, but that no one on her street or in her school knew that she was the subject of the CNN report since none of them had seen it. With this anonymity, she was able to live her life more or less normally. She had plans for continuing her education and seemed to be doing well. At the end of the interview, she said she was against circumcision and hoped it would be abolished. She vowed that if she ever had daughters, she would protect them from having the procedure.

As for me, my career teetered in the balance for longer than I would have liked. Overnight, Egyptians on the street went from welcoming us to despising us. CNN was the very first English-language network to be aired in Egypt, and for years we had enjoyed a fame that opened doors. Everyone knew and loved CNN, and they had been excited to speak with us. But now, CNN was regarded as evil, un-Islamic, and anti-Egypt. We removed the CNN logo from our car and when vigilantes accosted us, asking where we were from, we'd truthfully explain we were Cable News Network. Unfamiliar with the full network name, they would let us pass. It wasn't just our CNN crew—all of the international press suffered harassment. The Egyptian newspapers published stories of people vowing to attack American journalists and smash their cameras in retaliation.

Ed Turner and my boss Steve Cassidy flew to Cairo at the end of September to meet with Egyptian officials in an attempt to ease the situation. Ed was CNN's executive vice president and one of the first people CNN founder Ted Turner had hired in 1980 to run the fledgling network. The meetings Ed and Steve held with Egypt's top ministers helped make amends, but it was decided to discreetly get me out of town. Over the next few months, I bounced between Kuwait, Jerusalem, Damascus, Moscow, London, and the US. Then in February I took an extended assignment in New Delhi. It was an effective strategy by CNN. They were refusing pressure to officially remove me as Cairo bureau chief while still pulling me out of a heated situation long enough to appease the government. I was grateful for their support, and for the opportunity to live in India for a while. Our assistant Salah moved into my apartment to care for my cats, and my bureau office was taken over by James, who reported in my absence. Mary, too, was dispatched on assignments all over the map. We went dark.

By the end of 1995, passions had cooled enough for me to resume reporting from Cairo, although I never again lived in Egypt for any significant stretch of time. A gadfly Egyptian lawyer had filed a lawsuit against CNN for millions of dollars. Apparently, making Egypt look bad was technically considered treason.

One evening, more than a year after the circumcision story aired, James and I went to an Egyptian wedding in the countryside. It was a beautiful night with lanterns hanging from trees, and the female guests had turned out in their most colorful dresses. There were tables of sweet Sport Cola and piles of cookies. A troupe of musicians arrived with bendir drums and thin reedy trumpets—musical instruments that have been used since the time of the pharaohs. Belly dancing is ubiquitous in Egypt, and everyone does it. Men, women, children, old people. Just tie a sash around a random person's waist and they would start dancing, with encouragement from a boisterous crowd clapping in unison.

There is a little-known, and fairly uncommon, ritual in Egypt called the *layla al-dachor*, or "night of entrance." To ensure the bride is a virgin, the groom's mother or a female family member will wrap a white cloth around her index finger to see if the bride's hymen bleeds. Many women confided that since they know the test is unreliable, women from both families will help ensure there is some blood, not necessarily from the bride, on the cloth they show the men.

Having a great time at the wedding, James and I wondered aloud if we could film the ritual. We weren't serious. Still, a young English-speaking journalist overheard, and went off to ask the families if they would mind. He came back excitedly to say they were agreeable to letting an all-female CNN crew join them and videotape the event. I was floored. James and I looked at each other in horror, then burst out with inappropriate laughter. Again? No. No. Never again.

NINE

RELIGION

Jerusalem had been ruled by the Romans for centuries but became part of Odaenathus's realm as he gained power. The city's Jewish population had always chafed under occupation and struggled for self-rule, so it was not surprising that, after Odaenathus had died, a Jewish patriot was caught rebelling against Zenobia as she strengthened her hold over the region. The defiant patriot was captured and sentenced to death, but before his execution, two Jewish envoys arrived before the queen to plead his case. They argued that the prisoner was an honored rabbi traumatized by the death of his brother, who had died years earlier when Odaenathus first seized Jerusalem. They showed Zenobia the sword used to kill the prisoner's brother and asked that she spare his life. Zenobia recognized that sword—it belonged to her late husband. He was the one who had killed the prisoner's brother. She relented and set the rebel free.

The story comes from a brief passage in the Jewish Talmud and has been cited by some scholars who believe Zenobia might have been Jewish herself. They cite archeological evidence that shows the city of Palmyra had a vibrant Jewish community that included at least one synagogue. Jewish inscriptions have also been found in the remains of several homes and on funerary monuments, suggesting that the population was large and prosperous. Zenobia was also protective of the Jews who lived in Egypt during her rule. An engraving found in Cairo states that Zenobia granted refugee status to a synagogue so that Jews could have a safe haven from persecution. Even Saint Athanasius, a leading figure in early Christianity, stated she was Jewish in one of the many letters he wrote in the century after her death.

Others have suggested that Zenobia was actually a Christian. Syria was a hotbed of early Christian development in the centuries following Christ's crucifixion. The Apostle Paul was converted on a trip to Damascus and went on to spread the religion throughout the region, building the first Christian church in Antioch. Two hundred years later, Zenobia gave her protection to Paul of Samosata. He was a controversial bishop in Antioch who was slated to be deposed for heresy, but Zenobia overruled his condemnation.

Even Muslims have claimed Zenobia, although she lived three centuries before the birth of the Prophet Muhammad and the founding of Islam. She was however part of the pre-Islamic Arab world and was a respected historic figure. Both a wife and a daughter of the Prophet were named Zaynab, the Arabic version of Zenobia.

However, as a member of a nomadic Syrian family, Zenobia would have presumably worshipped her own community's gods. The Canaanite religion that dominated the

Middle East in her era had many regional variations, but most Canaanite gods were humanoid in form but linked to lions, bulls, camels, and other important animals within Syria. The gods were in control of major forces such as the weather, fertility, money, and military success. There are remains of temples in Palmyra dedicated to Aglibol the moon god, who was symbolized by a calf—hence the golden calf of biblical fame. The many images of camels carved throughout Palmyra are testament to the god Arsu, who protected caravans.

When I visited Palmyra, I loved spending time in the Temple of Baalshamin, a god of the sky. Four intact Corinthian columns framed a massive doorway. Inside, there was a curved altar along the entire back wall, set with smaller Corinthian columns. The floor was paved with marble, and sunbeams from high windows allowed small trees and plants to take root within the sanctuary, garlands of vivid green leaves against the warm brown stone.

There would have been a statue representing the god on the altar and perhaps benches and cushions along the walls. There were probably metal tripods for burning incense, the smoke curling gently to the ceiling, releasing scents of sandalwood and amber. Temples were calm and relaxing spaces—stirring music played on a lyre, soothing water, aromatic plants, chanted affirmations that have been lost to history. During feasts, the faithful ate roasted meat from sacrificed animals and drank wine together.

Syrians went to temples to ask the gods for their intervention in return for a prayer. They offered gifts; flowers for the altar, some coins, fresh figs, or perhaps a sacrificial animal such as a goat or sheep. It was a comfort to feel somewhat in control of life's challenges, as if it was possible to strike a bargain with fate. They believed that if they were pious the rain would come and fill the cistern, or the caravan that took their investment would soon return with earnings doubled, or that the fever gripping a favorite daughter would soon abate. Adherents came to meet friends and family, to gossip, to reaffirm their identity with their tribe. As a monarch, Zenobia would be a link between her people and their gods. She would have been regarded as half-divine, with one foot on the ground like a mortal and one foot in a celestial realm that elevated her above mere humans. She was a conduit for their bargains with the deities.

The citizens of Palmyra, with their many Canaanite temples, made room in their city for other religions, as well. It was a crossroad linking east and west, north and south. Merchants from Persia and India flooded into Palmyra, trading with people from Rome and Gaul. The Illyrians would have been bartering with Egyptians. Zenobia was familiar with many religions and included all of them in her empire. It was a benevolent, albeit shrewd, move common in antiquity. Religious tolerance appeased conquered subjects, allowing them to contentedly worship as they pleased as long as they acknowledged her as their ruler.

The Middle East today remains an epicenter of diverse religions. In Jerusalem, Jews gather to pray at the holiest site in Judaism, the Western Wall. The beautiful edifice of limestone blocks is all that remains of their holiest temple, which was destroyed by the Romans in 70 AD. It sits below the Dome of the Rock, where a blue and gold mosque encloses one of the holiest sites of Islam, a flat rock where it is believed the prophet Muhammad ascended to heaven. Nearby, the Church of the Holy Sepulchre is built on what is believed to be the site of Christ's crucifixion.

During my early twenties, I spent a summer in Jerusalem as a volunteer for an archeological dig called the "City of David," which was located on a sloping hill behind the walled Old City. I'd been intrigued by Jerusalem when I first visited during my backpacking adventure and had even studied some Hebrew. I always loved to be invited to a seder, the traditional Passover meal that celebrates the Jewish community, its history, its resilience, and its great food. My mother, a worrier and a Catholic, was convinced I was planning to convert to Judaism.

I stayed in a youth hostel in Mea She'arim, one of the oldest and most religious Jewish neighborhoods. Every morning, I'd wake before dawn for the long walk to the archeological site, entering the walled Old City through a giant stone archway on one side, continuing through narrow cobblestone passageways, and exiting on the opposite side through the Dung Gate. The dig would already be underway on the sloping hill below the walls, even though the sun was just breaking over the olive trees on the opposite side of the valley. It remains my favorite city.

After I joined CNN, I went to Israel frequently to help with coverage of the Intifada, the Arab uprising against Israeli restrictions in areas such as Gaza and the West Bank. Jewish families were moving into lands occupied by Palestinians and tensions were running high. One evening I found myself in a field next to a small stone house that looked like it could have dated back to Zenobia's time. There was a gang of youths. Their New York accents were strong and they spoke English, not Hebrew. They were ripping out olive saplings and stomping on the roots while singing and hugging, rejoicing that this was their land, given to them by God. The Palestinian family that had fled the house was gathered a short distance away, in tears, clutching paperwork they eagerly showed me, saying it proved their family had owned the land for many generations, hundreds of years. But, it was useless now.

In my mid-twenties, after the archeological dig in Jerusalem, I moved to Jamaica—and my mother feared I would become a Rastafarian. Such warm, gentle, and mellow people. Of course, the ganja helped.

One night I went to a massive political rally in Kingston for Prime Minister Edward Seaga who was speaking in advance of the upcoming election. The crowd pushed me to the front of the stage because they thought we were related. Not true, but an understandable mistake given that Seaga and I were pretty much the only people there who appeared to be White. A cloud of smoke hung overhead like a fuzzy blanket. The crowd went wild as Seaga came on stage, which he shared with a reggae band. I breathed deeply, because damn, the ganja was good. He spoke about his opponent Michael Manley. Boos. Hisses. He spoke about his achievements. Whistles. Cheers. But the crowd soon grew restless. The reggae band started up, cutting Seaga off mid-sentence. Everyone danced. Seaga danced, shuffling stiffly and unrhythmically just like me. It went on like this for hours. Seaga would speak, then dance badly, speak, then dance badly again, until we all went home. I wish American political rallies were like that.

But not all Rastas were good guys. A few months earlier, gunmen had entered the home of Peter Tosh, a founding member of Bob Marley and the Wailers. Tosh and two guests were killed. The three survivors identified the gunman as Dennis "Leppo" Lobban, a leech who had hung around Tosh, caging money and food and ganja. Tosh was generous to a fault but had been trying to cut Leppo off.

Leppo's trial was in a cavernous courtroom with floor-to-ceiling windows open to catch a breeze. As part of the Commonwealth, the Jamaican barristers wore black robes and white wigs as required in an English court. They picked a jury and Leppo pleaded innocent. His eyes were dark and cold, and he appeared uninterested in the testimony of the witnesses who identified him, one after the other. The jury was sent to deliberate, and the reporters went out to a balcony for a smoke. We'd only been out there for a moment when we were called back into the courtroom for the verdict. The jury had agreed Leppo was guilty while they were walking toward the deliberation room.

After Jamaica, I was off to Cairo, so my mother had to worry about me converting to Islam. I do love how the call to prayer is a gentle nudge to stop the humdrum drudgery and anxiety of daily routine, creating space for calm and gratitude. During the holy month of Ramadan, the city pretty much came to a standstill, as almost everyone fasted during the day. They experienced hunger together, rich and poor. Then they broke the fast together at sunset for *iftar*, a daily feast often paid for by the wealthy and open to everyone. I'd join them sometimes in Ataba Square, in the older part of the city. Thousands of people sat at long tables, quiet and subdued, until they heard the boom of a cannon perched on a cliff overlooking the city. It was the signal that the sun had officially set and the day's fast was over. Not a voice was to be heard—just the clatter of cutlery and the rustle of baskets as everyone dived into a meal of tart hibiscus tea, dates and almonds, roast chicken and discs of fresh bread.

Afterwards the narrow streets would be crowded with people smoking shisha from water pipes and eating sweets under strings of colorful lights, enjoying the holiday until the early hours of the morning.

It's hard sometimes to separate religion from culture, but almost all of the Muslims I met were kind, generous to a fault, quick to laugh at themselves, and rarely complained about what they didn't have. The whole region had low rates of crime in the 1990s, partly because they were military states but also because the populations were deeply religious. Americans would ask if I was scared living in Cairo, but the city felt safe, filled with families led by strong, principled women.

But there were extremists of course, launching terrorist attacks against tourists and assaulting Christians in Coptic churches. Mobs of non-extremist Egyptians were also risky—get a large group of men together and ethics fell by the wayside. A decade after I left, when President Hosni Mubarak was deposed, crowds of men attacked and molested women in Tahrir Square during anti-government protests. One mob chased a group of Coptic Christians from the square and into the Video Cairo building next to CNN. My friend Gohar, the owner of Video Cairo and a Muslim, immediately hid some of the fleeing Copts in his office bathroom and gave others props of cameras and clipboards so they blended in with his employees. Thugs followed the Copts up the stairs and demanded Gohar turn them over. He refused and the men finally left after a tense hours-long shouting match. At dawn, Gohar smuggled the Copts into cars the following morning and got them safely home. But he became the target of retribution and ended up fleeing Cairo for Canada, leaving his successful media empire behind.

The Muslim women I befriended loved their religion but were frustrated by rampant misogyny that they blamed on cultural norms, not on their faith. In Saudi Arabia, the prohibitions against women felt crippling. When I checked into an American-chain hotel in Riyadh, I was handed a long black abaya and told to wear it. As a woman, I could not wait in the hotel lobby, visit the business lounge, eat in any of the restaurants, or even enter the hair salon. I could not sit in the front seat next to the driver, and I had to maintain the fiction that the cameraman was my brother.

And then, I landed in India and was able to explore Hinduism. The CNN Delhi cameraman invited me to his house to celebrate the holiday of Holi and his wife thoughtfully sent me a pure white salwar kameez to wear on the big day. I tied the loose pants under the long tunic and wrapped the blinding white dupatta shawl over my shoulders.

When I got to their house, the wife gently took a small bowl of tinted powder and marked my forehead with pink and green. Then the children arrived and flung containers of dyed water and fistfuls of powder at me. Game on. I grabbed containers of the colorful water and powder and chased them squealing across the yard. This was a celebration of spring in the most vibrant country on Earth. No one was spared, and by evening, the entire city was stained. When the taxi driver dropped me off at the hotel, I saw a grim-looking Western man trying to brush orange powder off his suit. Inside the lobby, everyone was leaving footprints of yellow and blue. The mirrored elevator showed my face painted like a Scottish highlander and I had a large streak of green in my hair. What is not to love?

And yet extremists were in India, too, with Hindu militants attacking Muslim mosques. I tried to interview one extremist Hindu leader who was wrapped in vivid orange cloth, with a weathered deeply lined face and fierce white mustache. He was so intimidating and angered by my questions that the crew and I retreated.

A militant Sikh separatist movement was also active in the 1980s and 90s, bombing planes and assassinating politicians in retaliation for attacks on Sikh communities. I flew into the disputed region of Kashmir and experienced the toughest security measures I'd ever encountered at an airport. No water bottles, no purses, no shoes, no jackets, no bags of any kind. I was searched at least five times before I walked empty-handed onto the plane in flip flops.

Finally, I was transferred to Rome. My Catholic mother was ecstatic. I covered the Vatican and Pope John Paul II, the most traveled pope in history. We would fly with him on an Alitalia airliner, flanked by two cars of Italian military police that would race on either side of the plane as it sped down the runway. I never quite understood how that enhanced the pope's security, but it looked cool. The Alitalia stewards would gift each member of the press a carton of cigarettes, a large bottle of perfume, and a full-sized bottle of liquor. It seemed a bit incongruous for a papal mission, but still much appreciated.

Sometimes the pope would appear from first class to give us a brief blessing. He was elderly then, and often looked so frail and weak, almost on the verge of collapse. But when he was at a public mass, he would shuffle onto an altar, a massive crowd before him, and his energy would simply flow. More than once we would be outside for a mass on a rainy overcast day, and the moment he appeared the skies would clear. It was uncanny.

I went with the pope to Portugal where he was beatifying two of three people who were said to have received secret messages from the Virgin Mary in Fatima when they were children. The third child, Sister Lucia, was still living and took the opportunity to reveal the final secret; that Mary would intercept an attack on a bishop dressed in white. It was interpreted to refer to the 1981 assassination attempt on Pope John Paul II in Saint Peter's Square, when the pontiff was wounded by a Turkish gunman. The latest Fatima revelation was a major story, but I struggled because all of the children's prophecies were revealed years *after* the events they supposedly foretold. An editor in Atlanta wanted me to report the prophecy as a fact, an awe-inspiring revelation, a prediction that came true. He was disappointed by my on-air skepticism.

There was misogyny and extremism here too. There was a shortage of priests in Italy but devout women were barred from taking vows, even though they comprised the majority of Italian congregations and could recite the mass by heart. Opus Dei, Miles Jesu, and other ultra conservative and problematic lay organizations grew in popularity under Pope John Paul II, edging out more moderate Catholics. And while I met wonderful princes of the church, there were some who inspired dread. I was advised to avoid one handsy Vatican official, much like the Muslim prohibition in Egypt against a man and woman alone together in a room. Once, when the CNN team was negotiating permission to film from Vatican property, a prelate raised a hand bejeweled with gaudy rings and rubbed his fingers together in an almost cartoonish signal that he wanted money. It felt like I was in a Fellini film.

Over the years, I recognized the divide between religion and politics, the differentiation between faith and hypocrisy.

Personally, I never settled on any particular religion. I have a menorah I light every Hanukkah, and a Ramadan lantern that I pull out to mark the holy month. I bought an antique carved wooden frame in Cairo that once held polo trophies and turned it into a lararium, an altar that ancient Romans kept in their entryways to worship their household gods. I've placed within this arch my own pantheon of deities that I've collected over the years, including a small stone Buddha with his palm upturned, symbolizing enlightenment, next to a carved alabaster Ganesha, the elephant-headed Hindu god of prosperity. There is a stone Thoth, the Egyptian god with the head of an Ibis who protects scribes and writers, a small Muslim Hand of Fatima to ward off bad luck, a byzantine icon of the Virgin with Child, and a small iron figurine of a Roman goddess of journeys and adventure.

I often have a bud vase with cuttings of flowers and leaves in front of my lararium. Sometimes a ripe pear or peach. I place my fingertips lightly on the smooth stone of the gods, close my eyes, and feel gratitude for everything good in my life. It's also where I bargain when anxious, lighting a scented candle in exchange for serenity. Intellectually, I know my lararium doesn't possess divine power. It is, however, an excuse to pause and recapture those moments of peaceful solitude I experienced in the sunlit temple in Palmyra.

My mother got it all wrong. Perhaps like Zenobia, I've actually become an omnist—someone who sees value in all religions while despising those who manipulate it as a cover for greed, lust, or power.

TEN

WAR

The first time I ever saw someone get killed was in Jamaica in the late 1980s, when I was reporting for the *Daily Gleaner*. It was the run-up to elections and there were frequent violent clashes between supporters of the two political parties. I was covering election-related violence in a poor neighborhood of Kingston, where there were often protests or fighting or just general mayhem. That day, an angry crowd had gathered within the crossroads of two poorly paved streets surrounded by low-slung buildings painted turquoise and pink and other tropical colors that had faded under the intense sun. I didn't know exactly what was going on. People were growing increasingly agitated, and the situation had become chaotic. Someone—I'm not sure if it was a policeman, a soldier, or a bystander—fired an automatic weapon into the air, possibly to disperse the crowd of men, women, and children.

But, whoever he was, he didn't account for the recoil from his weapon, which yanked his extended arm downward. The bullet's trajectory was just over the top of the crowd and struck a tall young teen on the crown of his head. I didn't see the boy drop, but as the crowd scattered, I could see him on the pavement in his tattered khaki school shorts and white shirt. I realized then that lying next to him was his brain, perfectly formed and pink. Somehow, it had escaped perfectly intact from his shattered cranium. I kept blinking, thinking that couldn't be possible. Some men came over with a piece of cardboard. Two picked up the body and another used the cardboard to scoop up the brain.

That evening I had pizza with friends in the newsroom at the *Gleaner*. I couldn't believe I had an appetite, and that I wasn't trembling. It seemed then as if I didn't care. And yet, I *still* care. The young man died in the crossroads almost forty years ago, and I catch myself wondering whether his mother is still alive, or a family member, or a friend—someone who still remembers him, misses him, and mourns his passing. I hope that he wasn't forgotten. I haven't forgotten him.

I have never been in the middle of an open battlefield or on a warship that fired weapons for anything other than training exercises. Armies today seem to rarely fight in hand-to-hand combat as they did in antiquity. Enemies and innocent bystanders are now killed by missiles and drones operated by specialists in control centers half a world away.

But I've seen enough violent clashes and killings to have an idea what it might have been like when the armies of Zenobia and Aurelian finally met, and I think it must have been brutal. The chaos, the bewildering and sometimes contradictory orders, the moving forward, retreating, moving forward, pushing back. The comrade nearby that falls so fast and so hard it's clear that he is dead, the distinct metallic smell of blood, the heavy armor that restricts vision and hinders movement, screams of anger and shrieks of pain. Zenobia was a veteran of battles. It's not clear if she fought alongside her troops; she probably didn't. But, like me, she was a witness to deadly conflict.

Historians say that the queen accompanied Odaenathus on his Persian military campaigns along with their two young sons and the king's older son, Herodes. While there are historical accounts of wives accompanying their husbands to war, it was still an unusual arrangement in the ancient world, and perhaps more so in Eastern culture. Odaenathus was in no way assured of victory, so there was a great deal of risk to have his family members follow him into the heart of Persian territory. Yet Zenobia was reportedly fearless and able to withstand the hardship of a military march across the Syrian desert. She would have been at least on the periphery of battlefields and witnessed the carnage, perhaps walking among the bodies of vanquished victims as well as those of the Palmyrene troops who sacrificed their lives. When she became the ruler, she knew what she was facing when she ordered her troops into battle.

By mid-271 AD, at the start of her fifth year on the throne, Zenobia had carved out an empire that stretched from eastern Turkey to the borders of Persia and Saudi Arabia, across Syria and down further south to encompass the whole of Egypt. She was still nominally calling herself a regent to her son and maintaining that she was ruling in partnership with Rome, including the Emperor Aurelian's name on official documents, inscriptions, and coinage. But Rome was not impressed by her token gestures of goodwill.

Aurelian had reunified the western part of the Roman Empire, subduing the Vandals and Goths. The Aurelian Wall in Rome was nearing completion, expanding the city by encompassing the ancient Campus Martius, a field outside the city used for military training. It's now the heart of Rome, where the Trevi Fountain, Piazza Bernini, and Spanish Steps are located. As Aurelian wrapped up his military campaigns in the western end of the Empire, Rome was finally regaining its footing, expanding the city, and collecting more and more taxes far and wide.

At some point, Aurelian sent a clear message to Zenobia that she was next on his agenda. He didn't have spare troops to send east just yet, so he sent ships instead. An armada sailed to Alexandria to root out the Palmyrene soldiers stationed there. Zenobia took note and started to prepare for the inevitable clash that was coming. She must have realized Aurelian was intelligent and capable—she emulated him by building a wall around her own city. It was finished in time, but just barely.

By early 272 AD, both sides were mustering their forces. Aurelian had assembled a patchwork of Roman legions that had fought under a myriad of emperors and generals over the past decades. Now, they were united under Aurelian to fight a foreign foe. Morale was likely high, yet their ranks were thinned by the many years of combat. The emperor had between 30,000 to 50,000 troops to march against Zenobia—not an impressive number.

The queen had 70,000 troops to defend her realm. She also had special forces that looked like an early version of the knights who would someday define the Middle Ages.

They wore heavy body armor of bronze or iron, and metal helmets that covered their faces with only a slit to see through. Their horses too were draped in chainmail. Called Cataphracts, the heavily armored horses and riders were the tanks of the ancient world.

Zenobia had a few other advantages. The East was her home turf. Her soldiers, and hopefully their horses, were accustomed to the desert heat and scarcity of water. She also had capable generals under her command, including Zabdas, who was recognized by both Romans and Syrians as something of a military genius. He already had experience routing Roman troops in Egypt and Arabia, which led to the deaths of two Roman governors.

Both armies marched toward Antioch, the third-largest city in the empire that Zenobia had lured to her side only a few years earlier. According to historians, Zenobia rode on her horse and "frequently walked with her foot soldiers for three or four miles" at a stretch. She was dressed for battle, with one history noting her helmet was "girt with a purple fillet," meaning encircled by a thick purple cord, probably of silk. The helmet was encrusted with dangling jewels, and in the center above her brow was a golden colchis, a spiral symbol that was considered powerful in Syria. It's not known what headgear Aurelian adopted. On most of his coinage, he's shown wearing a simple wreath of laurel, an honor reserved for victorious Romans. But he was sometimes depicted with an intimidating helmet of radiating spikes in honor of his favorite god, Sol Invictus.

Despite having a smaller army, fewer armored horses, and a lesser helmet, Aurelian represented the might of Rome and had a reputation for brutally sacking every city in his path. Zenobia's allies were understandably on edge.

They were in favor of Arab self-rule when Rome was perceived as a blip on the horizon, but now a fearsome Roman general known for being testy with rebels was coming into their land with large, brutish, battle-hardened Roman soldiers. Aurelian and his troops crossed the Bosphorus, the narrow inlet of the Black Sea that separates the continents of Europe and Asia at what is now Istanbul. From there, they quickly encountered Palmyra's first stronghold—a small walled city called Tyana. The Roman emperor allegedly vowed that "not a dog would be left alive" once he conquered it.

The night before the battle, while residents of Tyana were likely sleepless with visions of impending doom, Aurelian reportedly had a pleasant dream about the philosopher Apollonius of Tyana, who had lived a century earlier and was revered across the Empire. He dreamed that the departed philosopher advised him to spare civilians rather than massacre them as he had in the past. The next morning, the Romans quickly subdued Tyana's forces, which seemed to have mainly consisted of farmers waving farm implements. The dream must have inspired Aurelian because he shocked Tyana's terrified citizens by announcing he would pardon everyone who renewed their allegiance to Rome.

His change of heart may have been triggered by the otherworldly message from Apollonius, or perhaps the dream story was cover for a more calculated rationale—if he pardoned Zenobia's allies then they would be more likely to ditch her and rejoin the Roman Empire without a fight. He still needed to save face, however, and told his soldiers, "I did, indeed, declare that I would not leave a dog alive in this city; well then, kill all the dogs."

It was still a slaughter of the innocents, but the men, women, and children of Tyana must have fallen to their knees in relief.

The only human casualty in the conflict was a rich local citizen who had betrayed his city by showing Aurelian where he could breach Tyana's defenses. According to historians, Aurelian killed the traitor but left the man's fortune to his heirs, so that no one could accuse the emperor "with having permitted a man who was rich to be slain for the sake of his money." Aurelian was a leader consumed by what others thought of him. Not just his reputation among the gossipy Roman elite, but also how he was perceived by the Syrians he was in the midst of conquering.

After Tyana was defeated and pardoned, city-states across the eastern empire that had been sympathetic to Zenobia started to switch their loyalties back to the Roman side. Aurelian's strategy seemed to be working well. But Antioch, the third-largest city in the ancient world, remained loyal to Zenobia. So, as her army marched to its defense, Aurelian and his legions raced to intercept them.

The two foes met in Emmae, about thirty miles east of Antioch's gate. Zenobia and her general Zabdas had hoped to fight Aurelian from a position of strength within the fortified walls of the city, but instead the Palmyrene army and Roman legions would duke it out on a field with nowhere to hide. Aurelian adeptly beat Zabdas by using the same tactic the Palmyrene commander had successfully deployed in Egypt. The Roman calvary broke rank and pretended to flee at a fast trot. The heavily armored Cataphracts gave chase, but the sun and heat were too much for the horses and men under the weight of metal mesh and hammered plates. They faltered, exhausted. Aurelian's forces then turned and charged, slaughtering the human-equine "tanks of antiquity."

Zabdas and Zenobia would have been metaphorically gutted, as well, when they realized their calvary was destroyed. While their infantry was still intact, they knew these less-seasoned troops would be overwhelmed by the battle-hardened Roman legions on an open plain. Rather than risk hand-to-hand combat, they chose to retreat, ordering most of their army to flee back toward Palmyra.

Zenobia and Zabdas fled the battlefield as well, but they made a speedy detour to Antioch. The general feared the citizens of Antioch would turn on Zenobia if they knew she had lost the battle, so he found some random man who resembled Aurelian and paraded him through the city streets as if he was their prisoner. It was an original, if desperate, attempt to trick their allies into believing the Palmyrene were the victors. When darkness fell, the general and the queen slipped out of the gate and escaped deep into Syria.

In the morning, the people of Antioch realized that Zenobia and her troops had fled and that the real Aurelian was very much still in command. A large Roman army was marching from the battlefield toward the city in the early light. The citizens quickly threw open their gates and declared their loyalty to Rome, probably trying to convince Aurelian they had been on his side all along. Once again, the Roman emperor, known for sacking cities without mercy, showed clemency. In fact, he stayed in Antioch for several weeks, dedicating a temple, attending civic meetings, bulking up his treasury with plunder, and bolstering his forces with troops from eastern city-states wishing to curry his favor. It was reported that Palestine sent a special detachment of soldiers armed with clubs.

By the time Aurelian was ready to face Zenobia again, she had consolidated her troops in Emesa, a Syrian imperial stronghold that stood between Aurelian and the capital of Palmyra. It was to this city that Zenobia believed her ancestress, Drusilla of Mauretania, the great-granddaughter of Cleopatra and Marc Antony, had arrived 150 years earlier to marry a Syrian king. Perhaps Zenobia contemplated the symbolism of taking her stand in the realm of her Egyptian ancestor, fighting the Romans much as Cleopatra had. She would have known by then that she was in a tight spot, that her allies were abandoning her, and that Aurelian's forces were stronger and more seasoned than hers.

Yet there was reason to hope. Emesa had been home to the families of Syrian kings for hundreds of years and was staunchly loyal to Zenobia. She still had the bulk of her army and she was on her own familiar territory, while Aurelian was far from Rome in a strange new land. The war was not over. Both sides were poised to win this decisive battle.

At the start of the clash, Aurelian's troops seemed to be losing ground. But then, as in the previous battle, his cavalry fell back and hers gave chase, leaving the Palmyrene foot soldiers at the mercy of the Roman infantry, not to mention the Palestinian clubmen.

Romans deployed the same military strategies for centuries. First, their soldiers weakened the opposition by chucking deadly spears known as pila into the enemy'vs ranks, breaking the wall of shields that formed a front line of defense. Once the line was broken, the Romans went into the fray with their shields and swords, hacking until they couldn't lift their arms. The first line of combatants would drop back when they were exhausted, replaced by fresh combatants who would continue the slaughter. They were disciplined fighters who knew the drill and were extremely strong after years of marching and fighting.

This time, Zenobia's retreat was not as orderly or calculated as her departure from Antioch. There was no time to gather provisions. She and Zabdas scrambled to Palmyra with the remnants of their troops, leaving her royal treasury behind in Emesa for Aurelian to plunder.

We don't know how many men were killed or wounded at Emesa. Ancient battles went down in history like mythic events, with the focus on the victor and perhaps some attention given to the defeated foe. Historians have little to say about the experiences of individuals in antiquity who were in the thick of the fighting—military or civilian. But, I have a sense of what it's like to experience carnage, and the way humans quickly adjust to unthinkable horrors.

At one point in the early 1990s, I was dispatched to Jerusalem following a string of deadly bombings throughout the city. I was en route to an interview with a CNN crew when we received a call on the car phone ordering us to race to an open-air market. A Palestinian suicide bomber had strapped a staggering amount of explosives under his clothes and had boarded a city bus. It detonated as the driver pulled into a crowded open-air market, blowing the bus and everyone on board into pieces. Many shoppers were also killed by the blast wave and shrapnel. A satellite truck would meet us at the scene so we could link directly to Atlanta.

When we arrived, the air was full of smoke and dust and bystanders were covering the remains of the victims with newspapers. This had become a ritual in Israel in the wake of terrorist attacks. The newspapers were to protect the bits and pieces of bodies, to direct the recovery teams where human remains were located, and to give the newly dead some measure of dignity and privacy. It was eerily quiet, except for the brief wail of ambulances as they pulled up to collect survivors. Victims and bystanders were in shock. We quickly set up our camera and satellite transmission. I put in my IFB—an earbud used for live broadcast—so I could hear the anchors in Atlanta and began reporting about the extent of damage and the unknown number of victims.

I gestured to the scene around me so the camera could pan a little and then glanced down at my feet. A sheet of fluttering newspaper had blown partially away, and I realized as I was speaking live on air that I was standing on the edge of a human rib cage. White bones, dark red flesh, skin. I looked up at the camera right as it panned back to me and continued my report.

When you are a journalist, it's drilled into you that you are a witness, not a participant. This mindset creates a barrier, an imagined safe spot. Cameramen say that looking through a lens feels almost like watching a video in real time, so they concentrate on getting the shot. Battle-hardened war veterans have described the same sense of distorted reality. It's how humans cope with unspeakable carnage and are able to function surrounded by death and destruction. It was only later that I could catch my breath and mourn the victims of that awful terrorist attack, the Israelis on their way to market, settled in their seats, perhaps preoccupied with a daily list of obligations, planning meals for those they loved, or excited about some future plan that would never be realized. Lives taken; bodies violated. The anguish of moms or husbands or sisters who had to collect shreds of what had been a body they longed to hug.

In antiquity, soldiers would patrol the field after battle, bury their dead, and finish off wounded enemies with the thrust of a spear or sweep of a sword. It must have been grisly and horrific, yet they moved forward and did it. I doubt they were all unfeeling psychopaths. The dead had to be picked up and buried. Zenobia likely lost tens of thousands of men in these battles, young and old. Because of their gender and socioeconomic status, they were sacrificed to the ambitions of the powerful. Many of Aurelian's troops suffered the same consequences, and were buried hastily in a land far from their homes. I remind myself that victims long ago, as well as today, were people with ideas and dreams and families and goals. They started the day with hopes, became part of history, and then simply disappeared. Individually, they were deeply mourned by those they left behind, until there was no one left to remember them.

On another assignment in Israel during the Intifada, I was out with a cameraman at a small village in the West Bank covering a fight between Palestinians and the Israel Defense Forces. It was a lopsided conflict. The IDF had firepower while the Palestinians, like their ancestors at Emesa, had clubs and rocks.

A young Palestinian was shot in front of us and dragged by his comrades to the side of a building where the cameraman and I were taking shelter. There was confusion, chaos, shouting. A car pulled up to take the boy to the hospital and the cameraman and I followed in our car close behind. We all pulled up to a small and stark cement hospital, spraying gravel from speeding tires and slamming brakes. The wounded youth was carried inside and then, somehow, we were inside as well. Everyone crowded into an operating room. There was no electricity but I was holding a light that was running off the camera battery. The room was dim and it was hard to see. The doctors called us over and asked me to hold the light high over the operating table so they could examine the boy's wounds. "Higher!" "This area!" I stood there like a grotesque parody of the Statue of Liberty, torch held high, trying not to look down at the misery beneath. But it was only for a moment, because the young man died as I stood there and couldn't be revived.

His friends and family wailed in disbelief, while the cameraman and I went outside to sit in our car. Within a few minutes, the others came out too, holding the boy in their arms like they had brought him in, but this time, he was wrapped in white plastic. They put him in the back seat of their car and took off. The cameraman and I exchanged a glance and followed. When we got to the boy's house, he was already inside on the dining room table. His mother and sisters were keening, their howls echoing off the bare walls. His mother must have been so worried when her sons had left the house to confront the IDF, and now her worst fears had been realized. The women bathed his face. They changed his T-shirt and removed his shoes. Someone took a key and a small wad of bills out of the pocket of his jeans. He was rewrapped in a sheet and then we were all off to the nearby cemetery where his friends had already dug a shallow pit. The men gathered and we stepped back while they prayed over his body and covered it with dirt.

It happened so fast. Less than an hour earlier, he was a young man with running shoes, a mom, friends, an unruly head of dark brown hair. Now he was being buried in the jeans and socks he had put on that morning. Palestinians buried their fallen as quickly as possible because they feared the Israelis would confiscate the body for an autopsy and families didn't believe they'd get them back.

As we left the cemetery, I caught sight of the boy's brother. Older brother, I think; the brother who had probably told his mother not to worry, he'd be there to protect the younger one and make sure he didn't do anything stupid. The older brother now started spinning like a dervish through the graveyard, yelping. His arms and legs flailed wide as he spun in great leaps across the weeds and dirt, between headstones. It was dusk now. The friends were in a group running after him, trying to catch an outstretched arm to slow him down. We pulled away. I don't know if they caught him.

At some point, the dead of Emesa were buried, probably without the care of their mothers and sisters who would have been waiting anxiously at home for news of the battle. Once again, Aurelian issued a blanket pardon. The city wasn't sacked and its citizens were not slaughtered. The Roman Emperor went to the local Temple of Elagabalus, his flamboyant Syrian predecessor who had started the Crisis of the Third Century that Aurelian was now ending. Historians say he wanted "to pay his vows as if by a duty common to all." Flush with Zenobia's state treasury, Aurelian dedicated gifts to the people of Emesa and promised to build more temples, bolstering his popularity not only in Syria, but throughout Zenobia's fast-crumbling empire.

Back in Palmyra, Zenobia and her subjects must have been seriously worried. By then, she had lost Egypt, as well. The Roman naval expedition dispatched to Alexandria was under the command of the esteemed general Aurelius Probus, who would become emperor a few years after Aurelian's death. He had landed near Alexandria earlier in the year and wrestled back control of Rome's vital grain supply.

Palmyra was now the last holdout of Zenobia's empire, her last stand. The city fortified its hastily built wall, then waited for Aurelian and his troops to march over the horizon. They did not have to wait long. The Roman general was not far behind Zenobia and arrived with a force that included Zenobia's former vassals who had turned against her. The troops set up camp and cut down all of the palm trees that surrounded the city, the ones that had given Palmyra its name. They secured the spring, the city's source of water. Caravans were stopped in their tracks and were prevented from bringing goods and supplies inside the gates.

Palmyra was under siege—the best strategy to take over a fortified city. Squeeze the adversary, terrify the population, and wait for the city to crumble from within. The gates will eventually crack open, enabling troops to storm through the gap and finish the job.

Inside the walls of Palmyra, the citizens must have been anxious about their fate, terrified for their lives, while still trying valiantly to complete routine daily tasks to care for their homes and their families.

I know what it's like. I've been there.

ELEVEN

KINSHASA

As I was checking into the Hotel Memling in Kinshasa, the chatty front desk clerk informed me that he was twenty-seven years old and would die when he was thirty-three. I asked how he knew that, and he told me all great men died at thirty-three—like Jesus Christ, Alexander the Great, and Bob Marley. I argued that actually Bob Marley had been thirty-six; when I lived in Jamaica I had reported on the disputes over inheritance initiated by the seven mothers of his thirteen children. Besides, I added, many great men lived to be quite old. But the young clerk smiled knowingly and said he knew his destiny.

Kinshasa is the capital of the very large southern African country then called Zaire. It was March 1997, and rebel forces, the Alliance of Democratic Forces for the Liberation of Congo, were several hundred miles outside the city and closing in fast. It had been relatively easy for me to book a flight into Kinshasa, but getting a flight out was becoming impossible. Wealthy families, expat workers, diamond dealers, diplomats, drug runners, and the wives and children of the military elite were escaping while they could. Those who couldn't get a flight out of the capital were taking a fifteen-mile boat ride across the width of the great Congo River to Brazzaville in the neighboring Republic of the Congo.

One person, however, wasn't going anywhere—President Mobutu Sese Seko, who had been in power for almost four decades.

Mobutu had deposed a democratically elected president in 1960, installed a military regime, and began amassing a personal fortune from purloined foreign aid and the proceeds from the country's natural resources of diamonds, copper, and cobalt. He renamed the country from the Democratic Republic of the Congo to Zaire, which means "mighty river" in the Bantu language. He also changed his own name from Joseph Mobutu to Mobutu Sese Seko Kuku Ngbendo wa Za Banga, which has been translated to "the all-powerful warrior who, because of his endurance and inflexible will to win, goes from conquest to conquest, leaving fire in his wake." Under his long rule, Zaire became one of the poorest and most corrupt countries in the world.

Known for his trademark leopard skin hat, Mobutu brutally suppressed challenges to his authority over the years, often with US and European support. This time was different. The well-funded rebels were supported by Rwanda and Uganda, and his own people were ready for change. In the past, he had relied on help from foreign governments, but this time no country was willing to send military aid to defend his government. He was also suffering from advanced cancer. People weren't wondering *if* his regime would fall, but *when*.

On big stories, the international press corps often gravitated to a single hotel, which made life easier. We could share resources, tips, drivers, videotapes, and snacks. It was safer to team up with other reporters as there is a higher likelihood that someone would notice if any one of us went missing. This was especially important for the safety of newspaper reporters, who were often on assignment by themselves. CNN, in contrast, usually had large teams of cameramen, sound techs, satellite operators, editors, on-air reporters, and off-screen producers.

Shortly after I checked into the Hotel Memling, a crew from Atlanta arrived with one of the network's "portable" satellite dishes—I put "portable" in quotation marks because it was huge. The dish was unpacked from heavy anvil cases and snapped together on the hotel rooftop. From this perch, the techs could feed video straight to Atlanta at any hour of the day or night, and reporters could do live shots with the city as a backdrop. By this time, we each had our own clunky mobile phone, but service was spotty so we also depended on satellite phones and landlines. The Atlanta-based techs brought power generators to run the satellite transmission and charge our phone batteries if the power failed—and to run the mini refrigerators they brought for bottled water. The rooftops of hotels, where the satellite techs usually worked across the globe, were either burning hot or freezing cold and almost always windy.

Our assignment was to stay in Kinshasa until the rebels breached the city and overthrew the regime. As the rebels grew closer, many of the city's inhabitants became frightened and panicky. A few years earlier, 3,000 of Zaire's paratroopers had mutinied over lost wages and sacked Kinshasa's commercial district with the help of civilian looters. That unrest was only quelled when France and Belgium sent troops to help restore order. But everyone knew foreign troops weren't coming to help out Mobutu this time, and his hold on his own military had eroded badly. Over the weeks, he would raise everyone's hopes for a peaceful transition by unexpectedly flying out of Kinshasa for peace talks, only to return again a few days later defiant and irritable.

Over the weeks of rebel advances and abandoned peace talks, transport in and out of the city tightened and commercial flights finally stopped altogether. The roads were dangerous and supply chains from the countryside were mostly cut off. Not unlike Palmyra, the city of Kinshasa was under siege, with a ruler trying to cling to power.

It was a waiting game. We reported stories about refugees fleeing into the city from the countryside ahead of the rebels. We staked out the airport waiting for Mobutu's private plane to depart and then return. We chartered our own plane and followed him to Brazzaville or to Johannesburg, South Africa, for negotiations that never ended well. Back in Kinshasa, we interviewed academics, disgruntled soldiers, and worried shopkeepers. Almost every day I went to the Ministry of Information, a stubby cement building that looked like it had already been through the war. Windows were broken, everything was dusty, and the carpet smelled. Only a handful of employees were at their desks. No one was getting paid at this point, but some workers, like Mobutu, were loath to give up their defunct jobs.

There was a lot of down time as the stalemate dragged on, creating a situation similar to the one I faced at the

Damascus Sheraton years earlier on my first CNN assignment. There was a hotel pool here, too, but the mood was decidedly darker. The African-based press corps were grittier and wilder than our lot from the Middle East. They were danger junkies, inspired by a group of legendary photographers from Johannesburg nicknamed The Bang Bang Club. They thrived on close calls and epic parties.

Kinshasa was filled with *shebeens*, private homes that served up alcohol and loud music. There was also a larger dance hall we called the Green Bar, because it had a green neon light around its front window. Inside, it was dimly lit and frequented by gorgeous women with waist-length braids and coral lipstick who danced to Afrobeats, a wave of 1990s pop that sounded a bit like American funk music. Many of them were prostitutes looking for clients among the rowdy press corps. The Green Bar opened its doors at midnight and closed them sometime around dawn.

Late one night, I headed over there with a group of colleagues and a translator. As we made our way down a muddy street of shuttered shops, we picked up a ragtag following of men. They lurked in darkness and then moved closer behind us.

How did I end up here?

Youssef was leading our little pack to the bar. He was the head of the European Broadcasting Union in Egypt; his home office was across the hallway from my office in Cairo. He was a big guy in a polo shirt, but not big enough to take on all the men surrounding us.

Youssef suddenly stopped in his tracks and nonchalantly turned to the most ominous-looking man who was closing in from behind—the one with a mean dog on a rope and a flapping shirt.

Youssef made eye contact and thrust his hand out with the equivalent of $20, casually instructing the translator. "Tell him this is all we have now, but we'll pay him three times more if he protects us."

The mood changed instantly. The big man drew himself up. The dog snarled. The others dropped back into the shadows.

"He wants to know where you're going," the translator said.

"The Green Bar."

We moved forward with our new protector, who took his job seriously. He picked up a large stick and swung it back and forth, scattering loiterers out of our way. When we were safely inside, we pooled the money we had been carrying and Youssef paid our new bodyguard, sharing a drink with him, or perhaps cigarettes. I'm not sure, because I'd already hit the dance floor.

By mid-May the mood grew more sober. Mobutu's army crumbled as the rebels reached the outskirts of the city. The rebel leader, Laurent-Désiré Kabila, was a wild card. He'd tried to overthrow the Mobutu government in 1965 with the help of Che Guevara, but Guevara complained that the then-twenty-six-year-old Kabila wasn't really serious about revolution because he spent all of his time in bars and brothels. Kabila re-emerged in the 1990s and convinced neighboring Rwanda to back his second attempt to oust Mobutu. Unlike Aurelian, Kabila did not personally lead his troops into battle. He stayed in a secure city on Zaire's border, as his rebel forces made their torturous march over poorly paved roads to the capital.

Finally, on May 16, with rebels massing at the edge of the city, Mobutu boarded his private jet and left Zaire for the last time. Peace talks aboard a South African ship with Nelson Mandela were abandoned and Kabila declared himself president from the safety of his compound. He ordered the rebel forces to take control of Kinshasa in advance of his arrival. There was no organized military force to block the takeover of the capital, but that didn't preclude violence. The civil war had sparked looting and ethnic violence across the country, with some assessments suggesting thousands of Zairians had already been killed by the time Mobutu fled.

The rebels announced they would start their march into Kinshasa in the morning, sparking rumors that were flying around the capital. It was said that international mining companies were already striking million-dollar deals with Kabila for rights to the country's copper and zinc assets. Mobutu's son had come to the Intercontinental Hotel with a squad of soldiers looking for revenge against military officials quartered there—or, in another version, he was seeking access to government money stashed in the hotel vault. But he left empty handed and fled by boat to Brazzaville in the middle of the night. The treasury was missing or looted or had been hidden somewhere.

Soldiers who had been loyal to Mobutu were left to fend for themselves. Some escaped, some ditched their uniforms and tried to blend in with the crowd, others were armed and ready to defend themselves. The impoverished residents we interviewed were fatalistic. There was not much they could do to protect themselves.

However, the elite who had been associated with the government were panic stricken. We heard that the plumbing at the Intercontinental Hotel had failed because so many guests, who had checked into rooms in an attempt to hide from the rebels, were flushing incriminating documents down their toilets.

I was personally on edge because the asshat CNN producer who had harassed me in Somalia was now in Kinshasa, disrupting our coverage and making my life hell. He'd revived his taunt that I was obsessed with being raped by black men, and tried to coerce me to put his bar tabs on my personal expense account. This was decades before the #MeToo movement, so I mostly ignored him. But his abuse got so bad that others complained to Atlanta on my behalf.

I also had a few embarrassing personal issues. I'd been having fun in Kinshasa, which included a brief liaison with a martial arts expert who charmed me by flipping me onto a bed. But now, the evening the rebels were poised to enter the city, I desperately needed some medicated cream. It is challenging to find a gynecologist who speaks English during the middle of a rebellion. I was also desperately trying to fax a signed contract with Trinity Pictures, which wanted to purchase the rights to a light-hearted screenplay I'd written a few months earlier about an Egyptian archaeologist and his kids. I was thrilled that the producer liked my script, but the timing was somewhat inconvenient.

And yet another problem: I did not realize then that I suffer from a condition that makes it hard for me to recognize faces. I'd given an envelope of cash to an itinerant rug dealer whom I thought was one of our drivers. Later in life I would spend an hour in an MRI capsule while scientists at the National Institutes of Health examined my brain for a study on face blindness. But, back then in Kinshasa, I thought I was just pathetic. There were hundreds of people milling in and out of the Hotel Memling and I couldn't keep straight who was who.

The night before the rebel invasion, journalists gathered in the cavernous, dimly lit lobby of the hotel. I can't remember why it was dim. Maybe the lights were running on generators, but the overall effect was like a renaissance painting with the patina of age. There was a grand piano and someone played The Beatles' "Let it Be," which seemed fitting and wistful. At this point, the airport was locked, all the boats had been taken, and there was nothing left to do but wait for the morning and see what would happen.

The siege of Palmyra was Zenobia's last stand and, like Mobutu, she was determined to cling to power. The wall that enclosed the city had been completed, but Aurelian had paused on his chase to gather a larger force and assemble siege equipment. He now had six Roman legions and numerous auxiliary forces donated by city-states looking to curry favor. There were 40,000 men outside the gates. At least some of them were likely Zenobia's former soldiers who had switched sides. Aurelian had also negotiated with Bedouins to supply his army with food and water. Even Zenobia's closest subjects, the tribes of her childhood, had abandoned her.

Aurelian came armed with scorpio, an early form of siege cannon. A towering triangular timber frame was fitted with ropes that were twisted tight and then released to uncoil with force. A net or basket at the end of the coil would fling large rocks or metal bolts. Some of this ammunition would be aimed at the city walls in hopes of creating a breach. Some would be lobbed *over* the walls and into residences, banks, and markets in hopes of creating mayhem. If needed, the Romans could follow up with a volley of weighted darts with sharp blades that sliced whatever they struck.

If the scorpio didn't create a breach, Aurelian also had battering rams he could use against the gates. But the rams would be a last resort because they exposed the men carrying them to the Palmyrene soldiers on top of the wall, who had the advantage of shooting downward. The Roman strategy was to weaken the forces by destroying as much as possible from a distance, much as we do today with drones and missiles launched from afar. In his efficient Roman camp equipped with water from the spring and provisions from the Bedouins, Aurelian was in an advantageous position.

The city's inhabitants realized Aurelian would take the city one way or another, and feared he was no longer in a lenient mood. He had been ambushed by a gang of Syrians during his march across the desert toward Palmyra, and there were reports that an arrow had struck his shoulder. He had survived, but the wound probably hurt a great deal. There was no guarantee that he would be as merciful toward Palmyra as he had been toward Tyana and Antioch. If Aurelian had to fight his way into the city, it was possible he would allow his disgruntled soldiers to sack homes and businesses and plunder whatever treasures they could find. Wealthy merchants and city officials would likely be killed, leaving behind wives and children who could be taken as slaves to boost the labor pool in Rome or used for sexual gratification.

These fears grew stronger after citizens offered the gods gifts in return for victory. They tossed silver and jewels and bolts of silk into a sacred cistern. But instead of sinking to the bottom, signifying the gods had accepted the bargain, the gifts floated away, an indication that the gods did not support Palmyra's defiance of Rome. It must have been a sobering moment to see that your goodwill gesture had been brushed aside by your city's own deities. It got worse; the Palmyrene were warned that their rebellion was doomed by several omens, including an oracle at the temple of Syria's most powerful goddess.

I imagine even a brave woman like Zenobia would be anxious, holed up in her palace within her beautiful city, receiving disturbing dispatches that her subjects were renouncing their allegiance, troops were defecting, and even the gods were turning their backs on her. Aurelian had brought her allies over to his side, as historians put it, "some by forcible means and some by cunning." Zenobia had lost Alexandria to the Roman armada; Palestine was no longer within her power; Antioch was lost; Arabia had switched sides. She was alone, pinning her hopes on backup troops from Armenia. But they never appeared.

After Aurelian flexed his imposing siege apparatus, he sent a letter over the wall that was addressed to the queen. In it, he ordered Zenobia to surrender and forfeit everything in return for safety: "You, O Zenobia, can live with your family in the place which I will assign you upon the advice of the venerable Senate. You must deliver to the treasury of Rome your jewels, your silver, your gold, your robes of silk, your horses, and your camels." It was a generous offer given the dire situation.

Roman historians say she responded to Aurelian's letter "with more pride and insolence than befitted her fortunes, supposedly with a view to inspiring fear." She began her letter: "From Zenobia, Queen of the East, to Aurelian Augustus." Bold opening, to call herself Queen of the East considering she'd already lost all of the territory she had seized from Rome. Zenobia went on to evoke the memory of her ancestress: "You demand my surrender as though you were not aware that Cleopatra preferred to die a Queen rather than remain alive, however high her rank." Like her ancestor, she would never surrender.

The rich mercantile population of Palmyra vehemently disagreed. They were not willing to bank on the remnants of Zenobia's army to defend them against 40,000 Roman troops with scorpio and battering rams. They wanted to follow the lead of Tyana and Antioch and open the city gates, beg for mercy, and plead for forgiveness. It's not clear how they confronted their defiant queen and her distinguished general. Did they send a delegation and speak calmly of their concerns? Perhaps a mob stormed the palace and demanded her surrender. Zenobia was running out of options, but was still not willing to give herself up to Aurelian. She knew she and her children would likely be taken to Rome and put on display, and her sons possibly executed.

So, the citizens sent her packing. Zosimus says they called a council and decided that the best course of action was for Zenobia to leave the city and head east to Persia for help, a curious plan given that the expected Persian reinforcements had already defected to Aurelian. But "having thus determined, they set Zenobia on a camel . . . and conveyed her out of the city." The historian doesn't say whether the queen agreed with this risky plan of action or whether she was ignominiously slung on the back of the camel like a sack of goods. Zosimus notes, however, that it was a "female camel, the fastest of its breed and faster than any horse." Not only did they want her out of the city, but they wanted her out as speedily as possible.

When he realized Zenobia had fled, Aurelian sent a contingent of troops to chase after her while he entered the city gates, which had finally opened in surrender. Despite his wounded shoulder, Aurelian maintained the same magnanimous persona he had developed in Tyana. He reassured the citizens that they would be able to return to business as usual after paying taxes *and* tribute to Rome.

The emperor took his time touring Palmyra, meeting with officials and leading citizens who likely expressed their admiration and support, given the Roman troops milling about the city. The emperor also visited the temple where the Palmyrene offerings had been rejected and publicly thanked the Syrian gods for favoring him over Zenobia. In a letter to Rome, Aurelian stated he wanted the temple to be restored to its former glory with abundant gold and silver. However, he did specify that the Palmyrene would have to pay for the project out of their city treasury and he would take the credit.

Kinshasa didn't have a wall or gates to fling open, but there was no opposition to the rebels who entered the city in the early morning. For the most part, it was peaceful, with some people lining the streets and cheering as the rebels appeared, guns in hand and their ammo slung across their chests in bandoliers. They were well armed, but many were dressed in ragged clothes and looked exhausted after long battles and marches through the countryside. Their eyes were red from drugs or alcohol or lack of sleep. Some smiled at the crowds, but most kept their heads down as they moved toward the city center.

There were a few skirmishes and pockets of resistance. Some soldiers loyal to Mobutu were captured. But, for the most part, the residents of Kinshasa went about their day, trying to earn some money and feed their children. Wars and civic strife are like that. Combatants will be shooting at each other in the street while a few blocks away a barber is giving someone a haircut and a woman is selling bowls of stew on the roadside. For the majority of Kinshasa's inhabitants, the day was stressful, but the day-to-day struggle continued at its monotonous pace.

At one point, a number of cameramen started to film the stoning of a man on a city street, perhaps by rebels, perhaps by a mob. The stones were supplemented by chunks of concrete and the victim was covered in blood, staggering and dazed. The journalists worried the perpetrators were spurred on by the cameras, excited by the attention, that they were going to kill him. It was mutually agreed to put down the cameras and walk away.

Later, one of CNN's star camerawomen returned to the hotel with video of prisoners captured by the rebels, who suspected them of being Zairean soldiers. The men were on the flatbed of a truck, dressed as civilians, begging to be freed. They said they were just residents of the city, working for their families. One of the rebels explained on camera their suspicions, showing minute evidence that the men had exchanged their uniforms for civilian clothes. They showed the faint marks on their ankles that may have been left by thick socks, and hair that may have been flattened by a military beret. The rebel was convinced that the captured men were part of Mobutu's disbanded army. The truck sped away with the prisoners, who were probably destined to be executed. There were no trials, just hunches.

Kabila, the rebel leader, arrived in Kinshasa days later once he had deemed it safe enough. He was a big man with a big smile. Like Aurelian, he assured the populace that they would prosper under his rule, leaving the citizens skeptical but resigned. Some business owners told me earlier that they preferred Mobutu to Kabila only because Mobutu and his family had already stolen billions from the country and his thirst for wealth was likely sated; there was not much more they could take. Kabila was new and would be looking for spoils for himself, his family, and his closest followers. It would be the start of a fresh round of corruption and theft. The Palmyrene merchants probably had similar concerns. Expansion and administration of the Roman Empire required a lot of money, and Aurelian would be looking for fresh sources of funding.

Kabila toured around the capital in a bid to reassure the populace that he was a benevolent leader. He met with people rich and poor, taking his first steps toward states-manship after a lifetime as a struggling revolutionary. Photos showed him happy and confident, but he had yet to hold a press conference or publicly outline his plans for the new government. It seemed impossible to pin him down. But several days after the takeover, we got word Kabila was touring a city hospital, so I raced there with a crew hop-ing to waylay him. We found him strolling through the hospital garden with doctors and bodyguards, so I went up to him to ask if he would answer some questions for CNN. He was imposing, tall and wide, with a grin that took up most of his face. He was delighted to be on camera at first, but his jovial mood dissipated as the questions got harder. When I asked him about calls for a free and fair election, he made veiled threats then stomped away.

There would be no elections. Days after our interview, Kabila was sworn in as president, head of the military, and head of state. Like Mobutu, one of his first acts was to change the country's name—from Zaire back to the Dem-ocratic Republic of the Congo. But he only ruled it for a few years. In January 2001 he was assassinated by a teen-age bodyguard in a murky plot that brought his son Joseph Kabila to power. As for former president Mobutu, after mere months in exile in Morocco, he died of advanced prostate cancer.

The story wound down, but the airport was still closed to commercial flights. Mary and I found ourselves on the city dock surrounded by CNN anvil cases, waiting for a boat to Brazzaville, where we would catch a flight back to Cairo. The dock was crowded with dozens of motor-ized skiffs lined up along the pier, loading and unloading people and baggage as passengers milled about anxiously. The Congo River is wide, and the wind whipped up little whitecaps in the muddied brown water.

I was thin as a reed and had lost a lot of my hair from stress. I think I was also partially hungover that chaotic morning. The incessant harassment from the CNN pro-ducer had worn me down, along with anxious days at the hotel. The nights dancing at the Green Bar were fun, but at heart I wasn't a party girl and drinking copious amounts of Simba beer had made me sick. I felt disappointed in myself; that I'd been too timid, that I hadn't stood up for myself against the producer, I had not been brave enough to actively seek out violent clashes.

But I was feeling a little giddy, too. Steve had called me that morning on the satellite phone from Atlanta. They were moving me to the Rome bureau.

TWELVE

PROPAGANDA

Following the siege of Palmyra, Aurelian wrote a letter about the immense challenges he faced in conquering the city. "It cannot be told what a store of arrows is here, what great preparations for war, what a store of spears and of stones." According to the emperor's version of history, he faced almost insurmountable odds and overcame great peril to defeat Palmyra and reclaim the eastern empire. He made no mention of Palmyrene merchants loading Zenobia onto a fast camel into exile, then throwing open the gates while groveling for mercy.

Journalists understand there are many sides to a story. But, ancient historians were not journalists; they needed to curry favor with those in power and viewed the world through a narrow lens of bias. Their narratives, while based on facts, have a spin that makes it almost impossible to discern the truth. After I left the Middle East and the internet was established so that I could look things up, I did my Master's thesis at Georgetown University on Aurelian and Palmyrene propaganda surrounding the life and times of Zenobia.

For Aurelian, who constantly complained about what people said about him, Zenobia was a potential liability to his carefully crafted reputation. Roman men did not perceive the defeat of a woman as a particularly noteworthy achievement. In the Roman epic the *Aeneid*, Helen of Troy is depicted as a manipulative queen who uses her legendary beauty to seduce and betray men on an epic scale. When Troy is sacked, the hero Aeneas flees the burning city while carrying his son and elderly father on his back, leaving behind his poor wife who stumbled and fell. Rather than save his wife, he debates with himself whether he should hunt down Helen and kill her for all of the trouble she has caused. But then he decides not to because: "There's no great glory in a woman's punishment. Such a conquest wins no praise."

Poor Aurelian wanted the Romans to laud him, not scoff at his accomplishments, so he was vested in crafting his own narrative about the vanquished Zenobia. He had to convince his critics that she was different, that she was a worthy foe and conquering her therefore made him powerful rather than pathetic.

But the emperor still had to toe the party line that women could not be great leaders—he didn't want to risk offending elite male sensibilities. Roman men had always wallowed in misogyny but by the third century they were suffering a longstanding existential crisis that made them even more threatened by powerful women. Before Julius Caesar crossed the Rubicon, elite Roman males vied with each other to become first among equals. A male born of a good family could expect to follow a "course of honor" that would raise him into a string of important jobs, including the Senate. Roman males from non-aristocratic families could also rise up through the course of honor, such as Cicero, who was lowborn but very clever. He also married into a rich and powerful family, which helped.

But when the Republic ended, power concentrated in the hands of the emperor and members of his immediate family. All military honors were reserved for the imperial family—by law, only *they* could receive a much-coveted Roman Triumph, a military victory parade. The spoils of war were deposited in the imperial treasury, and administrative power fell into the hands of well-trained slaves and professional former slaves known as freedmen, many of whom became extremely wealthy and powerful—some more powerful than the most elite Roman males. It stung.

Prolific writers, Roman men shared their angst with posterity. They were outraged that freedmen were richer than they were. They feared their slaves were insolent and disrespectful. They shuddered at the thought of their wives cheating on them with gladiators.

Roman women were traditionally expected to be chaste matrons who concerned themselves with the home and children. But they actually had quite a bit of freedom in antiquity, especially compared to Greek women who were typically confined to the house, barred from athletic competitions, theaters, even markets. In contrast, Roman women were able to watch horse races at the circus maximus, attend the many theaters around the city, shop in the marketplace, and even enjoy gladiator shows at The Colosseum. Many Roman women from rich families controlled their own fortunes, and poorer women established their own businesses. Women could—and did—divorce and remarry.

Men embraced misogyny in their effort to retain a sense of superiority and establish their rightful niche in the world, including control of politics and the military. A woman who seized power was threatening to the male elite—really the worst-case scenario, just as bad as losing your wife to a gladiator.

Rome's two most reviled villainesses were Dido and Cleopatra. Dido is perhaps a mythological character. She was the queen of Carthage who seduced Aeneas and delayed the journey from Troy he undertook on behalf of the gods to establish a Roman presence in Italy. Aeneas ultimately obeyed the gods and snuck away from Dido's North African kingdom without saying goodbye; in effect he ghosted her. The distraught queen threw herself on a burning funeral pyre and cursed the future Roman Empire as Aeneas sailed away, the smoke from her pyre drifting over his head. This early clash with Dido presaged the wars that later raged between Carthage and the Roman Republic. She may be a myth but Romans were still tetchy about that curse.

The other most-hated queen was Cleopatra. She was in a class by herself. Like Dido, she delayed Julius Caesar's military campaign by seducing him with a cruise up the Nile. Then, after Caesar's death, she deployed her womanly wiles on his favored general Marc Antony. Ancient Roman historians depicted her as licentious, amoral, and gluttonous. The great orator Cicero, who actually met her, summed up the opinion of most Roman men: "I can't stand that queen."

Rome's first emperor, Augustus, could afford to denigrate Cleopatra because he could justify his victory over her by arguing that, *actually*, he had defeated the great Roman general Antony—not Cleopatra. To Roman males, she was just Antony's sidepiece.

Aurelian didn't have that option. Zenobia was single and undeniably the ruler of her rebellious eastern empire. He had to convince Romans that she had been a worthy opponent, despite the failings common to all ambitious women. It was a balancing act that he mastered admirably.

Although he referred to her as a "mere woman" in his letters, Aurelian and his historians avoided portraying her as a degenerate like her ancestor Cleopatra. They never defamed her with the same vitriol, partly because they wanted to portray her as a worthy foe and partly because they were no longer writing solely for the benefit of elite males back in Rome.

The world of 272 AD was far different from the age of Cleopatra. During her era, citizenship was reserved solely for Romans who hailed from the city-state. Augustus didn't have to curry the goodwill of Egyptian foreigners; he only had to impress the men of Rome. Therefore, he could demonize Cleopatra without worrying about backlash from her supporters.

Zenobia, however, was a Roman. By the time of her birth, citizenship had been granted to families throughout the Empire for many generations. Aurelian himself had been born into an obscure family in the Balkans, and his long military career across the empire kept him out of the city of Rome for most of his life. Yet, he was accepted as Rome's leader, as were many other emperors who came from equally humble backgrounds far from the capital.

In addition, Syria had become an integral part of the Roman world. It was an important hub for commerce and the center of Christianity, which was spreading throughout the empire. At the same time Aurelian was launching his campaign against Zenobia at Tyana in 272 AD, the future emperor Constantine was born in the Balkans. Constantine would become Rome's first Christian emperor and move the capital east to Constantinople, not far from Tyana.

In the centuries after Cleopatra's defeat, the eastern territories had become populated with families of Roman citizens who paid taxes, helped raise armies, and supported the empire. They were proud of their heritage and likely protective of the reputation of their women, as Arabs are to this day. Zenobia was, at least initially, a generally popular and admired widow of a Roman hero—the man who had defeated the Persians and secured the Roman Empire against incursions from the Far East. Portraying her as licentious and amoral would play out well in Rome, but risked alienating potential allies in her realm.

Given all of the history, the sensitivities, and the realities of the empire in the 270s AD, Aurelian had to carefully weave a narrative that put him in the best possible light. He knew that critics were already downplaying his victory. In a letter, he gripes to a colleague, "the Romans are saying that I am merely waging a war with a woman." In another letter to the Senate, he complains, "I have heard, Conscript Fathers, that men are reproaching me for having performed an unmanly deed in leading Zenobia to triumph."

To counter the whiff of disdain, Aurelian started a public relations campaign to bolster the Syrian queen's reputation and ironically became one of her most steadfast champions. "In truth, those very persons who find fault with me now would accord me praise in abundance, did they but know what manner of woman she is," he wrote home to Rome. Aurelian goes on to enumerate Zenobia's unusual qualities. "How wise in counsels, how steadfast in plans, how firm toward the soldiers, how generous when necessity calls, and how stern when discipline demands."

Aurelian continued to spell out his version of history in a barrage of letters he sent post haste to Rome after his victory. In his telling, Zenobia was able to forge a new empire because eastern men were afraid of her: "Neither Arabs nor Saracens nor Armenians ever moved against her," he declared. The underlying message was that only a Roman such as himself possessed the strength and courage to challenge her rule. The emperor laid it on thick, going so far as to suggest that Zenobia was the real power behind the success of her late husband. "I might even say that it was her doing that Odaenathus defeated the Persians," he mused, publicly, so effusive was his praise of the Syrian queen.

Historians followed his lead. Aurelian's most credible biographer, Zosimus, describes Zenobia on equal footing with male rulers because she had "the courage of a man." He claimed the queen was exceptional in that she possessed masculine, and therefore admirable, traits. "Her voice was clear and like that of a male."

It was also important for Aurelian to cast Zenobia as a Roman, not a barbarian foreigner, because victory over a Roman citizen was much sweeter than victory over a dissolute potentate. Historians backed up the emperor's narrative by highlighting Zenobia's staunch Roman qualities. One wrote that she enjoyed some of the luxurious pomp of an Eastern potentate but was Roman at heart. "It was rather in the manner of the Persians that she received worship and in the manner of the Persian kings that she banqueted; but it was in the manner of a Roman emperor that she came forth to public assemblies."

Aurelian propaganda didn't stop there. The emperor and his historians spun about Zenobia the aura of the Amazons, female warriors of myth. Even in Rome, Amazons were widely admired for their strength and skill in battle, along with their chastity. Zenobia perfectly fit the Amazonian profile; she was a beautiful woman who hunted, rode on horseback, and marched with soldiers—and she was chaste! There are tales of Amazons lying with men only on specific occasions in order to beget children, just as Zenobia was said to have orchestrated sexual relations with her husband. What seems to modern readers of ancient history to be a gossipy tidbit about Zenobia's love life was likely a carefully crafted analogy that ancient readers would immediately understand.

They would perceive Zenobia as being cast from the same mold as Camilla, the legendary Amazon in the *Aeneid*, whose purity was perhaps only matched by what must have been her brute strength. The author Virgil somewhat breathlessly writes that she killed Aeneas's strongest warrior with an axe "as he begged and prayed desperately: The wounds staining his face with warm brain-matter." It was only with the help of the gods that Camilla was finally defeated by a spear thrust under her breast that "drank her virgin blood." Romans of Aurelian's time were raised reading this heroic epic.

Then there was Penthesilea, the Amazon of Greek legend who fought against Achilles at Troy. In some versions of the ancient story, Achilles pulled off Penthesilea's helmet as she lay dying from his fatal blow and fell in love when he saw her beautiful face. The scene was embedded in mosaics on the floors of Roman houses and depicted on their pottery. Aurelian's historians were somewhat obsessed with Zenobia's helmet: girt with purple fillet and dangling gems. It seems like an innocuous detail today, but the ancients would have understood that a woman wearing a helmet was connected to Amazons—and to the great deeds of heroic men.

Of course, not all Romans regarded Amazons in a positive light. The poet Juvenal asked testily, "What modesty can you expect in a woman who wears a helmet, abjures her own sex, and delights in feats of strength?" But by raising the specter of Amazons and praising her masculine qualities, Aurelian and his historians were able to elevate Zenobia into a noteworthy adversary. It was a position Cleopatra could only have dreamed about—her young descendant garnering Rome's respect, if not admiration.

However, Aurelian propaganda was often contradictory. In their effort to make the emperor heroic in every conceivable way, historians emphasized the skill it took for Aurelian to defeat the Palmyrene generals. They often bolstered the reputations of these men at Zenobia's expense. Zosimus named the Palmyrene noble Apsicus as the principal author of the rebellion against Rome, not the queen. Others heaped praise on her generals, especially Zabdas. These were the real powers behind the throne that Aurelian had defeated. His victory was not over a mere woman, but over clever and capable men.

Aurelian, too, vacillated on the subject of Zenobia. He praised her masculine qualities in one letter and described her as a weak, frightened woman in another. He scoffed: " . . . as if Zenobia alone was fighting against me, and yet, as a matter of fact, there is as great a force of the enemy as if

I had to make war against a man, while she, because of her fear and her sense of guilt, is a much baser foe."

Yet, in a way, it is fortunate that Aurelian and his historians had to pursue so many different narratives to fit their agenda. They ended up creating a more nuanced portrait of Zenobia's life, her personality, and motives. Most women in antiquity, if mentioned at all, were presented as one-dimensional stereotypes—the manipulative queen, the chaste matron, the degenerate harlot, the doomed Amazon. Zenobia emerges from antiquity as a fully realized human being with a fascinating childhood, a complicated marriage, and competent reign. It's why I was drawn to her as I read my purloined copy of Zosimus's history from the Cairo expat library. She seemed like someone I could relate to, and would have enjoyed hanging out with in the Middle East.

Aurelian may have felt the same way. Like many historical women, Zenobia became something of a footnote over the centuries, but in her day she was the most fascinating woman in the Mediterranean. People across the Roman Empire closely followed her trajectory and were fascinated by her exotic lifestyle, her vast riches, and her military triumphs. Aurelian not only wanted credit for defeating Zenobia, he wanted to bask in her fame and aura, and that of Cleopatra as well.

Aurelian and Zenobia both had much to gain by including the legendary Egyptian queen in their narratives. For Zenobia, it conveyed the power of an ancient ruling family that stretched back to Dido. She claimed to be a descendent of both women, since Cleopatra had claimed Dido was her ancestor. As one historian wrote: "Boasting herself of the family of the Cleopatras and the Ptolemies, she proceeded upon the death of her husband Odaenathus to cast about her shoulders the imperial mantle; and arrayed in the robes of Dido and even assuming the diadem, she held the imperial power in the names of her sons."

It was in Aurelian's best interests to emphasize Zenobia's connection to Cleopatra because, by doing so, he likened himself to Augustus, the greatest of Rome's emperors. Augustus ended years of turmoil and created the Pax Romana, a protracted era of peace and prosperity. After his death, he was declared a god and every emperor who followed took his name.

When Aurelian entered Palmyra, he was already known as Aurelian Augustus. In his view, history was repeating itself. He had saved the empire from Cleopatra's descendant and was ready to institute a new Pax Romana across a united Roman Empire. If Zenobia was cast as the "new" Cleopatra, then he could assume the mantel of the "new" Augustus.

His victory allowed Romans to relive one of Rome's greatest eras: Augustus versus Cleopatra. It was like the remake of a classic film.

But the ending this time would have a different twist.

THIRTEEN

FLIGHT

In 2011, shortly after I started working at the World Bank in Washington, DC, I saw a news flash on my phone that Muammar Gaddafi had been captured by rebel forces in Libya and was shot in the head. For months, his family and supporters had been begging him to flee the North African nation he'd controlled for forty-two years. Instead of giving up, Gaddafi remained in his country until the bitter end, eventually chased from the capitol Tripoli to the Libyan desert. Rebels discovered him cowering in a drainage pipe, bloodied and confused. Within an hour, he was executed by one of his captors who was too impatient to hold him for trial.

Like Zenobia, Gaddafi had been raised in a Bedouin family and was propelled into power at a young age—he was just twenty-seven when he led a coup d'état against Libya's King Idris. He turned the oil-rich country into a socialist state and generally irked world leaders for decades with secret plots and unpredictable political alliances, interspersed with overall wacky behavior that was frequently parodied on Saturday Night Live. Gaddafi may have been sometimes amusing, but he was dangerous. He was deemed responsible for the 1988 bombing of a Pan Am flight over Lockerbie, Scotland, that killed 270 people. He was also heavily criticized for human rights abuses.

Despite his dismal record, I was saddened that Gaddafi's end was so brutal. I'd spent a lot of time in Libya and frequently met with Gaddafi over the years. He was, truthfully, *very* odd, and Libya was unlike any country I'd ever visited. There were no restaurants, movie theaters, or coffee shops and only a few businesses in Tripoli's downtown district. Once, when I was walking along the main street, I was surprised to see a store and pulled open the door to check it out. There were several clerks standing behind a single display case of about two dozen batteries arrayed on a white satin cloth. I didn't need a battery so I bid the clerks goodbye in Egyptian slang and walked out. They stood rigidly throughout the whole encounter and never uttered a word.

Downtown Tripoli was quite beautiful because all of the old Italianate buildings were perfectly preserved. Every façade was painted a creamy white and uniformly trimmed in the same shade of pistachio green, said to be Gaddafi's favorite color. There were a few billboards, but they didn't advertise consumer products. They were images of Gaddafi's face, sometimes in Bedouin clothing and other times in a British-inspired military uniform and aviator sunglasses.

During one trip to Tripoli, authorities confiscated my passport so I couldn't leave. I was with a group of journalists staying at the main hotel on the waterfront, and we were informed that we were forbidden to venture outside. Our in-room telephone lines were cut and it appeared someone had rummaged through my suitcase and taken my birth control pills. Day after day we questioned our flustered minders: Were we hostages? Could we call the Canadian Embassy? Could we be escorted to the Tunisian border?

Finally, our minders hustled all of the journalists onto a bus, took us to the airport, flew us to the Libyan desert, and led us into a white tent that seemed to be pitched in the middle of nowhere—just a barren plain of sand and dirt with nothing on the horizon. After waiting more than an hour inside the tent, I was hit by the overwhelming scent of jasmine. Car doors slammed, and in marched a cadre of beautiful women in military uniforms and clutching rifles, their lower faces covered by black veils—Gaddafi's famous female bodyguards. He followed behind them, looked surprised to see us, and asked coyly, "They told me you came here. What do you want?"

He chatted with us for an hour about nothing in particular. At one point he alleged there was a conspiracy to hide the fact that William Shakespeare was not English, but an Arab from North Africa. Everyone around me was furiously taking notes. I looked up and saw that he snorted with a smile. He was playing with us.

The following year, the United States threatened a military strike against Libya after spy planes uncovered a secret chemical weapons plant outside of Tripoli. Gaddafi agreed to meet me for an exclusive live interview in the ruins of his former home, which had been destroyed by the US ten years earlier in retaliation for a terrorist bombing at a German disco. His toddler daughter had been killed in the 1986 bombardment and the house was abandoned.

Mary, James, and I were picked up from the hotel in a black town car and driven to the ruins of the leader's former compound. We tried to get out of the car, but they locked us inside until minutes before we were scheduled to start the live broadcast.

When we were finally released, we raced to get ready. The house was in shambles, with concrete walls stained by decade-old blood and covered with large, gruesome photographs. Somehow, we got a call through to Atlanta master control as Mary helped a Libyan crew set up cameras and microphones. The Libyans were providing the satellite, so they could cut off the interview if they wanted. Gaddafi was nowhere to be seen as she helped establish the link with Atlanta. Through my IFB earbud I could hear the CNN anchor touting my upcoming live interview after "a short commercial break." I stared at Gaddafi's empty chair and wondered, How short? I was grateful I had taken a Xanax earlier.

With literally seconds to spare, Gaddafi drifted in and sat down across from me, right as the anchors pitched: "We go now live to Correspondent Gayle Young in Tripoli." The CNN control room operator hissed "you're hot" through my IFB. It wasn't a compliment; it meant that I was on camera.

This was my first—and only—live interview with a world leader. The US was threatening to take military action against Libya within 24 hours, and I was told that State Department officials were watching the live broadcast in Washington. In answer to my questions, Gaddafi announced he would finally agree to US demands and allow United Nations inspectors into the suspected chemical plant. He probably had stalled so he could clean out the facility before inspectors arrived. But the crisis was averted.

Years later, when Libyans began protesting during the Arab Spring uprisings in the early 2010s, Gaddafi could have safely fled Libya and found asylum in any number of African countries where he had friends and allies. But he decided to stay put and ride it out, as did other Arab leaders in the Middle East. It was a losing strategy.

Only months before Gaddafi's death, Egyptian President Hosni Mubarak refused to resign until protesters took over Cairo and his military backers melted away. He was taken prisoner and given a life sentence for failing to protect peaceful protestors and later sentenced again for corruption. Yemen's President Ali Abdullah Saleh also refused to step aside. He clung to power off and on for months until his car was struck by a rocket-propelled grenade as he tried to flee the capital. He survived the grenade but, like Gaddafi, was shot in the head by an impatient rebel.

Zenobia, too, waited until it was too late, and she was unable to elude capture. She reportedly had a secret tunnel that led from the throne room of her palace to a spot in the desert far outside of the city, allowing her to initially evade Aurelian's forces. "Should something unexpected occur, I shall enter the tunnel and go to my fortress," she was quoted as saying by the Persian historian al-Tabari. He says she escaped with camels in what looked like a normal caravan. Inside the heavy sacks slung across the camels' backs were not exotic goods, but hidden soldiers—a desert version of the Trojan Horse. It was a desperate last-ditch effort. She may have had some loyal bodyguards, but she was vulnerable and without an army to protect her against the Roman soldiers in hot pursuit.

To paraphrase George W. Bush's proclamation about Saddam Hussein after the second Gulf War: She could run, but she could not hide.

The queen was discovered near the Euphrates River, which today flows across Syria's border and into Iraq. She might have sought safety in the palace she'd built on its banks, where she and her family could escape the bustle of city life. Her vacation home would be the first place a Roman posse would look, but perhaps it was her only option, or that her decision to go there was more emotional than tactical. Zenobia was a bold woman but she must have been desperate, even afraid, as the Romans closed in on her and her family.

The Euphrates twists and turns through a rocky brown landscape, mostly flat and edged by small carpets of bright green grass on heavily silted banks. There are few trees to provide cover for a queen in flight; her camel convoy would have been visible for miles in every direction. Historians say Zenobia was captured while crossing the river in a boat or possibly fleeing under the water through a tunnel. A tunnel may sound implausible, but the river is quite narrow at some points. Perhaps it was a conduit, like the drainage pipe Gaddafi was pulled from centuries later.

Aurelian had ordered that the queen be captured alive, just as Augustus had wanted to keep Cleopatra alive to display in his triumphal procession in Rome. For Cleopatra, being paraded before jeering Romans was a fate worse than death. She barricaded herself and her maids within a tower in Alexandria and was soon surrounded by Roman soldiers who tried to determine how best to extract her. It's said that she outsmarted them by arranging for a basket of figs to be pulled up to her window by a rope. Hidden under the fruit was the famed poisonous asp. Augustus's grand plan was thwarted.

Aurelian was more fortunate in that Zenobia was captured alive and brought before him in chains. His soldiers demanded that the vanquished queen be turned over to them for punishment. We can only imagine what that would have entailed. But historians say the emperor refused because he wanted to take her back to Rome, "wishing to show her to the eyes of the Roman people."

There's no definitive description of what had to have been an epic first face-to-face meeting between Zenobia and Aurelian. Some Roman sources contend that she broke down in tears, blaming the men in her life for manipulating her into war to advance their own ambitions. Historians say she was put on trial, possibly in Palmyra, before Aurelian started his long march home. By then, the Romans had rounded up Palmyra's defeated generals and advisors to stand trial alongside her.

Zenobia's kingdom was gone. The same queen praised earlier as having the "courage of a man" was now ridiculed for being unable to make her own decisions. "Zenobia coming into court pleaded strongly in excuse of herself and produced many persons who had deceived her as a simple woman," wrote one Roman historian. I'd like to think this was all an exaggeration on the part of Roman historians, that Zenobia, a woman who had demonstrated considerable composure in the past, would have been a little sassier, albeit prudent enough not to court death.

The life of the "simple woman" was spared so she could return with Aurelian to Rome. But historians say the men who had advised her to wage war on the emperor were immediately put to death. The brilliant general Zabdas was tried and executed along with her advisor, Gaius Cassius Longinus, a well-known rhetorician who was said to be "skilled in pointing out the faults of others." Zosimus, a fellow historian, found the execution of Longinus to be particularly tragic; writing that a man "whose writings are highly beneficial to all lovers of learning, Longinus suffered upon the accusation of Zenobia." Although Zosimus did add that the philosopher went to his death cheerfully.

In this era of history, the condemned were usually tied to a stake and beheaded with an axe. But crucifixion was still a common method in the Roman world. Often the bodies, or just the heads, were left on posts as a warning to passersby. Aurelian wrote to a friend his thoughts on the trials of Zenobia and her court; "Why say more? She fears like a woman, and fights as one who fears punishment."

Zenobia may have avoided execution, but she was duly punished. Along the long road back to Rome, the emperor stopped in Antioch and had her chained on a dais in the middle of the city's hippodrome, a spacious outdoor entertainment venue where crowds typically gathered for spectacles and horse races. Once, Zenobia had considered Antioch a seat of power, where she ruled from her luxurious palace and likely walked the streets with a retinue of attendants, accosted only by sycophants currying her favor. No doubt she had attended spectacles at the same hippodrome, in the best seat, shaded and cosseted.

Now, her former subjects came to gawk at her shackled and suffering in the sun. Perhaps they were sympathetic. Or maybe they still held a grudge for the trick she and Zabdas had played on them by parading a man disguised as Aurelian through the streets before slipping out of town in the night. The gawking and ridicule would have been a painful ordeal for the former queen.

Aurelian continued to humiliate Zenobia as they resumed their journey back to Rome with his legions, parading her on a camel through all of the Syrian cities he had conquered. Zenobia was noted for her impressive regal bearing, but it was a long and arduous journey after a bitter defeat—she wouldn't have been at her best on top of a camel. As with Antioch, it is unknown how her former subjects reacted to the sight of their vanquished queen. The crowds may have stood in respectful silence, or been angry that she had involved them in her relentless pursuit of power. Because of her, sons and brothers and husbands died on battlefields. Families had lived in terror that Aurelian would sack their cities. Their dogs had been massacred.

It's possible the people of Syria were disappointed that the rebellion failed and that they were returning to Roman rule. But it's been my experience that people in the Middle East, as a collective, gravitate toward strong leaders and rigid governments, especially after turbulent times. There is often a preference for peace and order, even over civic rights. After the giddy success of the Arab Spring that ousted Mubarak from power, Egypt eventually moved on to yet another military-backed government.

I've wondered if Zenobia regretted the insulting letter she sent to Aurelian during the siege of Palmyra. She would have been much better off accepting his generous terms rather than trying to escape the city. Like the modern-day leaders caught in the web of the Arab Spring, Zenobia had refused to relinquish her power and suffered for it. Like them, whatever bold and relentless qualities she possessed that propelled her into the spotlight must have also prevented her from leaving it voluntarily. The ancient Greeks called it hubris, excess pride or self-confidence that leads to ruin.

As for Palmyra, it faced its own challenges in the wake of Zenobia's defeat. The rich and arrogant city had enjoyed independence before the rebellion and was not prepared to be treated as a defeated vassal to Rome. Palmyra had hubris of its own, similar to what I witnessed in 1990s Iraq.

FOURTEEN

BAGHDAD

In Baghdad, I marveled at how efficiently the CNN team could swing into action when news was breaking. We would leap into cars and careen through city streets. Cameramen hit the ground running as I trailed behind lugging the tripod. They muscled into the thick of things to record what was happening on our heavy industrial grade analogue TV cameras. We grabbed people to interview, on and off camera. We'd shoot the standup. I preferred that we record me talking on camera in a quiet, shaded place where I could look calm and professional. But the camera operator would inevitably pull me in front of a burning car or a riot for a dramatic background, with the wind whipping into my face.

Sometimes, I'd only have minutes to write a script, usually in the back of the car as it was speeding to our satellite video feed point. I'd listen to playback of the tapes so I could find good soundbites from people we had interviewed.

We would send the script to Atlanta for a quick review, then I would record the narration in a closet, or under a bedspread, or anywhere we could cut down on background noise. The video editor would combine imagery and the narrated track, scrolling through the tapes on large decks, and miraculously finishing with seconds to spare. It cost a lot of money to book a time on a satellite, so we rarely missed a feed. The tape would be jammed into a deck that was cabled to a satellite dish. We'd rewind and play the story a few times until Atlanta had a good copy with clean video and audio. Master control would add text at the bottom of the screen indicating location, my name, the names of interviewees, and then put it on air.

CNN was legendary for its speed in reporting news as it happened. The first global twenty-four-hour news channel, it was an endless beast that consumed videotape and was only sated when technological advances allowed for inexpensive live transmissions from anywhere in the world at any time, day or night. Smartphones now enable everyone to see what's happening on the other side of the globe via live stream, but back then we almost always had to tape news events and then transmit them to Atlanta through a satellite link. There were live satellite trucks in Jerusalem and we could rent them in some major cities, but that was almost never an option in the places where I was dispatched.

Yet, when our ninja-like news gathering was finished, and Atlanta was momentarily happy, it was torture to get us all together to go out to dinner. Like herding cats. Muhammad Ali was in town on a peace mission and holding court at the Al-Rasheed Hotel bar, and some of the crew had started ordering drinks. Watergate journalist

Carl Bernstein was spotted in the lobby. The drivers had disappeared to eat their own dinner. Someone was still taking a shower. Someone else was talking on the satellite phone with his fiancée.

I'm whiney when I'm hungry, so I usually opted for room service or microwaved a potato from the potato stash in the CNN workspace. Dump some canned tuna on it and I was good. But one night I went along to a big CNN dinner with about twenty people at a Chinese restaurant somewhere in Baghdad. It was dark and I hadn't paid attention to where we were headed. The chaos continued once we were seated. Some ordered appetizers while others shared entrees and most hadn't looked at the menu yet. My colleague Jane Evans, one of CNN's star camerawomen, and I were kind of tired, so we decided to cut out early. Out in the parking lot, we realized all of the drivers had, once again, disappeared. So, we decided to take a taxi.

We walked through a few dark streets to a busy avenue with cars and trucks whizzing along and started looking for a taxi. We were jabbering and laughing together, non-malicious gossip about CNN and the press corps, when a thought struck me. "You know, Jane, most Western women would be kind of freaked out walking around Baghdad in the middle of the night trying to find a ride home."

She blinked at me. "You know, you're right!"

We dissolved into even more laughter. Not because we were so brave but because our lives were so absurd. Eventually, we did find a taxi and got back to the hotel. The mid-1990s was a relatively safe period in Baghdad between the first and second Gulf Wars when Saddam Hussein still ruled with an iron fist and every Iraqi was cowered into submission. But our late night adventure was still a reminder that crazy situations had become our norm. And Baghdad was a crazy place.

After his 1990 invasion of Kuwait, Saddam Hussein had been defeated by a coalition of troops from forty-two nations in Operation Desert Storm, also known as the First Gulf War. Within a span of a hundred hours, allied troops had driven Iraqi troops out of Kuwait, gutted Iraq's entire military, and advanced to within 150 miles of Baghdad before returning back to the Kuwaiti border to negotiate a settlement. Saddam wasn't booted out, but he did have to accept strict terms for a ceasefire. All international trade and financial transactions were banned except for food and medicine. He would have to work with the United Nations to destroy all of his weapons of mass destruction. He had to accept UN inspectors tasked with looking for hidden weapons or for the illicit manufacturing of new ones.

An international embargo on flights in and out of Iraq meant that we had to drive from Amman, Jordan, to Baghdad, usually in convoys for safety. The trip took a minimum of twelve hours—about eight hours of which were spent traversing a ribbon of Iraqi highway through the desert. No bathrooms, no rest areas, no bushes, and no trees. I carried a large shawl to shield myself during bathroom breaks on the side of the road. If we stopped along the highway at night, I could look up at the sky and see the Milky Way. There was no light pollution on that barren stretch, and few clouds. I could even spot satellites streaking across space, carrying news and entertainment and important communiques from here to eternity. Perhaps relaying news from Baghdad about Saddam's ongoing machinations.

After his defeat, the Iraqi leader had to accept the presence of a United Nations Special Commission, known as

UNSCOM, specifically created to seek out and destroy Iraq's famed "weapons of mass destruction." This included missiles Iraq had modified to carry both chemical and biological agents capable of killing whole populations.

Centuries earlier, Palmyra, too, had to accept the systematic destruction of their ammunition and weaponry. Aurelian described in detail what he discovered when he was able to enter the fortified city. "There is no section of the city wall that is not held by two or three engines of war," he wrote to the senators of Rome. "And their machines can even hurl fire."

These "engines of war" were the weapons of mass destruction in the ancient world. Aurelian was likely describing catapults and ballista, which could be modified to heave highly flammable material wrapped around rocks. The Palmyrene would have used them to attack Roman battering rams or wooden siege towers. If the Roman camp was close enough, the Syrians could have burned down tents and temporary wooden structures. Ancient armies sometimes used these catapults to hurl diseased cows or human corpses, in the hopes they would spread plague within the enemy's ranks. It is the earliest recorded form of biological warfare.

Aurelian ordered the engines of war destroyed, along with all of Palmyra's weapons. Its army was disbanded. The emperor even stationed peacekeepers, like UNSCOM, to ensure that Palmyra was completely demilitarized. A Roman garrison of 600 archers was in charge of collecting a veritable mountain of spears, the main weapon of Zenobia's military force. They would have broken or burned the shafts and perhaps collected the deadly spearheads to send to Rome for recycling. The garrison also dismantled the towering sling shots and catapults that Aurelian had described. Perhaps these devices were also burned to ensure they couldn't be reassembled.

In Iraq, UNSCOM was tasked with searching and destroying Muthana, a mysterious complex in the desert outside of Baghdad. Saddam staunchly maintained Muthana was just the State Enterprise for Pesticide Production that churned out fertilizer for farmers. But intelligence during Desert Storm pinpointed the site as Iraq's main production and storage facility for weapons of mass destruction. In this secret lab, in the precise center of the country, Iraqi scientists worked to create some of the deadliest weaponry in the world. A supersized complex spread across hundreds of acres, Muthana produced chemical gases that were used in a long-waged war against Iran and were deployed in the Halabja massacre that had killed thousands of Kurdish people in Western Iraq in 1988. The arsenal included mustard gas, an old standby that has blistered the lungs of casualties since World War I. The World War II successor of mustard gas was the nerve agent sarin; one tiny whiff could kill an adult within minutes. Newer lethal chemicals included a nerve gas called VX that was thick and viscous enough to stick around and kill multitudes, rather than dissipating into thin air.

Scientists at Muthana also experimented with biological agents that could potentially infect and spread deadly viruses and bacteria throughout populations. Anthrax, which kills slowly over several weeks; poisons like aflatoxins that quickly cause cancer; and lethal forms of botulinum toxin that can unleash botulism severe enough to paralyze the heart.

I negotiated with the United Nations and the Iraqis for CNN to have exclusive permission to travel to Muthana with the UNSCOM team. The UN weapons experts had been in Iraq for months by then, dismantling the secret facility weapon by weapon. I would go as a producer with CNN's international correspondent, Brent Sadler and Jane, who would shoot the video. Karen was the sound technician and video editor.

We arrived at a military airbase at dawn to join the UNSCOM team for their daily commute from Baghdad to Muthana, boarding a transport helicopter for a thirty-minute ride south into the desert. The UN team was a genial multinational group of about two dozen weapons experts, many from England and Australia. Although they never admitted it, some were likely members of the SAS, the Special Air Service in Britain that trained secret operatives, or from covert military units in other countries. They were a secretive lot.

The chopper dropped us at a landing pad at the edge of the vast military complex. It was stifling hot. The four of us from CNN were kitted out with full hazmat suits and gas masks and taught safety protocols. We were required to rinse off our boots and suits throughout the day. But, because of the heat, we didn't have to wear the gas masks at all times, only when signaled to do so.

On the ground, Muthana appeared to be a maze of large flat rectangular bunkers and low-slung buildings. But from above, it was designed to look like a small factory complex. Many of the large hangers were topped with dirt and rocks to blend into the landscape, and there were decoy buildings to ward off air attacks. But those measures didn't work. The Iraqis who were hunkered down within the complex during the Gulf War told us that unmanned Tomahawk Land Attack Missiles would slam into the hidden bunkers that contained Iraqi weaponry, leaving the decoys untouched. The US cruise missiles, they said, were surprisingly low and slow, so the Iraqis on the ground could watch them as they approached and maneuvered toward their intended targets, like a floating bus headed for its parking space.

UNSCOM and Muthana's workers had removed Iraq's arsenal from the bunkers and stacked it outside—rows upon rows of dun-colored warheads and missiles and shells stretching into the dun-colored landscape. Iraq had manufactured thousands of surface-to-surface ballistic missiles known as SCUDs. Most of them were al-Hijarahs, short-range SCUDs with warheads capable of carrying and dispersing loads of chemical and biological agents. They'd been deployed against the Iranians and the Kurds for years, killing thousands of victims.

These terrifying weapons had ushered in a new form of warfare aimed at civilians. At the launch of Desert Storm, residents of Israel and other surrounding countries targeted by Iraq were issued gas masks and even provided with special baby carriages that created a safe air bubble for infants. Fortunately, Iraq only lobbed one known al-Hirajah missile at Israel during the conflict, and its warhead did not contain chemical agents. Instead, Iraq pelted Israel and Saudi Arabia with SCUDS carrying conventional explosives that inspired more fear than damage. The Iraqi-made missiles wobbled badly and couldn't stay on course because the gyroscopes needed to keep them stabilized were defective. They routinely missed their intended targets, or failed to detonate.

At the Muthana facility, the UNSCOM team was working with Iraqi weapons experts to methodically destroy the entire arsenal, which would take months, if not years. Jane recorded them carefully unpacking crate after crate of sarin-filled missiles. Steel drums were cut in half lengthwise and filled with gasoline, then the missiles were positioned in rows across the top like kabobs on a grill. The team duct-taped charges on the contraptions and then drove off to high ground about a half mile away. The detonator looked like one from the Bugs Bunny cartoons of my childhood: a box with a plunger. It created a fireball, triggering a massive black mushroom cloud of smoke and debris that drifted off over the Iraqi desert. All of the sarin was burned off instantly.

There was also an iconic evil laboratory filled with giant vats and drums, its tubes and flasks snaking up to the ceiling. It was here that chemical weapons were perfected and pro- duced. A sweet white-haired Iraqi scientist showed us how he was neutralizing hundreds of liters of chemical agents a day. When Brent asked him what would happen if we came into contact with the gases, he responded in broken English, "You will be died!" and gave a maniacal little laugh.

The Iraqis had given us permission to shoot video of Muthana because they wanted to show the world that they were serious about destroying chemical weapons, as agreed at the ceasefire. But, in reality, they chafed at the UN's pres- ence and were irritated by the constant supervision. They expressed their displeasure in a multitude of ways. The Al-Rasheed Hotel where we stayed had a giant mosaic of President George Bush on the floor of the lobby. Anyone entering or exiting had no recourse but to tromp across his earnest, smiling face. In the Arab world, showing some- one the bottom of your shoe is a grave insult, on par with flipping someone off with a middle finger. Stepping over

Bush's face with dusty footwear was the greatest indignity Iraq could lob at the United States. A giant "fuck you."

Under the thumb of a frightening dictator, Baghdad may have been relatively safe enough for us to stumble home from dinner, but it was an intimidating city where Americans were the enemy, and everyone spied on everyone else. It is common in dictatorships for images of the leader to be displayed as a sign of loyalty, but Saddam Hussein took it to a whole new level. His face was everywhere; on television twenty-four hours a day, in murals painted on the sides of buildings, on billboards hovering over traffic, and in framed photos prominently placed in every store, office, and in private homes. Larger-than-life statues of Saddam were installed throughout the country. There was a ten-story-high victory arch in the center of Baghdad with a replica of Saddam's hands holding two crossed swords. Most Iraqi men tried to look like him as much as possible, with big bushy mustaches and identical haircuts. Iraqis were constantly reminded of Saddam's power, even when they looked into a mirror.

Because informants were everywhere, Iraqis trusted no one, especially us. And we didn't trust them either. It was rumored that there were cameras behind the TV screens of our rooms at the Al-Rasheed. I'm not sure if that was true, but every time I threw a scarf over the screen, someone from housekeeping would arrive and remove it. It's the only hotel I've ever encountered where the doors could be locked from the outside so that you could be trapped inside the room, with no way out. Our drivers and translators were constantly questioned about what we did, what we said, and where we went.

There was an abundance of rules and protocols to make our lives difficult. For example, we had to adhere to the artificially inflated official exchange rate for the Iraqi dinar, although we were billed in US dollars. Once while moving some furniture in our workspace, we accidentally made a small scratch on the glass covering a framed poster. We were told we had to pay to get it fixed. Fair enough, but with the inflated exchange rate they calculated the damage at several thousand dollars. We had to pay cash for our rooms, and the damaged poster, in crisp hundred-dollar bills. I once went into Iraq with $100,000 in cash stuffed into a fanny pack under my shirt that made me look pregnant. When it came time to pay the hotel for our stay, I'd sit in the office with the hotel accountant who examined each bill by hand. There were certain sequences in the serial numbers that they would not accept. They also would not accept any bill that was bent or frayed. The process took hours. I couldn't be angry, though, because the poor workers weren't being obnoxious, they were simply terrified of accepting a suspicious bill and getting into trouble.

I was in Iraq frequently over the first couple of years at CNN, sometimes staying at the Al-Rasheed for weeks or even months at a time. During one visit, I decided to tag along with our translator to the Ministry of Sports, where he was going to pick up a spare video deck from their production department. This particular ministry was under the domain of Saddam Hussein's son Uday, who was perhaps even more evil than his father. We were told Uday would cruise the city's big hotels on Thursday nights, a hotspot for middle-class Iraqi weddings. At every venue there would be a dozen brides in heavy makeup, wearing long white dresses and veils, holding silk flowers, and looking terrified. They would consummate their marriages for the first time that night. I'm sure rumors that Uday was lurking about made them even more anxious. Witnesses swore that he would pick out young brides to rape in a hotel suite before turning them over to their new husbands. Some of these women would disappear or "accidentally" fall out a window or were just left dead. It may have all been exaggerated rumors, but my gut instinct told me that it was based on at least some truth.

I did not expect to see Uday when the translator and I went into the sumptuous Ministry of Sports in search of their video production studio. The building was bright and pristine and modern, but hardly anyone was in there. I felt a little spooked walking down the massive main hall with its blinding overhead arc lights and polished floors. Our footsteps echoed into the void. We found only one person in the video studio and he, too, was ill at ease. He gave us the heavy deck and we hurried to bring it back to our tape editors.

CNN was required to work out of the Ministry of Information so authorities could keep tabs on us. Our workspace was a large room inexplicably crammed with a dozen heavy brown armchairs that we couldn't seem to remove. Almost as soon as I returned from the Ministry of Sports with the deck, a Ministry of Information official urgently called me to come upstairs to see him. Usually, we chatted while sitting at a coffee table in his office, drinking glasses of sweet tea brought by an assistant on a metal tray.

This time, he indicated I was to sit in a chair in front of his desk. He demanded to know why I had gone to the Ministry of Sports. He specifically questioned why I had walked down the main hallway. *Why did you do that? Do you know who controls the Ministry of Sports? Do you?* I stuttered as I explained about our broken video deck and the need for a temporary replacement. He kept asking why I walked down the main hallway, the empty hallway that echoed with each footstep. His freakout was starting to freak me out.

"Leave Iraq immediately," he said, glaring at me from across his desk. "I'm telling you this as an official, not as a friend. Get out."

I went back to the hotel, jammed my things into a suitcase, arranged a car and driver, and headed out on the twelve-hour trip to Amman. There was no congenial convoy of cars that day, with snacks and books and witty conversation with friends and colleagues. I was the only one leaving and I didn't let the driver stop until we reached Jordan. By then, it was the middle of the night. The driver was illiterate and couldn't read a map. He was not one of our usual drivers and was only vaguely familiar with Jordanian roads. I could read Arabic, but didn't know what all of the words meant, so I read street signs to him phonetically and we managed to find our way to the Amman InterContinental sometime before sunrise.

I lay on the bed in the Jordanian hotel thinking about the Ministry official in Iraq and his threat, "I'm telling you this as an official, not as a friend." He was never my friend, of course, but we had met often over the past few years as I came in and out of Baghdad. He had always seemed outwardly sympathetic to the foreign press, and tried to help us get the video we needed for our stories. But he wouldn't have the job if he wasn't a vetted loyalist to the Saddam regime.

Once, he had given me a long lecture about how the United Nations, in general, and the United States, in particular, violated Iraqi sovereignty. He startled me by pounding his fist on the table, exclaiming that no country should be disarmed by another. It was an insult that UNSCOM was dismantling Iraqi weaponry and flexing their authority over Iraq's own military leaders. I wanted to say to him, "But you lost the war!" Iraq agreed to the very conditions he was railing against. The terms of the ceasefire called for the destruction of the weapons, for Iraq to compensate victims, and to accept economic sanctions. Most international observers thought Iraq got off too easily after Desert Storm and that Saddam should have been removed from power. But I didn't say any of this to the ministry official; I kept my own counsel. Freedom of speech is beloved in America but comes with unpleasant consequences in oppressed countries.

Seventeen centuries earlier, Palmyra too clearly chafed under the Roman occupation of their city-state, even with all of Aurelian's kind words and temple visits and civic deeds. As with Iraq, Palmyra's weapons were not only destroyed, but economic sanctions were enacted that interfered with their ability to trade. They were losing money and losing face.

In 273 AD, almost a year after Zenobia had been carted away to Rome, the Palmyrene staged a second rebellion led by a well-born citizen named Septimius Apsaios. The rebels first appealed to the Roman governor of the region, Marcellinus, making him an extraordinary offer. They said they would crown Marcellinus emperor of the East if he helped them restore the Palmyrene army, manufacture new weaponry, and to once again profit from the caravans by levying their own taxes. The offer was not at all tempting, but Marcellinus was in a bind. He had only a small force of Roman troops; he wouldn't be able to easily quell the rebellion by force. So, like Penelope holding off her suitors in the Odyssey, he chose to play for time. He told Apsaios that he was intrigued by their generous offer but would need to give it some thought—lots of thought—for a few months, at least. Then he sent a secret message to Aurelian to gather troops and return to Palmyra post haste.

Palmyra grew impatient as the months slipped by and decided to move ahead with their own king. A Roman child named Septimius Antiochus was declared Augustus, the title that Zenobia had used. Very little is known about little Septimius, but it is speculated that the boy king may have been a relative of Zenobia's or even one of her sons. There is a controversial Palmyrene inscription on which the name of Septimius's mother is scratched out. Scholars have suggested the erased name might have been Zenobia, and that Septimius was the Romanized name of a younger brother to the heir Vaballathus. Zosimus recorded that the boy was only five years old at the time he was named king, so he would have been born after the death of Zenobia's husband Odaenathus. Perhaps she was in an early stage of pregnancy when her husband was killed, or, far less likely, Septimius was her son by another father. I always wondered if he might have been Zenobia's nephew, a son of her much-loved sister.

Aurelian must have been furious when he received word from his governor that Palmyra was once again in revolt. Perhaps he was also irritated with the deceased philosopher Apollonius of Tyana, who had convinced him to bestow leniency in his pivotal dream before battle. In any event, in 273 AD, he once again marched against Palmyra.

This time, Roman troops sacked the city. Citizens were killed. Their homes, temples, and storehouses were pillaged.

Anything of value was hauled back to Rome and used to glorify the cult of Sol Invictus, or Invincible Sun, Aurelian's preferred deity.

Iraq, too, would attempt to throw off the yoke. Four years after Brent's CNN report on the destruction of weapons in Muthana, Iraq announced it would no longer cooperate with UNSCOM weapons inspectors, and the team was forced to leave the country. The United States Congress countered by passing the Iraq Liberation Act of 1998, which supported the overthrow of Saddam Hussein. After the 9/11 attack on the World Trade Center in 2001, the act was used to shape policy for the Second Gulf War.

Although Iraq was not involved in the 9/11 terrorist attack, Saddam became a focal point of the George W. Bush administration. Many US officials believed Iraq still had weapons of mass destruction, that some of the chemical and biological agents and al-Hirajah SCUDS had slipped through the net. In the spring of 2003, a US-led coalition returned to the region and, like Aurelian at Palmyra, invaded Iraq once again. It would later be proven that the weapons were destroyed, but by then Saddam Hussein had been overthrown and was later executed.

After decades of lethal civil conflict and economic turmoil, Iraq has slowly stabilized. Although I have no plans to return to Baghdad for Chinese food, a recent poll showed that the percentage of Iraqis who feel safe walking at night has risen from a low of 34 percent in 2009 to around 75 percent in 2022.

Palmyra, however, never recovered. It ceased to be a commercial trading hub and slowly disintegrated into a sparsely populated Roman outpost at the edge of the empire, housing a Roman garrison and whatever citizens remained to profit from their presence. Palmyra's unique language, and the specific gods they worshipped, disappeared. The last known Palmyrene inscription was from 280, just a few years after the second revolt was suppressed.

After the fall of the Roman Empire, rulers in the Middle Ages would rediscover Palmyra and use the site as a trading outpost, though it remained small in scale. By the 1400s, the ancient city's temples, palaces, theaters, and markets had crumbled into ruins and were bleached white by the relentless sun. The site was called Tadmor, the Semitic word for palm tree, after the small village outside its walls.

In her bold move to expand her empire, Zenobia instead caused it to be wiped out of existence—the city, the people, their language, heritage, and religion. Perhaps she suffered from hubris, unbridled ambition. Or perhaps she was just an ambitious mother who wanted to ensure her little prince was set for life.

FIFTEEN

HEIRS

While we know a lot about Zenobia's sex life, we know almost nothing about her role as a mother. There were few women leaders in antiquity, so that may explain why Zenobia's children were hardly mentioned in historical records. But to be fair, ancient historians didn't mention the children of male leaders either, except perhaps to impart the name of an heir. That's led to speculation today that ancient royals rarely saw their offspring, sons or daughters, except perhaps for a few moments out of their busy days. They were occupied with expanding empires, mustering armies, and quelling rebellions. Attendants kept the children seen but not heard.

But surely parenthood impacted people in antiquity as much as it transforms young parents today. Not only the rhythm of daily lives, but also perceptions about the future, the reassessment of what's important in life. And there is

209

plenty of evidence that Roman children were cherished. Their images are carved on tombs, with epithets praising their short lives. Children are depicted playing with toys and pets, picking flowers, and helping their parents with tasks. At The Metropolitan Museum of Art in New York, there is a marble engraving of a round-faced young boy with a puppy at his feet. The legend reads: "To the departed spirit of Anthus. From his father Lucius Iulius Gamus to his sweetest son." Girls were loved and honored, too. Little Soteris was not yet six years old when she was "devoured by pitiless death." Her monument recorded that her mother was inconsolable: "The grief which the daughter would someday feel for the loss of her mother, is now the mother's grief for the loss of her daughter."

Even in antiquity there was an expectation that parents would die before their children, not the other way around. It's true that childhood mortality in antiquity was higher than it is today; an estimated twenty-five percent of babies died before their first birthday. But it was still a heavy blow, a violation of the natural order of things.

We know Zenobia had at least one son, her heir Vaballathus, and there's evidence she had a second boy who may have been called Hairan. His image and name were inscribed on an imperial seal alongside that of his older brother. But given the great pains she took to conceive through her regimented sex life with Odaenathus, Zenobia may well have had multiple pregnancies and more children who survived infancy. One historian, writing long after her death, noted that she had daughters who married into wealthy Roman families who perpetuated her lineage. It's plausible that Vaballathus and Hairan had a few sisters to boss them around.

According to ancient accounts, Zenobia and her sons followed her husband to Persia during his military campaigns. The boys would have been very young, both under ten years old. However, it was not unusual for boys to tag along with their fathers to the battlefield. The young sons of Roman generals were often clad in modified military armor with pint-sized swords, so it's possible that Zenobia's youngsters also wore little uniforms while on the march. The Roman emperor known as Caligula, meaning "little boots" in Latin, got this lifelong nickname from Roman legionnaires when he was a toddler following his father around miliary camps under the watchful eye of his mother who, like Zenobia, accompanied her husband into war.

Once she was queen, Zenobia attended her court wearing the garb of Cleopatra with her young sons dressed like emperors. It must have been a great show of royal pageantry, the queen sweeping into the audience chamber in a heavy headdress, trailing masses of purple silk and emblazoned with jewels. Padding behind her, two little boys trying to behave in their scratchy purple robes. A family destined to rule, with an heir and a spare, regal and rich.

It's a given that a queen would have vast numbers of servants to care for her offspring. But the few historical accounts of Zenobia and her sons, in court and on military campaigns, suggest she was a hands-on parent. She clearly wanted her boys to experience as early as possible the life of a ruler, to understand their destiny as heirs to an empire, and the complexities of rule. They would be taught how to behave with regal bearing, how to handle petitions, how to render judgment, and how to settle disputes.

If so, Zenobia was following the Roman custom of including children in civic life from an early age. Every day was a variation of our modern "take your child to work" day. Girls were expected to learn weaving and domestic arts from their mothers. Boys were expected to dog the footsteps of their fathers and learn about the family business. Sons of the Roman elite would hang out in the Senate chambers or watch the training of troops on the Field of Mars. Their fathers were close by to correct their behavior and explain what they were witnessing. *This* is how you take down an enemy with a sword—or with a well-worded legal retort on the Senate steps.

Zenobia's children, whether boys or girls, would have been well educated. Age seven was regarded as the "age of reason" in the Roman era, when children from wealthy families would begin their formal lessons. Parents would engage tutors to instruct one child, or a whole classroom of children, including siblings, cousins, and loyal family friends within the family home. These educators were often enslaved Greeks, from the land of rhetoric and philosophy. They taught reading and writing, languages, mathematics, and history. The alphabet was engraved into wooden boards and children traced the outlines with a stylus through a thin layer of wax. Roman discipline was based on the proverbial carrot and stick. Tracing the letters properly could garner a pat on the head or, better yet, a sweet treat. Clumsy children would get their ears wrenched.

The oral tradition was strong in Rome. Children would memorize book-length ancient poems, such as the *Aeneid* in Latin and Homer's epics in Greek. The assignments helped them learn grammar and phrasing that could be replicated in writing their own compositions. Their arithmetic lessons would include little songs to memorize simple equations, and there were rhyming ditties to remember the sequence of historical events. Girls would usually drop out in their early teens, the age of marriage, but many would be literate enough to read and write.

It was possible that Zenobia's children were tutored by the famed rhetorician Longinus, who was executed after the queen and her advisors were captured. Zenobia initially brought Longinus to Palmyra to help perfect her mastery of the Greek language, and it's plausible that he taught her children Greek, as well. As a noted rhetorician, Longinus may have helped them learn how to speak in public and express themselves with clarity and elegance. The cheerful, well-spoken tutor became one of the queen's closest advisors.

Just as today, children of wealthy Roman families were not expected to spend all of their time learning gender-specific tasks and tackling philosophy. They were allowed to play. We have stone carvings that show youngsters spinning tops, shooting marbles, and flying kites. They had pets: dogs and cats, but also ducks, birds, and monkeys. Stone carvings show there were games for adolescents that involved balls and bats, although the rules of play have been lost to history. Little ones even played on seesaws and swing sets, like modern children on a school playground. They had board games, too, carved from wood or limestone, and they played with dice carved from ivory or bone. The objective was to strategize and beat your opponent, but with the added element of the luck of the dice—an apt guide to navigating adult life. There was an early form of backgammon, a game that is still wildly popular in the Middle East, especially Syria. I have a backgammon set from Damascus made of inlaid wood that we played for hours on end at the Sheraton hotel while waiting for a hostage release.

Zenobia's children must have roamed through the villa she built for her family on the Euphrates, along with their cousins, the children of the queen's sister Zabibah. They could have gone swimming in the shallow parts of the river, splashing and jumping like the little boys I'd seen playing in the pool in Damascus. Maybe the girls would have been allowed to get wet, as well, soaking their tunics, messing up their hair. Their mother, after all, was known for her unconventional youth as the adventurous daughter of a nomadic tribal leader.

The children could have played games of tag and make-believe on the grassy riverbank or climbed poplars and date palms in search of fruit and flowers. Perhaps they learned the Egyptian language from their mother. She may have enjoyed spending time with them when she was not consumed by the business of running an empire. I can imagine Zenobia helping her children craft little boats from bark with parchment sails, floating them in the garden fountain, blowing puffs of air that sent them skittering across the ripples of water.

Zenobia was certainly in a position to spoil her children with an abundance of toys and games and special treats, but I suspect she didn't. Ancient Romans loved their children, but they also had a civic duty to raise them for their proper place in a structured society. Zenobia was conscious that her children would hold power someday, which was why she would dress them in purple at royal events— to get the children, and the populace, accustomed to their intended destiny.

She was Roman, but she was also ethnically an Arab woman in the pre-Islamic Arab world, which likely influenced her views on parenting. In Egypt in the 1990s, most of the parents I encountered had a much more pragmatic view of children compared to what I experienced in the United States. Egyptian children were a fact of life, a part of the human experience. I'd walk into someone's home with no inkling that a child was even living there. No toys piled in the living areas. No highchairs encrusted with pureed carrots. I'd note a swaddled baby asleep on a bed while the rest of the family bustled around noisily.

Egyptian families in the '90s also lacked baby containers—strollers, carriers, car seats, bouncy seats, backpacks, highchairs, rockers, bathing tubs, pack-n-plays. Instead, everyone in the family, aged eight and older, took turns carrying the baby until he or she could walk on their own. I'd see toddlers milling around the legs of family members as a group strolled along, like the littlest elephants trying to keep up with the herd. No fussing and no crying. Sometimes the little human would headbutt an adult or older sibling who would swoop them up and carry them for a while, give them a peck on the top of the head and then set them back down. Children were not always the main focus of attention, but they were a much-loved fact of life.

Birth control had reduced the average family size in Egypt from seven children in the 1960s to about four children in the 1990s. It's now down to three. Having smaller families has given Egyptian parents the opportunity to give their children a better start in life. In the 1990s, the national school system was flailing with underpaid teachers and inadequate infrastructure. So, as they did in antiquity, parents hired tutors. Our CNN soundman Ali and his wife were determined to give their son and daughter the best education possible. He told me once that half his salary went to pay tutors. He was especially proud that his children were learning English, and asked Mary and me to come to dinner to meet them so they could practice. His wife had laden the table with some of the worst food I've ever encountered in my life; rancid oil-soaked pasta and stringy camel meat on a bed of unripe tomatoes. The children were adorable and sweet-natured, but their English was almost non-existent and grammatically questionable. They repeated over and over with gusto, "Welcome in Egypt!" When I tried to gently note that it should be "Welcome *to* Egypt" they politely informed me that I was wrong. Ali was so proud, ruffling the hair of his son. I would never criticize his tutor's competence or his wife's cooking.

Of course, not all children get tutors and toys. In the Middle East in the 1990s, as well as in antiquity, many had a much harder life. Poverty almost always rends families apart, and children suffer the most.

There were so-called "carpet schools" on the edges of Cairo where children spent the entire day weaving kilims on large looms. Tourists were told the schools were teaching the children a skill along with educational subjects. In reality, their little fingers were well-suited for carpet weaving; they received little education, and even less pay that went directly to their desperate parents. When youngsters grew too old or their hands too large, they were kicked out so that younger children could take their places at the loom. The parents were not evil, just impoverished and without a safety net.

Late one night as I was walking downtown in Cairo, I saw a garbage collector with a handcart urging a little girl to wade into a large pothole of filthy water to pick up some discarded cardboard. She could not have been older than four. It was a cold winter night and the little one didn't have shoes. When she sloshed back with the trash, her father cradled her into his arms and gave her a kiss. They both laughed, the little girl's face alight with the joy of making her father happy. That encounter spurred an ongoing fantasy in my head to help children escape the ugliness of poverty with the same level of love and encouragement.

Even the poorest families tried as much as possible to help their children prepare for a better life. No group valued education more than the Palestinians—I believe they would go without food if they could buy textbooks. I once visited a two-room Palestinian home that didn't have running water and only a few bare bulbs hanging from the ceiling. I could see a small canister of tea on a shelf next to a few discs of bread wrapped in cloth. The children wore clean and mended clothing. The parents didn't speak English but were delighted to know I was from America. Their oldest daughter was in America attending school! At university! "Do you know which school?" I asked in Arabic. They nodded and carefully pronounced the name: Harvard.

In antiquity, Zenobia was probably vested in securing the best possible future for the children she had painstakingly conceived. She was most assuredly ambitious in her own right, fulfilling her destiny as a descendant of Cleopatra, a princess of the desert, the widow of a great king. But perhaps Zenobia's determination to throw off the yoke of Roman rule and conquer the East was also motivated by her desire to leave her children a better world. She was setting up her son Vaballathus for success, clearing a path to glory!

Yet, in hindsight she set him up for annihilation.

Zenobia would have known the fate that befell the sons of rebellious royals. They were almost always executed, just as Cleopatra's heir Caesarion was killed after her defeat. It was a brutal practice but considered prudent. Allowing the sons to survive into adulthood could create a potential catalyst for rebels of the future to rally around, a temptation to restore the "rightful heir" to a vanquished throne. Sometimes sons were killed outright in public. Other times, they would quietly disappear, poisoned or smothered, or allowed to succumb to a fever. They would simply vanish from history, never to be mentioned again.

This could explain Zenobia's arrogant letter to Aurelian, refusing surrender. At that point, when it seemed all was lost and her defeat certain, she could have been focusing on the safety of her sons. Surrendering to Aurelian would put their lives at risk. Perhaps she left Palmyra and headed east hoping to hide them from the Roman conqueror, a mother's desperate flight to save her offspring.

It didn't work. Zenobia and her son Vaballathus were captured, and presumably her other children, as well. As a mother, she must have been anxious about their fate, even more than her own.

I know I would be—from my personal experience.

SIXTEEN

MOTHERHOOD

In early March 1997, I did something I'd never done before. I wrote "Bad Things that Happened Today," followed by a list: Atlanta had nixed my feature story on pet pigeons; there was a misunderstanding with a former boyfriend; my refrigerator had stopped working; the waiter at lunch had accidentally knocked a glass of Sprite into my lap and then charged me for it. At the bottom of this list, I added a single "Good Thing" that happened that day. "Went to US embassy and picked up Form I-600A—looks doable." I folded the list and stuck it in a notebook.

Form I-600A is the Application for Advance Processing of an Orphan Petition. It's an American citizen's first step in a long and complicated process to adopt a child internationally. When I stumbled on this list years later, I realized that I'd taken that first step to becoming a mother exactly nine months to the day before my daughter was born. I regarded it as the date of her conception. On the day of her birth, I, knowing nothing of her existence, was having lunch at an Indian restaurant in Bahrain.

When I made the list that fateful day in March, I was not really sure what I was getting into. I just figured I'd take the adoption process one step at a time and see where it led, and the first step was to fill out Form I-600A. This was not something I could do in a day. It was a months-long process that involved travel back to the United States. But once the form was completed and approved, the US would grant me permission to adopt internationally if I found an eligible child and completed the process within eighteen months. So, step one: Complete the form. Step two: Find a child. Countries that allowed Americans to adopt their orphans required the I-600A before they would match families with a child. The I-600A was so exhaustively thorough that it usually sufficed to assure governments that the American who had State Department approval was a worthy candidate for parenthood.

I never made a separate list of the pros and cons of adopting. I never ran the numbers to see if I could afford a child. Never dwelled on what could go wrong. Never really considered how motherhood would impact my career as an international television correspondent or how it would impact my tangled love life. I was moving into my late thirties and adopting just seemed like a good idea.

In retrospect, the pragmatic attitude toward children in Egypt spurred my decision to start the process. I was also influenced by Jenny, who had a baby girl with Khaled, CNN's freelance producer. Their daughter Aysha was adorable, with a shock of dark hair and big, brown eyes that looked at the world with perpetual amusement. The baby spent a lot of time in the Cairo bureau, babbling along with the office's pet cockatiel. Sometimes I would bounce her in my lap when I was conducting a phone interview or writing a script. Like most Egyptian families, Jenny would bring her offspring almost everywhere. A few spare diapers in a bag along with a bottle and maybe a rag to clean up spit. During a party, Jenny would put her to sleep on a sheepskin tucked into a corner somewhere safe. It seemed so easy.

One day, James took me for lunch at the home of elderly Italian Egyptian friends whom he visited often in a small town far from Cairo. After a fabulous lunch of cacio e pepe, one of the women at the table beckoned me from the dining room. I trailed after her down a corridor and into a sparsely furnished room. A newborn girl lay on a cot. The woman shut the door and explained in whispers that the baby had been born out of wedlock by a young girl in the neighborhood. She had hidden her pregnancy from her family and left the baby in the care of her elderly neighbors. They were incapable of raising the baby themselves, and they didn't want to turn her over to the state. If they did, the baby would be placed in an orphanage without hope of finding a new family, as adoptions were prohibited in Egypt.

Instead, they wanted me to take her and pretend that I gave birth to her. They told me they knew a doctor who would forge a birth certificate so I could get her a passport to the United States and raise her there. The woman picked up the soft little bundle and tried to put her in my arms. She was so tiny, with little curled fists and her eyes shut tight. I so wish I could have agreed. I would have loved to walk out the door with her and climb into the car.

But it was illegal and unethical. Even though DNA testing was not yet widely available, Egyptian officials would absolutely know it was not my baby. CNN was broadcast throughout Egypt and everyone who knew me had seen me on air, clearly not pregnant. I explained to the earnest lady that I couldn't break the law. We wiped away tears as the baby was placed back on the cot and we returned to the dining room.

The next day, I was taking a long car ride to the Western border to do a story on Palestinian refugees who had been kicked out of Libya but were not allowed into Egypt. They were stuck in limbo between the two countries, in a camp of donated tents in the middle of nowhere. At some point during that long ride across the desert, gazing at the eroded landscape of the Qattara Depression, I decided I was going to adopt a baby girl, somehow, from somewhere.

Egypt was not an option. I'd been once to a state-run orphanage in Cairo although I don't remember why I went there, and I haven't been able to find any story of mine that featured it. The facility was massive. One room was the size of an auditorium, with dark polished wood paneling and high ceilings. The floor space was crowded with cots and beds and cribs of all shapes and sizes for the many children of all ages. Most of the orphans seemed to be under twelve years old, but it was hard to tell. It was dimly lit, and kids were everywhere, trying to get as close to me as possible until they were gently shooed away by the director who was giving me a tour. There were little girls peeking at me from behind pillars and doorways, looking hopeful. Little boys trying to tug the hem of my skirt. All of the children were clean and nourished, but so desperate for attention, for acknowledgment. Islamic Shari'a law does not allow for children to be adopted, even if their parents are both deceased. Instead, Muslims can foster or become guardians of orphans under *kafala*, or sponsorship. *Kafala* is considered a good deed, a blessing in Islam. But a child cannot take the name of the adoptive parents and is not fully considered their offspring.

Years earlier, Egyptians sometimes took in children on their own, without a legal contract, to be companions or servants. I knew of a family that long ago had brought a little orphan girl into their home as a playmate to their daughter, and later an unpaid maid as she matured. For decades, this woman had worked for the family, cooking and cleaning, running errands and witnessing births and deaths, marriages and divorces. Now, she was very old and the family members who knew her when she was a child, and perhaps even loved her, were dead. The younger generation was in a quandary over what to do—she was infirm, and they wanted her out of the family home. They didn't know her well and were not attached to her, nor beholden to her as an elderly relative. She was just a maid. But she had nowhere to go, no family, not a single friend.

As an unmarried woman, and a non-Muslim, I was not eligible to take in an orphan under *kafala*. And even if I was, it would be questionable whether I could get the child a passport, let alone a visa to the United States. Documentation was a hurdle for many orphans in the Arab world. As they aged out of the system, they had trouble obtaining legal IDs needed for work or marriage. If the father was unknown or their births were undocumented, they would not have a proper paternal name on record.

Despite my love for the region, I would have to look beyond the Middle East for a baby. But first things first:

filling out Form I-600A, which required traveling to police stations and court clerks and doctors to get records, reports, and affidavits. Everything had to be notarized, not by a simple notary public but with an apostille, a big stamp with a red ribbon that was beloved by all international bureaucrats. Apostilles could only be issued by the office of the US Secretary of State and I had to make appointments through the mail and appear in person in order to obtain one.

I treated the I-600A like a hobby that I worked on in my spare time, gathering bits and pieces whenever I had the opportunity. It took almost a year, in part because I was sent on assignment to remote places like Kinshasa and Kashmir, but mostly because I was not yet connected to the fledgling world wide web. I had to figure everything out by tracking down people to answer my questions, just as I did when reporting my stories. Fortunately, the I-600A didn't come with a deadline.

When I went back to Connecticut for my annual home leave, I spent an afternoon at my hometown's police department getting fingerprinted and then waiting while they ran my PD Form 70, or Criminal History Request. I brought a book but spent most of the time chatting with officers at the front desk about the hidden felonies of Westport. I also had to pay a visit to the family accountant to get paper copies of all of my tax records for the previous decade. I had to provide proof that I wasn't married, proof of citizenship, proof I hadn't changed my name.

There were medical checkups to determine if I was in good health, and free of AIDS and other infectious diseases. At some point, I was required to get an X-ray to prove I didn't have tuberculosis. My dear Egyptian doctor Boutros Ghali—cousin of the UN Secretary General—looked at my X-ray image and started pointing out all the TB lesions on my lungs. I was shocked—I had tuberculosis!? "Gayle, everyone in Egypt has had tuberculosis." He gave me a clean bill of health because the lesions were small and already healed. I breathed a sigh of relief and checked that requirement off my list.

It occurred to me that I could go through this long, expensive, complicated process to show that I would be a worthy mother to a baby—or I could just go to a bar one night and get lucky. After some thought, I decided to continue with the adoption route.

I needed multiple home visits by a certified US social worker, which was the trickiest part of the process given that my legal home was in Cairo, not in the United States. In a brilliant stroke of luck, I found a certified social worker expat living in Cairo with her husband, who was stationed there on a work assignment. She came to my little roof-top apartment overlooking the Nile and we drank tea and talked about my childhood and my reasons for wanting a child. It was a wonderful experience because I hadn't examined my motives before meeting with her. I am the opposite of introspective; I just go with my gut instinct, which usually—although not always—works out. I'd not even told my family, nor any of my friends other than Jenny, that I was filling out the I-600A. So, until I met with the social worker, I didn't have much of a chance to talk over my thoughts and concerns and hopes and fears. Our conversations helped strengthen my resolve.

She inspected my apartment as part of the certification process, joking that she was on the lookout for open containers of lead paint, caustic cleaners stored in soda bottles, and hypodermic needles lying about. Nothing about my lifestyle was that disturbing. Then she leaned over the part of my balcony that abutted the building's airshaft and gazed down the eight-story drop to the garbage pit below. "You're going to move, right?" Yes. I was already preparing to transfer to Rome. I was trying to get the social worker component of the process finished so that I wouldn't have to redo all of the paperwork when my residency switched from Egypt to Italy.

After the I-600A was approved and I was settled in Rome, I had my allotted eighteen months to find a baby. It was time to call Eileen O'Connor. She was the CNN bureau chief and correspondent in Moscow and was a whirlwind of accomplishments. She ran one of the largest international bureaus in CNN. She had given birth to four daughters. She smocked their dresses by hand. She learned sign language. She scooped major news stories. And she pioneered the international adoption of children from Russia.

Eileen and her husband John had adopted a fifth daughter in the early 1990s, becoming among the very first Americans to adopt a Russian orphan. The obstacles were enormous: She was in the thick of reporting a coup against Boris Yeltsin, and because Russian authorities had previously prohibited Americans from adopting their children, it was a point of national pride that young Russians should not be shipped off to a long-standing adversarial nation. But Eileen had bonded with a spunky little nineteen-month-old while filming at an orphanage and was determined to bring her home. She managed to convince high-level authorities to change the rules and had been helping other Americans to adopt from Russia ever since.

Before I spoke with Eileen, I let my boss Steve know what I was up to. "I'm here for you, babe," he told me. He sent me on assignment to Moscow to help the bureau with a rush of news coverage, but also so I could track down a baby. Eileen quickly arranged for me to meet with a lovely Russian official who ran the Moscow orphanage system.

Under Russia's newly enacted laws, I could adopt as a single mother, and I was still young enough to qualify for an infant. However, I told the director over coffee that I was open to adopting an older child or a mixed-race baby. There were migrant workers from Africa and Asia in Moscow, and their offspring were abandoned more frequently than Caucasian children. The director waved an elegant hand. "I have the perfect baby for you already." She had me write down a name: Small World Adoption Agency of Mount Juliet, Tennessee. "Register with them," she said cryptically.

My friend Susan from *Newsday* had been reassigned from Cairo to Moscow and I was staying with her in her high-rise apartment. That night, I looked out at the city from her narrow balcony. It was spring by then, and the air was cold but not too harsh, soft with rain. The sky was pitch black and the lights of Moscow stretched far into the distance, yellow and white with a hint of red.

The Chinese have a belief that two people can be born connected by a very long, invisible red thread looped around their wrists. Over time, the red thread gets shorter and shorter, drawing the two people together. Through the twists and turns of time and fate, they become closer and closer until they finally meet, seemingly by chance. The belief was originally meant for lovers, but was adopted, so to speak, by the adoption community.

Somewhere out there in Moscow that black night, there was a baby. That child was my daughter. I didn't know where she was or what she looked like. But I knew that she was there, and we were drawing closer and closer, the thread that connected us was pulling us together. Soon, I would meet her, pick her up, and hold her close, and we would be a family. That evening was the first time I felt the enormity of what I was doing.

The Small World Adoption Agency was a small, Christian-focused agency run by a big guy named Jimbo. I don't think I would have ever thought to hire them on my own. However, I later learned they were the only US agency registered with a specific orphanage in Moscow known as Baby House No. 2, where my future daughter was located. Small World was therefore the sole agent able to complete the adoption process of this particular child, whom the director had chosen for me. Jimbo and his team, which mostly consisted of his own family, were helpful and experienced.

In the late 1990s, there were an estimated half a million registered orphans in Russia, most of them living in more than 1,000 orphanages. The number of Americans adopting from the country was increasing, but they only took a proportionately small number of the children available; in the year I was there it was maybe 5,000 out of the 500,000, or one percent.

Following the instructions given to me by the Russian orphanage director, I called Small World, signed up, and paid a fee. I filled out more forms, sent more documents, and then waited for my referral. A few months later, a package was delivered to my office in the Rome bureau with a VHS tape. I popped it in the deck and watched a thirty-second video of a girl staring into the camera and drooling. She was neither mixed race nor an older child. She was a blond-haired, blue-eyed months-old baby.

Later, the orphanage director told me they picked my daughter because they thought she looked like me and they wanted people to assume she was my biological child. There was a great stigma at that time in Russia against internal adoptions, and many Russians along the way advised me to never reveal to anyone that my daughter was adopted.

After watching the VHS tape about a hundred times, I called my colleague, Elisa, who was working in the Moscow bureau, to share my news. We arranged for her to go to the orphanage and take more photos and video of my future daughter. She called me a few weeks later while I was in the Sistine Chapel showing around some CNN executives who were visiting Italy. I slipped out to the colonnade in St. Peter's Square to take the call and leaned against the base of a pillar as Elisa told me that if I didn't adopt this baby, she would. She sent me the cannister of film from her camera, which I raced to get developed at a drugstore near the Rome bureau. I flipped through dozens of images of my daughter leaning against the bars of her crib. She looked unsmiling at the camera, intrigued but calm, her cheeks flushed pink. Her hair was sparse and reddish from malnutrition, and her eyes were an arresting shade of light blue and gray.

The next step of the process was to visit Moscow to meet her in person. Then I would sign an agreement of acceptance with the Russian authorities and head home to Rome to wait for an assigned court date. I would then return to Moscow for the court hearing, after which I would take my daughter out of the orphanage but would be prohibited from taking her out of Moscow for ten days. The holding period was designed to give new parents time to ensure they were happy with their decision and fully committed to the adoption. Parents who balked after spending a few nights with a confused and possibly frightened child could change their minds and return the baby to the orphanage. After the ten days passed, I would be given my daughter's revised birth certificate and her Russian passport. I'd then take that passport to the US Consulate in Moscow, which would issue her a travel visa to America. This would allow me to take her to Connecticut at Christmas in hopes of securing her US citizenship—the final step in the process I had started eighteen months earlier.

I flew to Moscow for the first meeting and took the long drive to the outskirts of the city where the orphanage was located. Baby House No. 2 was an innocuous squat white building in a crowded residential area. It looked like it could be a school or an office building or an apartment block. There was a small, weed-covered play area with a metal slide and swing set surrounded by a tall chain-link fence. I arrived bearing gifts for the orphanage caregivers: a stack of colorful scarves from Rome, boxes of chocolates, and fruit. I wore a red chenille sweater because someone had told me babies loved the softness of chenille.

It was very early because the babies were awakened at six in the morning and were put down for their first nap at ten, so the window of opportunity to finally meet my daughter was narrow. I bounded from the car, the metaphorical red thread pulling me through the door, into the lobby and up the stairs behind the orphanage director. I had a feeling that my feet didn't quite touch the ground; I floated.

The room was the size of a modest cafeteria with white and green walls and a linoleum floor. There were bookcases along the longest wall with a handful of plastic toys behind glass. In the center of the room were a pair of extra-large playpens, each holding a dozen babies crawling around like puppies or sitting up staring at each other.

The caregivers whisked up my daughter and shooed me back. This was a big occasion, and they wanted her to be appropriately dressed. All of the babies were wearing sleeveless flannel onesies tied at the shoulders over long-sleeved cotton T-shirts. The caregivers quickly changed her into a poufy red polyester dress and pulled out a pair of white patent leather shoes, even though she was too young to walk. Her little face was pinched with confusion, but she didn't dare cry. Finally, they handed her to me. She grabbed a fistful of red chenille and nestled in my arms, gazing contentedly at her small, confined world. All I could see was the top of her head as I paced from one end of the room to the other. When I tried to put her down to get a better look at her, she wailed, so I picked her back up and resumed pacing.

There were around 115 babies in the facility, from newborn to about eighteen months. The room my daughter stayed in was for babies that could crawl and sit up but not walk. I thought of them as the "quadrupeds." Once they started walking, they were moved to the "biped" section.

The quadruped sector was mostly this one large room. To the left, there was a smaller room with wall-to-wall metal cribs. On the right was a tiled room with a small kitchenette at one end and potties on the other. My daughter had been in this facility her whole life. She had been one day old when Russian officials brought her here from the hospital where she was born.

Then my phone rang. It was CNN. I had to put my new baby down and step to the far end of the room to take the call. She wailed and the caregivers and director hovered around her, murmuring. With the phone jammed in my ear, I watched as she wriggled to look between the cluster of women straight at me. We locked eyes and she stretched out her arms begging to be held. Here she had just met me, a stranger, and she had known her caretakers her entire life. Yet it was me she wanted, as if she somehow knew who I was.

I visited the orphanage as often as possible while waiting for my court date. Steve had sent me back to Moscow to help cover Russia's 1998 economic crisis, which led to the collapse of banks and widespread social unrest. It was a busy time in the bureau, but I would wake up before dawn and a car would pick me up for the drive across the city. I spent as long as I could at the orphanage walking around the quadruped room with my daughter while looking at the top of her head. Then I'd hand her back to her caregivers and the car would take me to the CNN bureau in time for morning assignments.

The babies spent most of their time sleeping or in the pens with the other babies and a couple of toys. All of them were sweet and adorable. I once made the mistake of picking up a little boy who very much wanted to be held, and my daughter threw a jealous fit. She wanted one hundred percent of my attention. I brought her a book of colorful illustrations printed on thick cardboard pages that she promptly tried to chew. I realized it was the first book she'd ever encountered; it took her a moment to look at the pictures and follow my finger as I read her a story. The communal toys were well loved. Like the rest of the babies in the shared pen, she was most fascinated by a hard plastic clown's head about the size of a grapefruit with a grotesque red, blue, and yellow face.

Although the babies were quite young, they were no longer bottle-fed. The caretakers would put cups of water to their lips that mostly spilled down their shirts. Because of the financial crisis, food had become very expensive and the infants were usually fed a porridge of buckwheat groats known as *kasha*, sometimes with a dollop of applesauce or sour cream. The growing babies did get a little meat once or twice a week and the director told me the caretakers were sometimes jealous because they could not afford meat for their own families. I brought food on every visit, including bananas, bread rolls, applesauce, crackers, cheese—always enough for the ladies to take some home.

There was a matron named Olga who I thought was unnecessarily stern, maybe even a little harsh with the babies. She didn't tolerate nonsense and could change a diaper at lightning speed. But once I caught sight of her before I came into the room, when she thought she was alone. She was doing a little mock striptease dance with her apron, twirling it over her head, and the babies were gazing at her and giggling with delight. I came to realize they loved Olga most.

I was only allowed to visit early in the morning, so most of my time was spent working in the Moscow bureau. Russia was having a moment of intense turmoil. The government had devalued the ruble and defaulted on loans. The oligarchs, who had snatched up former state-run industries a decade earlier, were losing their fortunes and were not happy about it. The lobby of my luxe hotel along the Moskva River was a scene out of a spy thriller. Russian businessmen in dark suits arrived for meetings in a dark bar, accompanied by chiseled bodyguards said to be Israelis. The guards stood, feet apart, hands close to the waistbands of their designer jeans, sizing up everyone within firing distance. There were women, too, with thick blond hair and impossibly high heels, looking simultaneously languid and hyper alert.

One day, I was sent out to do a story on how the financial collapse was impacting rural populations. I spent time with an older woman who earned the equivalent of $35—a *year!* She grew her own food in a compact garden and traded with her neighbors for anything she was lacking. Every item in her home was reused and recycled. Coffee cans became buckets to draw water from the well, thread was unraveled from rags and used to sew scraps, a yogurt container served as a cup. She had a wonderful sauna she'd made out of twigs and rocks and stocked it with handmade soap. She said the main things she purchased with her scant pension were sugar and tobacco. She laughed when we told her about Russia's economic crisis, because she had no money anyway. Our CNN car got stuck in the mud on the way back to Moscow. The village roads were just tracks made by people and cows.

My court date for the adoption was set for early November and the weather had turned cold. At this point, Elisa and I traded places. She was in Rome, where her family lived, waiting to give birth to her second daughter. Her husband and older child were with her. I was staying in their apartment, a short walk to the CNN Moscow bureau. Their home had all the baby containers I would need. There was a crib and highchair and toys and electrical sockets that were baby-proofed.

I usually had very light periods that only lasted a day or two at most. But the morning of my court appearance I woke up sopped in blood and with a raging headache, shaking as if I had a fever. I dragged myself into the shower but cut it short and lay on the bathroom floor, shivering and sweating simultaneously. If it had been any other engagement, appointment, or assignment, I would have canceled. But I had no choice. If I didn't show up to court, the officials would write me off and I'd lose my daughter. I'm sure giving birth is more painful, but I had to wonder as I lay there, my cheek pressed into the cold tile floor, battling waves of pain and blood, if this was some sort of divine symbolism of the suffering women must go through to become mothers.

I managed to put on a dress and tights and drag myself outside to the pickup spot in front of the apartment. I reclined on a snowbank, grateful for the icy cold that formed crystals in my sopping wet hair. Perhaps I could freeze my headache. The representative for the Small World Adoption Agency pulled up in a Lada with my newly hired lawyer riding shotgun. Neither seemed unduly concerned by my condition. They hustled me into the back seat of the car, where I flopped like a fish. We took off, the two women babbling merrily in the front while I lay prone in the back. We had errands to run. We needed to pick up food for the children, then collect the director of Baby House No. 2, and then drive together to the courthouse in the judicial center of Moscow. It took a couple of hours, which allowed me to slowly regain consciousness, and for my hair to dry. They passed me bottles of water and some crunchy biscuits. Later, I wondered if they just assumed I was hungover after an all-night vodka fest. It was Russia, after all.

The courthouse was massive, the epitome of neoclassical Russian architecture. The hallways could accommodate four lanes of traffic. Ceilings were tall enough to fly a kite.

I was ushered into a room where a judge sat behind a long wooden desk on an elevated dais. My daughter's lawyer and my lawyer had desks in front of floor-to-ceiling windows, where bright sunlight, reflected by white snow, beamed through dusty panes. The orphanage director sat with the lawyers, and I sat on a pew-like bench with the Small World representative on one side of me and my official interpreter on the other. Everyone in the room was female.

There was a hearing. The director of Baby House No. 2 testified that my daughter had already bonded with me, since I visited so often. The judge asked if any Russian family had shown interest in taking her instead, and the director lifted her hands up in a gesture of defeat. The economic crisis had destroyed the finances of many families. The judge nodded, conceding it was unlikely. She asked me a few questions about my job and plans for childcare and then asked if I had anything else to say.

I'd given this a lot of thought. I told her that my daughter would be raised to know and respect her Russian heritage, the rich history of her land, its art and literature. She would know that from the moment of her birth she had been in good hands; that she had never been abandoned, never cast aside, but instead cherished and protected. I said I would always be grateful to Russia and the Moscow orphanage system for taking care of my daughter until I was able to take her home.

There was a moment of silence, the beams of cold light from the windows illuminating our little tableau. I wondered if I'd come across as condescending instead of deeply sincere. I felt as pathetic as I must appear, with no makeup, hair barely combed, pale and weak. The judge finally said thank you and asked us to leave the courtroom.

I'd been advised that it would take hours before the judge's decree, so I'd come with a book. But I'd barely settled onto a bench in the four-lane hallway when I was summoned back into the courtroom. It reminded me of the Peter Tosh trial in Jamaica when the verdict was reached as the jury walked out to deliberate. We all stood as the judge returned to her desk on the high platform. She looked me in the eyes and said, "Congratulations. You are a mother." I'd expected approval of my request, but somehow that simple statement felt like such a shock. I couldn't help it; tears filled my eyes and I let out a sob. My nose was starting to run. The director of Baby House No. 2 handed me a tissue and I realized she was teary, too. Just like that, I was a mom.

The next morning, when I arrived to pick up my daughter, I brought a complete set of clothes, along with a diaper, a jacket, and shoes. The shoes were very important. I was firmly advised they would not release her unless she had shoes. For the last time, I entered the quadruped room on the second floor. The tiny comrades watched curiously as the ladies undressed my daughter completely and changed her into the clothes I had brought—even her clean orphan-issued disposable diaper was whisked off and set aside to use on another baby. My daughter came without a single accessory. She owned nothing. The last thing they did was pull the Russian pacifier out of her mouth and pop in the new one I'd brought for her. Then they handed her over to me for good.

As we left the room, we ran into her caretaker, Olga, who was just arriving for work. She realized I was taking the baby far away and she'd never see her again. Olga reached out to hold her one last time, tears streaming down her cheeks, her lips on the crown of my daughter's head. I took a photo so my daughter would someday know how much she was loved.

It was probably the first time my daughter had left the orphanage building since she had been brought there as a newborn. She sat on my lap in the back seat of the car, looking out at traffic and buildings and road signs and people and stores and stoplights. There was a whole world she'd never seen, sights and sounds she'd never encountered. I was prepared for her to freak out, but she just gazed quiet and wide-eyed at everything.

We spent the next ten days at Elisa's Moscow apartment. I gave the baby a bottle of milk and she didn't know how to grasp it, so she maneuvered it onto the edge of the highchair tray and lowered her head until the liquid flowed downward. I had to teach her how to hold the bottle upside down. She loved the new foods, toys, the trips outside, music, the snow, the rain, books, baths, and walking barefoot on carpet while holding onto my hands. I took her to Red Square in a soft falling snow that made her cheeks rosy.

On her first birthday, the Russian women who worked at the Moscow bureau made her a cake that seemed to lack any kind of sweetener and had the consistency of damp sawdust. But the local CNN staff loved it. That day, we had our appointment at the US Embassy to get her visa and the packet of documents she needed to obtain her green card in America. At that time, American parents of an internationally adopted child still had to apply separately for US citizenship for their new offspring, it was not automatically granted. The Russian government had provided me with her Russian passport, her original birth certificate, and a new birth certificate with her new name and listing me as the mother, with no father. They advised me to destroy the original birth certificate, along with other documents that included the names of her birth parents, so that she would not be able to find them. I would never do that.

There was one glitch on the flight home to Rome because it had never occurred to me that I would need to buy the baby a separate ticket. This was all new to me. Alitalia got everything sorted and we were able to make the flight. I'd prepared a small room for her in my Rome apartment with Jenny's help. In truth, it was a large walk-in closet attached to the second bath, but it had a big window overlooking a courtyard, a small built-in bookcase, and a nook that was the perfect size for a crib. I'd kitted it out all blue and yellow, with art and books and stuffed animals from the Italian version of Toys "R" Us. I got one of those cool Italian strollers that folded up like a tripod with a strap that I could wear over my shoulder, the same way I carried the tripod for our CNN camera.

Once in Rome, my daughter pretty much hit the ground running. She practiced her first toddling steps on cobblestones in Piazza Navona, learned to swing on the playground at the nearby Castel Sant'Angelo, and splashed in a wading pool on our terrace when the weather warmed.

She didn't speak for a long time. I figure it was because she was suddenly bombarded with Italian and English as well as Polish from her new nanny. When she heard people speaking Russian on our long walks through the city, she would whip around to listen. Her first word was *da*, or yes in Russian, her second was *up* and her third was *cornetto*, an Italian croissant.

She retained a lot of her Russian heritage. She'd wave around her bottle of juice like a bottle of Smirnoff, take a big swig with her head tilted back, then wipe her mouth with the back of her hand. She thrived in snow and sleet. She was sometimes quick to anger and always quick to laugh, especially at herself. To this day she is a Russian beauty with a sardonic sense of humor and an awesome resting bitch face.

Adopting my daughter was the best thing I've ever done.

SEVENTEEN

JOURNEY

On a spring day in Rome, I stepped aboard my waiting chariot. Overhead, masses of floating white clouds scuttled across the sun, shining bands of silver light. The chariot too was trimmed in silver, a U-shaped platform with a waist-high barrier open at the back. The heavy wooden wheels were thick and studded with iron.

The charioteer in front glanced over his shoulder, his face leathered by the sun, his eyes squinting. He wore a short tunic of white trimmed with gold under a black leather jerkin adorned with imperial medallions at the shoulder. His bandy legs were encased in soft leather boots that laced up his calves. He nodded and turned back to the horses, raised his whip, and braced himself at the front of the platform, while, behind him, I grasped a thin metal handrail with both hands. Four matching pure white horses took off with the synchronization of ballet dancers, their tails and manes a blur of soft silky white as they picked up the pace.

The thick wheels hit ruts and rocks and jolted every bone in my body. We turned fast and I braced against the rail, trying not to slide backwards off the platform. The wind whipped my face, blowing bits of sand into my eyes. As we raced across a field of rubble, I finally caught my breath, found my voice.

"Basta! Enough! Stop already!" I shouted above the thunder of the wheels. The charioteer looked over his shoulder at me and clicked his tongue in disappointment. He brought the equally disappointed horses down to a slow walk.

It was not a daydream. The chariot was a prop from the 1959 film *Ben Hur* and the charioteer had supposedly been a stunt double for Charlton Heston. The four white horses were the direct descendants of the equine quartet used in the movie's most iconic scene, a chariot race between Ben Hur and his former friend, the traitor Messala. The ruthless Messala tries to kill Ben Hur by ramming spikes into the wheels of his chariot, but Ben Hur recovers and defeats his rival in the end. The movie was made before CGI, so the producers had to create real chariots and train actual horses for the gripping and dangerous scenes.

Thirty years after the movie's debut, I was on the edge of a parking lot, racing along a strip of land near a motorway. The CNN crew was somewhere behind us, obscured by a cloud of dust. It was not exactly like transporting back in time to ancient Rome, but it was a taste of what travel was like in the 270s AD.

Zenobia's long journey to Rome must have been excruciating, bumping and jolting over vast stretches of land in chariots or carts for hours a day. Palmyra is roughly 2,300 miles overland from Rome, so the trip with Aurelian's legions would have taken months. Each day, she would be stepping farther and farther away from her homeland, from the palatial halls of her palace, the palm trees that rustle in desert wind, the soft plodding sound that camels make as they trudge under their loads. Behind her was the world she was born to, that she conquered, and lost. She must have realized she would never see it again. Ahead of her, growing closer, was a world unknown. Perhaps her hands were bound, perhaps she had to beg for water. In cities and towns, she was paraded through the streets, an object of ridicule, possibly assaulted.

The fate of her sons was uncertain and likely tragic. Historians say the fourteen-year-old heir Vaballathus died shortly after he and his mother were captured, or possibly on the journey to Rome. It was never clear if he was executed or succumbed to illness. Her younger son Hairan was never mentioned again, suggesting he, too, had died quickly and quietly. The heartache must have been unbearable. The loss of a child, a shock that numbs the brain and an anguish that creates physical pain. I know Zenobia must have been devastated, even catatonic.

Many years after I left Cairo, my friend Jenny's daughter Aysha died unexpectedly at age seventeen. The baby who had brightened the Cairo bureau with her gurgling smiles, and grown into a quirky, kind, and intelligent girl. I sat on her hospital bed as she was removed from life support, my lips on her forehead, murmuring that everyone loved her. Jenny was crazed with grief and tried unsuccessfully to kill herself. I laid beside my dear friend that night, listening to her deep gasping breaths and sobs, my own pain engulfed by a mother's.

Zenobia's mourning would have been as vast. Her sons would have been only a little younger than Aysha, on the cusp of an adulthood never realized. The queen would mourn for her male progeny, her lost kingdom, the slaughtered soldiers, the forfeited treasures, her descent from power to helplessness. Perhaps she was comforted by a daughter, or daughters, who may have been allowed to live, but the emotional pain would have been heavy. Jolting along at a relentless pace, the days slipped into weeks and months. She had much time to replay the horror and rue her mistakes.

Zenobia's own fate would have been uncertain at this point. Zosimus wrote that Aurelian was "much pleased" when she was captured and brought to him in chains, but that "he became uneasy at the reflection that the future ages would not honor him for having conquered a woman." With his public image foremost in his mind, he was conflicted over what to do with her, whether she should live or die. He must have turned over different scenarios in his mind on that journey, wondering how people would judge his actions, in which direction the gossip would flow, sullen and resentful at the thought that his triumphant procession might be tarnished by his foe's gender.

Perhaps during that long, jolting, uncomfortable chariot trek from Palmyra to Rome, Aurelian and Zenobia had moments of connection, frank exchanges from one leader to another. Perhaps they built a nascent friendship—two Romans who grew up far from Rome and seized the opportunities that unexpectedly came their way. He had won, she had lost, but they both stepped forward as leaders and warriors in a chaotic time. Perhaps, too, once she'd regained her composure, she'd argued it was all a big misunderstanding, that she was simply securing the empire during Rome's crisis, that her coins and decrees *had* included Aurelian's name. She was just trying to create a strong and united East for her Roman son, who was the rightful heir to a celebrated client king.

It would explain why at some point on the journey, Aurelian changed his opinion of Zenobia. In a letter, after they had returned to Rome, he wrote that "she did a great service to the Roman State" when she and her husband secured the empire against the Persian invaders. He acknowledged that his predecessor, the Emperor Claudius Gothicus, wisely allowed her to rule unchecked in the early years, when he was preoccupied with his campaigns against the Goths. Aurelian no longer referred to Zenobia as a mere woman. She had become someone he quite admired and to whom he was somewhat grateful.

The end of Zenobia's long journey would be in a city unlike any on earth, a jumble of narrow streets radiating from a too-small forum. There were close to 1.5 million people living in Rome by the 270s AD, a mixture of the original Italianate Romans, and those granted citizenship from across the European continent, through North Africa, and along the Middle East.

Rome would have been crowded and the housing shortage acute. Even a wealthy man's home would have had rows of shops and fast-food kiosks along the perimeter, with the front door wedged somewhere between the basket seller and a fishmonger. Step inside and the house opened up into a maze of atria and open courtyards, filled with sunlight and cooled air. Windows faced inwards to gardens, not out toward the chaotic streets. These rich houses were known as islands, floating like a little bit of paradise in a sea of noise, stench, crowds, and jostle. But most Roman families crowded into small apartments or single rooms, like that of my former Egyptian tutor Hanan in Cairo. Cushions were thrown down at night for sleeping and stacked in the daytime so family members had somewhere to sit while they ate. There were blocks upon blocks of apartment buildings in ancient Rome as high as eight stories, with shops on the ground level, similar to the apartment blocks in the city today.

Rome's celebrated forum originally comprised a large open space, but that, too, was now crowded; arches and monuments to past emperors, secure housing for the Vestal Virgins, the senate building, a half dozen large temples, the records office, and several shrines that were so old that everyone had forgotten why they were there, but which nevertheless were still preserved and venerated.

The narrow city streets were dirty and noisy—too noisy to sleep, according to the poet Martial who lived there in the first century AD. "Who can enumerate the various interruptions to sleep in Rome?" he wrote petulantly. "One cannot live for schoolmasters in the morning, corn grinders at night, and the incessant hammering of charcoal burners." The poet also complained that Roman street food was disgusting, leaving diners looking as pale as a corpse with gouty feet. "Mighty Rome exhausts me."

For Zenobia, who struggled with Latin despite her citizenship, it was as far from the wide nomadic desert of her youth as she could get. After months of travel, she arrived in Rome with her fate still uncertain. She was there for one purpose only—to make Aurelian look good in a city that he himself had rarely visited before becoming emperor. They were both outsiders, with their fates riding on a big parade.

On a cool but sunny day in 273 AD, Rome witnessed what historians described as a "most brilliant spectacle," a Roman Triumph on a lavish scale not seen in generations. Aurelian was perched in a magnificent gold chariot said to have belonged to the King of the Goths, parading past cheering throngs lining the city streets. The chariot was pulled by four matching white stags with antlers tipped in gold and guided by expert handlers who apparently could keep four wild hooved animals bound together and moving in the right direction.

The emperor was followed by 800 pairs of gladiators who would fight in victory matches over the coming weeks in the city's celebrated Colosseum. Behind the gladiators came twenty elephants and hundreds of exotic beasts. Presumably a cleanup crew trailed behind.

Roman Triumphs were once-in-a-lifetime events that dated back centuries, staged for successful Roman generals who had saved or expanded the empire. The procession was massive and slow, giving Romans plenty of time to take measure of their latest emperor. They would have seen a weather-beaten soldier pushing sixty, with a furrowed brow and close-cropped hair. Following custom, he would wear red leather boots and a toga of purple and gold—the regalia of kings. But instead of a golden crown encrusted with jewels, the Triumphator would wear on his head a simple horseshoe-shaped wreath made of laurel leaves. It was symbol of victory associated with the gods and the ultimate prize for ambitious men.

Yet, despite his considerable accomplishments and awesome chariot, Aurelian was not the star of the show.

Somewhere between the white stags and the gladiators, the plodding elephants and husky legionnaires, there was Zenobia, bound with heavy chains. Aurelian was the victor and she was the vanquished. But it didn't quite look that way to the Romans lining the streets. Her personal chariot, hauled to Rome from Syria after her defeat, was just as magnificent as the one owned by the King of the Goths. The chains around her slender waist were made of solid gold, meant to show the crowd the rich spoils Aurelian had captured in his triumph over Palmyra. But glittering in the Roman sunshine, the chains served to wrap Zenobia in an aura of wealth and divinity. The parade planners had compounded the effect by draping the queen with her jewelry of iridescent pearls and multi-colored gems. Having ruled one of the richest cities in the world, she had enjoyed ample opportunities to get first pick of the finest and most beautiful adornments from Asia. She was so weighed down with mind boggling wealth that attendants had to help hold up the chains and jewels so she wouldn't topple under the weight of her bounty.

Zenobia represented everything that was held despicable by the ruling male elite of Rome. She was a foreigner, an Arab, a woman who had thrust herself into military and political spheres, the bastions of masculinity. It would follow that Zenobia of Syria would be the subject of the same caliber of contempt, pelted with filth and spit, jeered and catcalled.

Instead, the crowd turned in her favor.

Tall, dark haired, bold. She must have stood with grace under the weight of her wealth, never wavering, gazing back at the crowd benignly as they looked upon her slack-jawed and breathless. Had she been either haughty or humiliated, she would have lost the esteem of the crowd. Somehow, she struck a balance, regal yet feminine. She was the image of a spectacular goddess alit in a grimy city.

Aurelian, too, was under pressure to appear divine yet humble. A living god but also a modest guy. There was an ancient Roman tradition that an attendant would follow behind the chariot of a Triumphator and remind him throughout the parade that he was only human. Romans were a people who seemed to have big emotions that were often contradictory; they loved to hate yet somehow loved those they hated. They perceived leaders with a mixture of mirth, adoration, irritation, scorn, awe, and fury. It's why they both despised and admired Zenobia. They scoffed at Aurelian as a typical Illyrian yet cheered him on.

The Triumph, held weeks after their arrival, would have been a long ordeal for Zenobia and Aurelian both. It's said some Triumphs took days. Participants would break for dinner and an exhausted sleep before reassembling the next morning where they left off. There would be tableaus similar to modern-day floats with people or effigies dressed up as the emperor's vanquished foes or as gods granting Rome their favors or as soldiers in mock battle. Carts would be heaped with the spoils Aurelian had captured: statues, silks, gold goblets, chests of coins. Foreign weapons would be on display to underscore that the victory was hard-earned and well-deserved.

Captives marched in groups wearing native costumes with placards identifying their lands of origins, like the modern-day Olympic opening ceremony. Aurelian's procession included a group of ten women "who, fighting in male attire, had been captured among the Goths after many others had fallen." In front of these Germanic women was a placard declaring they were Amazons. Aurelian was playing the gender card for all it was worth; he was the modern-day equivalent of Aeneas or Achilles, fighting women warriors left and right.

The procession would also have included unusual animals, such as camels or Syrian ibex, alive or dead. I imagine stuffed carcasses rolled on little wheels like a life-size pull toy. There would be two very-much-alive oxen, pure white, their necks ringed with garlands of flowers, their horns gilded with gold, destined to be sacrificed and barbecued at the end of the parade. Animals would frequently bolt or a wheel would fly off a cart, and the procession would grind to a halt, mayhem averted, repairs made, then start again.

Incense would fill the air, possibly to mask the odors from anxious animals and crowded humans. There would be flowers and garlands. Wine, honey cakes, cheese tarts, figs, melons, grapes, and pomegranates would be distributed to the throng. Tipsy and well fed, the crowd would be excited to see their emperor in all of his glory, perhaps literally singing his praises and tossing back at him the flowers, if not the fruit, that had been so generously distributed. Aurelian's troops marching behind him would likely be drunk and singing bawdy songs at their general's expense. It was a raucous day of celebration combined with deep religious significance.

Aurelian was vindicated. His Triumph was legend. Even a thousand years later, a Byzantine monk would breathlessly describe that spectacular day in his brief history of the emperor—the jewels draping Zenobia, the four white stags, the throngs of admirers, the elephants and all the rest. The image-conscious emperor would have been thrilled.

But for Zenobia, it must have been a tiring and humiliating experience. Her sons were likely dead by then, or they would have been included in the procession. If traditions were followed to the letter, she too would be facing a grisly fate. After marching in a Roman Triumph, a vanquished leader was usually thrown into a pit dug under the Forum. Large paving stones were dragged over the top and the once-powerful enemies were left without food or water, buried alive beneath the feet of Roman citizens going about their business. Guards and passersby could peek into the dungeon through a few narrow grates to ensure the vanquished were duly suffering before their inevitable deaths. The rotted corpses and bones were left as they were until the next foe was thrown on top of the heap.

Zenobia's fate rested in Aurelian's hands, and the emperor may have been in a quandary about what to do. Killing her would potentially sour the mood of the crowds that had unexpectedly cheered her appearance. Letting a woman rot under the Forum could tarnish the reputation he had just earned. Aurelian may also have been impressed with Zenobia, even grateful. She had played her part well.

In the end, Zenobia was granted a reprieve. The emperor had most of his prisoners executed, but his captive queen was not thrown into the pit of slow death. Instead, he allowed her to live the rest of her days peacefully in a villa outside Rome. Perhaps he hoped she would continue to enhance his prestige, just as Augustus had attempted to bask in the fame of Cleopatra.

Poor Augustus had failed to bring Cleopatra home alive to parade in his Triumph. It's said he had to make do with a wax effigy of the Egyptian queen propped on a cart, clutching a stuffed asp. It was probably as lame as it sounds. But the wax effigy wasn't the only image of Cleopatra that Augustus displayed. He allowed statues of the Egyptian queen to remain standing throughout the empire, and her image was depicted in mosaics and murals in upper-class homes. Worship of the Egyptian goddess Isis spiked in popularity. "Thus Cleopatra, though defeated and captured, was nevertheless glorified, inasmuch as her adornments are dedicated within our temples and she herself is seen in gold in the shrine of Venus," wrote one ancient historian.

Why would Augustus allow such honors for a woman he hated? Perhaps he wanted to constantly remind Rome of his great naval battle in Actium. The story of Antony and Cleopatra was one of the greatest events in Roman history and Augustus did not want people to forget how it ended.

Aurelian, too, capitalized on his female foe's fame and mystique, and appropriated some of her beauty, aura—and, certainly, riches—for his own use. He built a new temple in honor of Sol Invictus, the invincible sun god, and filled it with Zenobia's treasures for all to see. Historians called the temple "sumptuous" and "ornamented with all the sacred spoils that Aurelian brought from Palmyra." Within the inner sanctum, Aurelian placed a cult statue of a Syrian sun god he had confiscated, and displayed fabulous garments taken from Palmyra that were "encrusted with jewels." The emperor seemed particularly intrigued by these royal robes as he unsuccessfully searched for the source of the dye that gave the cloth a deep purple hue that had never before been seen in Rome.

To draw a crowd, the emperor offered free wine and pork to anyone visiting the temple, which was conveniently situated near the city's wine market. The temple no longer exists, but its ruins fascinated the architect Andrea Palladio in the 1500s, who sketched its symmetrical columns, semi-circular apses, and arches. It heavily influenced Palladium architecture, which means this temple's homage to Palmyra lives on in suburban mansions in the US today.

Zenobia no longer needed her purple, jewel-encrusted robes, nor her golden goblets and finely wrought weapons, as she settled into her new villa outside the city walls. I'd like to think she might have kept in touch with Aurelian, but their time together after the Triumph would be limited.

Over that following year, Aurelian quelled unrest and worked to reform Rome. He introduced new, standardized coins that shored up the empire's economy. He improved the centuries-old practice of distributing free grain to the poor by adding free bread and olive oil, salt and pork— which became the mainstays of today's Italian cuisine. He also continued to fortify the Aurelian wall around the city and restore temples and government buildings that had fallen into disrepair. He rooted out corruption and prosecuted government officials on the take. He had treasury money to burn, thanks to Zenobia.

And then he was killed. In October of 275 AD, he marched east once again to battle Persians in Zenobia's former homeland, retracing the route he had taken in his campaign to subdue her. Before he could cross the Bosphorus into Asia, one of his close aides betrayed him. Afraid he would be punished for corruption, a secretary convinced the emperor's guards they were slated for execution. Believing the lies, the guards stabbed Aurelian in his tent.

Although he only ruled for five years, Aurelian accomplished so much that he is credited with bringing stability to Rome and ending the tumultuous Crisis of the Third Century. In the end, Aurelian earned the reputation he so eagerly pursued. After his death, the Senate quickly declared him a god. To this day, he is considered among the Empire's greatest emperors, alongside his hero Augustus.

EIGHTEEN

ROME

One afternoon James called to tell me that an Egyptian judge had issued a final ruling in the million-dollar treason trial launched against CNN over the female circumcision story. Our CNN lawyers were prepared to lose the case since Egyptian courts tended to favor Egyptian citizens over US corporations, but James excitedly relayed that the court ruled in our favor, with the judge noting we had simply reported the truth with no falsehoods or misrepresentations. James and I were elated because it meant the Cairo bureau would not be closed.

At some point during the conversation, we realized that he was speaking to me from the Pyramids in Egypt while I happened to be in front of the Pantheon in Rome. Mobile phones were still relatively new, so I believe we were the first to establish a direct telecommunications link between the Pantheon and the Pyramids. It would have taken the ancients many, many months to exchange news between these two points, and here we were speaking in real time on our boxy phones with heavy brick battery packs in our bags that needed to be switched out every few hours.

The Rome that Zenobia experienced was markedly different from the city I lived in during the late 1990s and into the new millennium. Yet it's called the "Eternal City" for a reason. Much had changed by the time I arrived, but the vestiges of the ancient world and native customs remained.

Most evenings, I would take a long walk from the Renaissance piazzas and winding streets of the historic center to the remains of the Roman Forum. I would skirt around the Capitoline Hill where the greatest temples once stood, swing by the ruins of the Senate, check out the Colosseum, and then make my way down to the Circus Maximus fronting the Tiber River. My own little triumphal route. Upward facing lights bathed the columns and arches in white so that they glowed against the dark sky. The air was cooler than during the day and there were far fewer people milling about.

I was not the only person in Rome who was infatuated with Roman history. The city was teeming with historians and archeologists and artists. Once I did a story about Italian men who attended gladiator school—an informal gathering where they could stage reenactments. They put down leather briefcases, slipped off Gucci loafers, and shed the work shirt and tie. They'd don simple tunics, maybe a helmet, and Roman sandals, lacing the leather cords up their shins. From tote bags, they would pull their weapons of choice: a short sword, a three-pronged trident, or a weighted net. They were not as lethal as in days of yore since these weapons were wooden and blunted. Still, the neo-gladiators attacked each other with a vengeance, sweat and spit flying. Then they would limp home, contented.

The poet Martial would not be surprised that Rome is still a noisy city. My evening walks were punctuated by a cacophony of horns from the Via dei Fori Imperiali, a four-lane highway that Mussolini built in a straight shot across the remains of ancient Rome's most historic sites. We did a story about archeologists who were tunneling beneath the roadway, uncovering treasures that had been paved over decades earlier.

"Would you like Rome to tear down the Via dei Fori Imperiali?" I asked one Italian professor.

He grimaced, countering, "The city would come to a standstill."

True. Rome must balance the need to preserve the past with the realities of a modern city in which people live, work, crave coffee, call ambulances, get their children to school, enjoy cable television, or require handicapped accessibility.

My apartment was on the top floor of a residential building, a block from the Tiber River on the west side. The neighborhood, called Prati, was considered new because it had been built in the early 1800s. The buildings were spacious and airier than those in the historic center, yet it was located just across the bridge, a block from the Castel Sant'Angelo. My unit was U-shaped with rooms wrapped around three sides of an extensive private terrace that had a view of the Castel and the Vatican in the distance. When the dome of St. Peter's was lit up at night, it hovered over the rooftops and terraces like a celestial UFO. I spent a lot of time puttering around my potted plants on that terrace, sometimes watering them and then hiding when the café owners on the street level came bounding upstairs to yell at me for spilling water on their patrons dining on the sidewalk below.

In ancient Rome, food shops spilled out onto the streets, just as restaurants in Rome do today. There are other amusing similarities. Certain streets of the ancient city catered to the well-heeled crowd, with luxury cloth from Asia and well-crafted sandals. It was like shopping for designer clothes and shoes on the Via Condotti. The ancients even had multi-story markets that were configured a lot like modern shopping malls.

There was no ancient equivalent to a 7-Eleven, though. Most shops in antiquity were only open from dawn to midday. When I lived in Rome, shops were also restricted to certain hours, both by custom and by law. Rome required similar types of shops to close one day each week, in addition to Sundays; so, the butchers would be closed one day during the workweek, produce sellers another day, and so on for each category of shop. It was a strategy that allowed small mom-and-pop shopkeepers to have a day off, to rest and run errands, without losing business to competitors. On days when I ran out of milk and the little dairy shop down the street was closed, I'd pop into a neighborhood coffee bar and ask them to fill my daughter's bottle with *latte*, which just means milk in Italian, not a caffeinated drink.

Our CNN bureau was also located in the neighborhood of Prati, but further back from the river on Piazza Mazzini, where Italy's RAI television operations were based. I'd walk to work whenever I wasn't traveling. On the ground floor of the CNN bureau was a well-loved bar named Vanni that sold gelati, coffee, and very cold prosecco.

They also had tea sandwiches and slabs of dark chocolate. It was my happy place.

We had a bureau car, but I walked everywhere because it was easier and faster than getting stuck in traffic. The same would have been true in ancient times. The streets were so narrow in antiquity that a runner had to be dispatched ahead of a chariot or cart to stop traffic at the intersection. If two carts met in the middle of a narrow street, one or the other would be forced to laboriously back up, just like taxis still do in the older parts of Italy. In Zenobia's era, Rome had banned vehicular traffic during daylight hours; visitors had to park their chariots outside the city gates and enter on foot or they could be carried by slaves inside a litter draped with curtains for privacy. When I moved to Rome, the city had recently revived that practice by restricting vehicles within the historic center. Vespas were the exception.

It's not known if Zenobia spent much time exploring the city. There were prohibitions against vanquished rulers entering Rome except in a Triumph, so she may have been exiled to her villa twenty miles away. The ruins of Zenobia's home are located on the grounds of what is now a private estate, so I could never visit them in the 1990s. However, the estate was recently listed for sale with a brief description of the remnants: "A bath complex, a peristyle with a breathtaking mosaic floor, a cryptoporticus, a sacred sanctuary, and even a viaduct." Photos show a long room with a barrel vault ceiling painted with alternating blue and red squares separated by a grid of white and gold. It is faded and crumbling but still standing.

The countryside surrounding Zenobia's former villa is lush with pine trees and Italian cypress, the tall narrow evergreens that populate Italian Renaissance paintings. It would have been a sharp contrast to the Syrian desert, but perhaps Zenobia tried to recreate some of the ambiance of the palace she had built along the Euphrates, the former sanctuary for her and her family. Colorful mosaic floors and Palladium arched doors and windows. Pots of palms, along with figs and pomegranate trees sheltered from the winter cold. Although her Roman villa was likely pleasant, it must have felt confining after all of her travels throughout the East, marches with soldiers, pitched tents in military camps, and horses racing into the horizon.

Zenobia reportedly married a nobleman who may have been a senator—a Roman man of means, undoubtedly rich and hopefully devoted. With her new husband, she may have been allowed to venture into the city, perhaps to attend the Theater of Marcellus, so well preserved today that people still live in apartments on its upper floors. Romans were particularly fond of slapstick comedies in Latin featuring wily slaves, domineering housewives, and clueless husbands. The couple might have also joined a throng at the Colosseum where gladiators battled for their adoring fans, sometimes for their lives. And the Circus Maximus for exciting chariot races, where she could see horses from Arabia displaying their speed and endurance.

There were reports that Zenobia and her distinguished husband were popular on the party circuit and that she held soirees in her villa. I imagine invitations were highly coveted. Rome's elite were probably eager to hear about her adventures with nomadic tribes, the battles she'd witnessed with her first husband, the exotic riches she accumulated from the Silk Road, and her personal encounters with the late, great Aurelian.

During my first years in Rome, I spent most of my time covering breaking news in other countries, but after I brought my daughter home, I didn't travel quite as much and was able to enjoy Rome as I had enjoyed Cairo. I mostly reported on Pope John Paul II and the Vatican, but there were other stories in Italy, as well. The Italian government collapsed several times. A US marine jet severed a ski lift cable in the Alps in an accident that killed twenty people. There was an ongoing refugee crisis with thousands of people from Africa and the Middle East coming ashore along Italy's 5,000 miles of coastline, then dissipating throughout Western Europe through the open border policy that had been recently adopted by the new European Union.

It was also the Jubilee, the two thousandth anniversary of Christ's birth. For more than a year, much of historic Rome was shrouded by scaffolding and canvas, passages blocked by cranes and power washers that sprayed marble facades with a non-acidic cleaner. The city looked awful as the year 2000 approached and everyone shrugged; it was clear it wouldn't be ready by December 31. And then in the last week of 1999, seemingly overnight, all of the unsightly mess disappeared. Saint Peter's was so clean that it glowed. For the first time in centuries, it was possible to see the marbles' natural colors of pastel pinks, greens, and yellows. Churches, piazzas, and parks sparkled. Streets were cleared of debris and floodlights beamed brightly. It felt like a magical kingdom.

On New Year's Eve, I was on the roof of the massive colonnade that frames Saint Peter's Square, with a sea of people in the streets and plaza below, ready to welcome the new millennium. There wasn't a big clock or ball drop to signal midnight. One section of the crowd was counting down "*quattro, tre, due* . . ." completely out of synch with other segments of the crowd who were still at "*dieci, nove, otto* . . ." It was two thousand years, so what did a few seconds matter? This was Italy, where being late was a given and everyone cheered at some point after midnight. White and gold fireworks streaked through the sky as the Pope appeared at his balcony, lit by floodlights, to bless the crowd. I walked home in the early hours of the morning, stepping over people asleep on the sidewalk wrapped snug in blankets—teenagers, elderly nuns, pilgrims, and tourists alike.

My daughter attended a public preschool that was near our apartment and was named after the poet Dante Alighieri. It was a wonderful school, but it would have caused headlines in the United States. There was an older man tasked with sitting on a chair in the coed bathroom, helping the little boys and girls pull up their underwear, which no one but me thought was remarkable. I was once asked to provide my daughter with a specific type of grape for a class project. I thought it was for a snack, but they had three-year-olds making wine as a fun educational activity. I tried a glass and it wasn't half bad.

In the mornings, parents would rush their children inside the school gate before heading off to work. The kids were usually unruly, tugging against their parents and whining. In the afternoon, they were picked up by their grandmothers and transformed into completely different children. Quiet, respectful, and exceedingly well-behaved as they marched home, their little hands slipped into that of a no-nonsense Nonna. There were no daycare centers that I could find in Rome at that time; parents told me that grandparents would only agree to look after one child, which contributed to the rise of single-child families.

Italy at that point had the lowest birthrate in the world. We went to cover a story of a village that had recorded only one birth in the previous four years, so the mayor was offering a stipend to any resident who would marry and procreate. It was a lovely, bucolic town filled with older people everywhere—in the shops, in the bars, and strolling through the streets arm in arm with friends. Many of the houses and apartments had been abandoned as their owners died off, and the only new construction was at the cemetery where workers were expanding a mausoleum.

It was a concerning trend because Italians loved children with a passion. Walking with my daughter in Rome was like accompanying a celebrity, so many people would stop to pet her hair or gently pinch her cheeks. Random ladies would lecture me if they thought she wasn't dressed warmly enough. Or told me that she shouldn't be chewing on an apple because it would upset her stomach. I was scolded that she needed sturdier shoes and a hat that tied under the chin. Once, she was being restless while I was eating lunch with a friend at a trattoria and the waitress picked her up and took her back to the kitchen. She was returned to me when I went to pay the bill, her mouth stained with tomato sauce as she clutched her new favorite toy, a wooden spoon.

The best part of being a parent in Rome, though, were the playgrounds, which had kiosk-sized bars attached. Parents could sit at bistro tables drinking coffee or sipping wine while their offspring played together without adults hovering over their shoulders supervising every move.

Perhaps that's not a promising segue to my experience taking my daughter to the hospital emergency room. In my defense, I was only two feet away when she unexpectedly pitched forward and banged her forehead on the school coatrack. I hustled her to Bambino Gesù Hospital inside Vatican territory, where they gave her a stitch. No waiting, no paperwork, no insurance information required, no fee. I also had her pediatrician's personal number on speed dial; I could bring her into his office at any time, no appointment necessary. The office visits cost about $20-$30 total—not worth processing through my CNN insurance plan, which required I spend the same amount on copays. Once, in the middle of the night when my toddler was feverish, I telephoned the city's on-call emergency doctor, who showed up at my door within half an hour. She recommended some medicine and then went herself to retrieve it from the all-night pharmacy because I was alone with my daughter and had no one to watch her if I went instead.

I was nowhere near as rich as Zenobia, but in Rome I could afford a nanny who stayed with my daughter when I worked or traveled. Ewa was a Polish immigrant who left her own family for months at a time to work in Italy. I didn't speak Polish, and she didn't speak English, so we communicated solely in Italian. I believe we created our own dialect.

These were the many benefits of living in Rome. The drawback was the crime—specifically theft. True, the criminals rarely hurt those they robbed, but they were out of control. Our TV camera was stolen off the street; our driver's brand-new car disappeared within twenty-four hours of purchase; my apartment was broken into twice. One time, they pried open the front door and the second time they came across rooftops and entered through the terrace. They took computers, cameras, clothing, and the gold bracelets I'd bought in various Middle Eastern souks.

Every time I went to the bank to make a cash withdrawal, I traveled by car and driver for safety. Once, I was making a particularly large withdrawal—$30,000—to send to our CNN team in Sarajevo. The tellers made me sit and wait for more than an hour. Only later did I realize it was part of a plan to give the thieves time to assemble. The driver took me back to the office and didn't notice the motorcycles following us. When I got out of the car, they were on me in seconds, twisting the bag of money out of my hand, then roaring off on their bikes into heavy traffic. The police sighed heavily when I went to make a report. The bank director was irritated when I demanded we meet. It's not our problem, he said, bored. I asked him how much his cut was. He looked at me and snorted. At least I only suffered a sprained finger.

In all, though, I loved living in Rome and learning how to be a parent. It was even better when Jenny came to live with us for part of the year with four-year-old Aysha. That August, we led the kids down to the Castel Sant'Angelo for Rome's summer festival. Organizers had put up netting to enclose a large play pen under a canopy of pine trees and filled it with geometric foam blocks. That's all that was needed. Children played in that pen for hours, romping with teenage volunteers while parents sat under the trees. I read my book, sipped wine, and inhaled pine-scented air. Life was indeed sweet.

Ideally, Zenobia, too, had some of her children with her during her Roman exile. The historian Zonaras says she had daughters who grew up to marry into high-ranking families that bragged about their link to the famed Syrian queen for several centuries. It's possible these were children she had with her new Roman husband. She was in her thirties when she arrived in Rome, still young enough to start a new family to somewhat ease the loss of her sons. Perhaps she even had grandchildren as she grew older and regaled them with stories about riding camels and hunting wild asses.

The villa on the outskirts of Rome would be her home for the rest of her life, and hopefully she made peace with it. At least she could get a good night's sleep far from the chaotic din of the city streets that drove the poet Marital insane.

Given her history, her verve, and her ambition, I have to wonder if she ever missed being in the center of action. She probably did. I, however, would not.

NINETEEN

EXIT

I am trapped in the back of a purple stretch limousine, an East European dream ride with faded velvet seats and sticky shag carpeting. The upholstery has been frayed by a succession of brides sliding across the seat in white polyester dresses; the air is thick with mold and dust. Outside it's raining so hard that the water sluices across the windows with the intensity of a car wash. But through the flowing curtain of water I can discern the distorted outline of a goat a few yards away. It's impervious to the downpour, munching diligently on a black cable that is connected to a CNN satellite dish, and I am frozen with horror. Trying to scream, but nothing coming out of my mouth; trying to open the door, but my leaden legs refusing to move. I am somehow suspended between wakeful panic and overwhelming exhaustion.

It's 1999 and I'm parked in a field in Turkey in this ridiculous limo. It was one of a fleet of cars I'd scrambled to procure for the CNN team in Istanbul the day after a powerful earthquake had destroyed entire towns on the eastern side of the Bosphorus, killing many thousands of people. The international press corps was pouring into the region along with rescue teams, aid workers, and frantic family members searching for loved ones. Every vehicle, every translator, every bottle of water was up for grabs.

The purple stretch limo had rattled up to the front of the hotel, completely blocking the entrance. Horns blared from all directions.

"What the hell is this?" I asked.

"Only thing available," the Turkish fixer replied, shrugging. "You don't want it, I give it to someone else."

The CNN camera crews refused to use it, so I was stuck with the monstrosity. It had a full tank of gas and a driver and it could carry a lot of equipment in its cavernous interior. So sure, I'll sail into a doomsday landscape of death, rubble, and dazed survivors while perched in the back seat of a purple stretch limousine with velvet seats.

Now, after a grueling week of twenty-four-hour news coverage of the tragedy, I was sitting in my limo, waiting out a torrential downpour in a temporary Red Crescent refugee camp. A sea of white nylon tents were lined up in precise rows along a gently undulating hillside, providing temporary housing for thousands of people who were made homeless by the earthquake. At the edge of the camp, CNN had constructed its "fly-away," the giant satellite dish capable of beaming live reports back to Atlanta so that master control could broadcast them to the world.

The opportunistic goat had chosen the stormy interlude to vigorously chew the satellite's power cable, which could bring the whole delicate "live broadcast" link crashing down. I was stuck in the back seat, trying to rouse myself from my half-sleep state. I managed to heave open a car door that was the length and weight of a kitchen table and stomped through mud and stinging rain toward the goat that, not unexpectedly, barely acknowledged my presence.

"Go away. Stop."

The goat continued chewing.

"Fuck you, goat. Stop it!"

I looked for a rock in the soggy bog of grass. Nothing. Finally, I grabbed the cable with my bare wet hands and tried to yank it from the goat's mouth, but the goat did not want to give up its prize. So, there I was playing tug of war with an ungulate and flirting with electrocution, one of the many times I have risked my life in service to CNN.

A technician from Atlanta sitting under a tent next to the satellite saw my ineffectual goat management and came over with a bright red CNN umbrella. The misogynist goat spotted him and skittered off to join the rest of its herd. As a teenager, I lived in a Connecticut town, a suburb of New York City, that was home to celebrities who were roped into attending local events. Every Memorial Day, the town had a parade that often included an aging but popular comedian named Rodney Dangerfield, whose whole shtick revolved around the line, "I get no respect." I thought of him fleetingly as I flopped back inside the limo.

This assignment in Turkey had been particularly brutal. The magnitude 7.6 earthquake struck before dawn near the city of Izmit, about one hundred kilometers east of Istanbul. People were sleeping snug in their beds when the ground beneath them jolted up and down, rather than side to side, the signature move of the deadliest type of earthquake. An estimated 60,000 buildings collapsed, 18,000 people were dead, 45,000 injured, and 150,000 made homeless. The quake and its aftershocks were so severe that part of one village was lifted from its foundations and slid under water. As I made my torturous way around the disaster zone I saw giant cracks in the earth, jagged like lightning bolts.

Moving through the rubble was a nightmare. There were electrical wires on the ground, debris everywhere, bridges were broken, roads were shattered. For the first few days, we covered rescue operations as people tried desperately to dig out their families and neighbors from under heavy beams and mounds of concrete. I'd purchased a dozen queen-sized sheets in Istanbul for our crew to use as awnings against the brutal August sun, but we handed all of them out to families who needed shrouds to wrap their dead.

Several times, frantic victims had come up to me, grabbing my hands and begging me to help find their children, their spouses, or their parents. Because I was an American, they thought I was part of a rescue team, that I had resources, some sort of power. I offered them bed sheets and whatever provisions we had, a warm clasp of their outstretched hand, a murmur of deep sympathy. Even now, when I close my eyes I can still see shrouded human forms laid by the road next to a distraught loved one, sitting on the ground cross legged, holding vigil, waiting for someone to come help. They'd just sit and rock gently back and forth.

By the second week, the search and rescue wound down and the focus shifted to the multitude of people who had lost everything—their homes, families, and livelihoods. Like the survivors in Durunka, the Egyptian town destroyed by flood and fire, the Turkish people in the tents were so much calmer and resilient than I would have been. Perhaps they were numb from the shock and the tragedy would hit them later, played out over a lifetime of repressed memories and nightmares.

Back in my hotel room that night, I had a bit of a breakdown. I'd temporarily lost a very expensive satellite truck. International cell phones were still dodgy and mobile networks were overwhelmed by the number of people desperately trying to connect with each other in the aftermath. I couldn't contact the truck driver or crew, and Atlanta was irritated. Half of the CNN team that had been sent to cover the story were packing up to go home with the usual excuses. "I promised my wife I wouldn't be gone more than five days." "I have a doctor's appointment." "My son's game is this weekend." Meanwhile, I was a single mom with a toddler at home. She was safe with her nanny, but I hadn't seen her in two weeks and FaceTime wasn't a thing yet.

Istanbul is one of my favorite cities. I'd been on assignment there a few years earlier, just when news of the Monica Lewinsky scandal broke. Suddenly, no story we were reporting from overseas was going to make it on air. I nestled in bed with a pile of pillows in my luxurious room at the Hyatt, ordering room service, watching CNN's nonstop coverage of the intern and the president on one of the first flatscreen televisions I had ever encountered. Outside the big plate glass window, snow was falling fast and silent, blanketing the city in white. I was so grateful for my job, for the nice hotels, the business-class flights, the unexpected perks, the adventure, the feeling that I was part of something special.

But now I was curled in a fetal position on an acrid carpet, sobbing because I lost a satellite truck, and I was a horrible mother. Also, I could have been electrocuted because of a goat. I called Steve in Atlanta and he told me to catch a flight out. He would go to great expense and trouble to find another producer to come in from Paris and wrap up the last few days of coverage.

It was on that flight home to Rome that I toyed with the idea of quitting. It was not lost on me that the site of the earthquake was within driving distance to ancient Tyana, the first city Zenobia lost to Aurelian, the beginning of the end of her ambitions.

Over the next few years, I tried to cut down on my travel for CNN, although I couldn't stop altogether. The pope was my excuse. He was elderly and ailing and I would hint that it might not be a good time to leave Rome, although I thought he would actually be around for many more years to come. He was Polish, like my relatives who pretty much lived forever. Right before the Jubilee, I went on what was supposed to be his last trip to Wadowice, his hometown. It was a very poignant visit, with many tears and reminiscing. But he lived so long that, years after I left Rome, he went back to Poland for yet another farewell tour.

Preparing for the inevitable, though, we worked to secure a place for CNN to cover his eventual demise and the election of a new pope. There were delicate negotiations and site visits and contracts to keep me busy. Our editor worked to compile video clips of all of the cardinals, one of whom would someday be chosen as the next pope. We also compiled a "greatest hits" reel of John Paul II with images of him in all of the countries he'd visited, along with the celebrities, world leaders, and small children whom he had blessed. The clip reels would make it easier for editors to find the best video imagery when the pope eventually passed.

Ongoing strife in the Balkans also kept me busy. Italy was the base of NATO's Operation Allied Force that was launched in response to Serbia's campaign of ethnic cleansing of Kosovar Albanians. Fighter jets, B-52s, and reconnaissance planes flew hundreds upon hundreds of missions out of NATO bases across Italy and from naval aircraft carriers off the coast. I was told I was the first to report live from a USS battleship. Utilizing a satellite onboard an aircraft carrier, we created a fuzzy video link from the middle of the Mediterranean Sea.

Advances in technologies were revolutionizing international newsgathering and, despite my live reports from an aircraft carrier, I wasn't quite keeping up the pace. CNN had been sold to Time Warner in 1996 and then Time Warner was sold to AOL in 2000. The emphasis was increasingly on hard news, back-to-back live shots, and extensive analysis by talking heads in the United States. CNN was facing a lot more competition as other networks adopted the twenty-four-hour news format, including Fox News, MSNBC, and the BBC. Our international monopoly on breaking news coverage was over, and ratings became increasingly important.

I am good at reporting breaking news. I can write scripts quickly, accurately identify the lead, and coax great soundbites out of reluctant interviewees. But edited news packages were being replaced by back-to-back live shots of correspondents speaking to camera, and I was never comfortable reporting live. I'd stumble over my words and my heart just wasn't in it.

I preferred my quirky feature stories about different cultures, history and animals, discoveries and exploration. In Egypt, it had been the camel-mounted police, a waterpark in the Sahara Desert, ancient cat worship. In India, I'd done stories about sea turtle conservation, the increasingly higher ratio of baby boys over baby girls, and an impoverished magician reviving the Great Indian Rope Trick. In Rome, I would produce stories about the rise of agrotourism, a café run by singing nuns, and efforts to straighten the Tower of Pisa so that it still leaned, but not as precariously. I actually produced and aired a story about ancient Roman porn.

When I joined CNN, the network needed these types of stories to fill the interminable twenty-four-hours-a-day format, but the demand for features was waning fast. I was also turning forty and CNN was taking more interest in our on-camera appearance. New hires tended to be younger and more telegenic in addition to being able to speak multiple languages fluently.

My stock was slipping. When Christiane Amanpour got married in a castle outside of Rome, dozens of CNN VIPs descended on the city for her wedding. An executive in Atlanta announced he needed to meet with me to discuss problems with my reporting and my on-air appearance. He insisted he had to fly to Rome, even though I was scheduled to visit Atlanta within a few months. After trashing my reputation to justify his haste, he conveniently booked his trip to coincide with the big wedding and surrounding events.

I didn't hear from him the entire week he was in Rome until the day before he was due to fly back to Atlanta. He must have realized he'd never actually made an appointment to see me, which was the purported purpose of his trip. I should have blown him off, but I sat with him for twenty uncomfortable minutes while he basically told me he didn't like my reporting or my appearance. I asked for examples and he said, "Well, in general." Then he raced off to the airport. I went back to my apartment where a lot of CNN friends had crashed for the duration of the wedding festivities and drank prosecco on my terrace, shrugging and thinking "whatever dude." But the damage was done.

I rode it out for as long as I could. When I got the call to come immediately to Atlanta, I called Steve to ask what was going on. "You're out," he told me. I wasn't surprised. But then he added that he was leaving, too. We were among dozens of staffers being offered either new assignments or buyouts. I couldn't imagine being at CNN without Steve, so suddenly I wasn't quite so upset .

I was offered an assistant bureau chief position in Washington, DC, but there was no way I could take that job as a single mother. I could make it work in Rome because I had my wonderful nanny Ewa, but it would be prohibitively expensive to hire an on-call, all-hours caregiver in the United States. Instead, I took a generous buyout.

CNN shipped all of the furniture and housewares I'd collected from India and the Middle East, along with my daughter's stash of toys, to Washington, DC. I found a sweet little house in Georgetown near a nice public elementary school and decided to chill for a few months. Like Zenobia, I was retiring to my home on the outskirts of the capital. I had some treasures to remind me of my former life, oriental carpets, and a modest collection of art, some wooden carved furniture, and a heavy marble Corinthian capital from a Roman column.

I was still getting settled when I got a call one morning from a Secret Service agent I'd gone out with a few times.

"Just letting you know I'm all right," he said.

"Uhm, okay. Why wouldn't you be?" I was just back from walking my daughter to kindergarten and was starting to hang some art on my bare walls.

"Aren't you watching the news?" he asked, incredulous.

In fact, I didn't have cable. I only had a little thirteen-inch portable television with a built-in VCR deck so my daughter could play her collection of taped cartoons dubbed into Italian. She loved when the Teletubbies waved and said "Ciao."

I tuned the television to a staticky terrestrial channel to discover the attacks on the World Trade Center and the Pentagon. That explained the sirens I had been hearing all morning. I'd gone from being the first to know, to the last to know within a matter of months.

The next call was from Steve. As of that day, he was back at CNN working as a consultant. They couldn't manage without him. He was assembling an A-team to go to Amman, Jordan, to create a super bureau that would cover the backlash against the Arab world. There were already calls for retaliation and a military response. Demonstrations, accusations, and conspiracy theories were brewing. He told me I could bring my daughter with me to Amman and get a nanny to watch her in the hotel. Could I start driving down to Atlanta? Did I have a cellphone number for James in Cairo? Did I know of any good fixers in Jordan?

I asked for a couple of hours to think it over and walked back to the elementary school to collect my child. There was an armored military vehicle parked in front, and she was one of the last ones left in the building. I was really behind the curve here.

My mind was in turmoil. Should I return to the thick of the action, to the Middle East I've always loved? It was such a dilemma. I was conditioned to jump when Steve called, because I owed him so much—he had always been my champion. My gut instinct was to lock up the house and load up my car for the drive to Atlanta, and from there eventually head to Amman. I still had my abaya, my military boots, my pre-packed toiletries kit. My child was still young enough to be portable.

In 273 AD, less than a year after Zenobia was defeated, Palmyra rebelled for the second time. Did they reach out and ask her to return to lead them? Doubtful, as communications were too slow. It would take months of travel to reach her with a secret message, months to bring her surreptitious answer back to Syria. It would be next to impossible for her to elude capture on the long trek home. She was world famous.

The revolution proceeded without her. But who knows? After Aurelian's death, she may have had opportunities to return to her homeland. Zenobia could easily have lived to see a half dozen more Roman emperors seize power and could conceivably have been alive when Constantine the Great ascended into power in 306 AD as the Roman Empire's first Christian emperor. Her former milieu, the eastern part of the Mediterranean, would become the seat of Roman power, the birthplace of modern religions, the focus of history.

But, it's likely she remained on the fringes of the capital. It was said that the former queen lived with her new husband "in the manner of a Roman matron." This unconventional woman had become a proper Roman wife, a mother of daughters. Far from becoming another

Cleopatra, she had become another Octavia, the paragon of female virtue. We don't even know when she died. She was no longer a ruler, no longer of consequence. Just a Roman lady with a fascinating past.

Here I was, seventeen centuries later, with an opportunity to return to the same world stage. I took my daughter to the park near our house where families were gathering. Men and women carrying briefcases had walked home from their offices because public transportation had come to a standstill. Children were taken out of school. The park was crowded with neighbors who had an aching need to bond with others experiencing the same feelings of shock and horror.

I pushed my daughter on a swing, twirled her on the little merry-go-round with its four horses: Blacky, Brownie, Whitey, and Grayey, her favorite. My head was full of the images on television, of the people jumping from the towers to escape flames. White shrouds in Turkey. The dismembered body parts in Jerusalem beneath my feet. The skeletal humans in Somalia. The boy who had his brain clipped out of his skull in Jamaica.

I missed the dry air and the grit, the soft light in the evenings, the calls to prayer, the aroma of spices and jasmine, the lines of laundry flapping across rooftops, and kites made of newspaper sailing overhead. I missed it. I missed the adrenaline of being in the middle of the action, the camaraderie forged in danger, seeing world leaders sweat under hot lights, the careening car rides to adventure.

But I was just an urban mom now. A grocery list was on the kitchen counter and my kid needed a bath. I still had to figure out the new insurance forms for her pediatrician. I could use a haircut. Friends had invited me to a cookout on Saturday and I was going to make a salad because I still didn't know how to cook. I should probably learn how to do that at some point.

I called Steve back to say I would not be coming back. The awards and statuettes were stashed in a closet. I, too, was no longer relevant, no longer in the middle of history; and that was okay.

EPILOGUE

When I was on assignment in India, I once encountered a man and a parrot sitting on a blanket along the sidewalk. The parrot was a fortuneteller and for a small fee would select a card that would reveal one's fate. I paid the fee plus a large tip. I didn't really want to know my future; I just wanted to help both of them. The man said I must ask a yes/no question. Nothing much came to mind, so I blurted out a standard: "Will I ever get married?" The world-weary parrot dutifully trudged across the blanket and flipped a card. It revealed the Hindu word for yes.

I inwardly snorted. I never wanted to get married. Almost none of my friends were married. It wasn't in my cards. So much for the all-knowing parrot. When I left CNN and moved to Washington, DC, I relished my role as a single mom by choice. My daughter shared my penchant for exploration, so we went to historical re-enactments,

Lego festivals, aquariums, trade shows, county fairs, sheep herding competitions, and whatever events that sounded even mildly interesting. We discovered a mutual love for those really big waterparks where you swirl around a multi-story, toilet-esque cone and get spit out into a plunge pool. We traveled, too, for long visits with the grandparents and back to Italy to hang out with friends, to Egypt to join Gohar and his family on a Nile cruise, and back to Israel, Turkey, and Tunisia. We also trekked to countries I'd never been to before, on continents I'd yet to explore. My daughter was a travel pro, traversing the world with a favorite stuffed animal peeking out from the top of her backpack. She led me through crowded concourses to the correct departure gate. She'd ask for her allowance in zloty and dinar.

Shortly after I returned to America, I was hired to develop documentaries for National Geographic's acclaimed Explorer series. I didn't often travel for work since my daughter was young and I needed to be with her, but it was still a fascinating job. I developed a film called "Hogzilla" about giant feral pigs, another on an extinct species of Hobbit-sized humans discovered in the Philippines, and one on the recovery of ancient Mesopotamian treasures from a Baghdad vault after UN troops finally ousted Saddam Hussein. National Geographic also had an employee enrichment program that paid for most of my master's degree from Georgetown University, just down the street from our house.

A few years after I submitted my thesis on Zenobia, the remains of Palmyra were all but leveled by the Islamic extremist militant group ISIS. They toppled my favorite temple, destroyed statues and carvings, and demolished the columns and buildings that had stood for 1,700 years.

They then beheaded chief archaeologist Khaled Al-Asaad in the middle of his beloved ruins. He had refused to tell the terrorists where he had hidden the ancient gold and the valuable artifacts he had spent his life protecting.

One by one, many of my best friends moved from the Middle East to Washington. James moved to DC more or less permanently, then Jenny too, temporarily. I have a half dozen friends and neighbors from Cairo who are now my friends and neighbors in Washington. My college roommate, Carol Rosenberg, became a renowned reporter based in Miami, covering Guantanamo Bay for *The New York Times*. The CNN camerawomen I worked with—Mary Rogers, Jane Evans, Cynde Strand, Maria Fleet, and Maragaret Moth—became legends, the subjects of several major documentaries. My best-ever boss Steve Cassidy, who is my daughter's godfather, moved on to revolutionize the United Nations' dissemination of broadcast and media content. Gohar fled to Canada after running afoul of the Egyptian authorities and then purchased a villa in Guatemala that is always open for guests.

When I was able to travel more, I moved from National Geographic to a new job as manager of the World Bank's multimedia production studio. James and Jenny were there, too. For a while, we were all working together again, decades after meeting in Cairo. The Bank is an international development organization and we produced mini documentaries about people pulling themselves out of poverty across the globe. Once again, I was flying to remote airstrips in far-flung countries. To Haiti for a story on young women training for traditionally male occupations. To Morocco where village women had started a business producing honey. To Azerbaijan for a project providing clean water and sewage services to cities. To the middle of Borneo where remote villages were practicing sustainable logging.

I missed CNN, but I was happy with this chapter of my life. Sometimes I would be reading on my bed, and my daughter would lie next to me with her own book or her Gameboy and we would be joined by both of our cats, Oliver and Matilda. I'd feel like I was safe on a raft, floating serenely through life with our little family.

Of course, life is always filled with disappointments and abject failures, stupid mistakes that kept me up all night, ruing the day I was born. I would mourn the passing of people I loved with all of my heart. Glorify the past and worry about the future. Struggle with medical issues and job loss. But I try, more or less successfully, to be profoundly grateful for the unexpected twists and turns of fate and circumstances.

When I dropped my daughter off for her freshman year of college, I ugly cried the whole way home. However, I had found an additional travel partner—a smart, tall lawyer with a dry wit and a disdain for clutter equal to my own.

Then, when I was sixty-two years old, there was an unexpected development witnessed by Steve and Gohar, Jane and Mary, Jenny and James, and many other friends and colleagues from around the world.

I married him.

ACKNOWLEDGMENTS

I am so grateful to the friends and colleagues named in this book, and to the many more who are not, especially: Carol Morello, Anne Cronin, Caryle Murphy, Stefano Kotsonis, Andrei Brauns, Carol Cassidy, Mark Bauman, Francesca Lucci, Jim Garber, Carol Slatkin, Aliza Spiro, May Ying Welsh, Fran Basche, Pierre Kattar, Susan Sachs, and Cate Carroll.

My brilliant thesis advisor at Georgetown University, Charles McNelis, helped me shape my perception of Zenobia and antiquity. Etta Kosi steered me to Bold Story Press, where I was inspired by CEO and founder Emily Barrosse to write this book. I'm grateful to her team, especially editor Karen Gulliver, who provided profound guidance and insight, and designer Karen Polaski for the awesome cover.

I also deeply appreciate the Lighthouse Writers Workshop in Colorado, The Writer's Center in Bethesda, MD, and the Byrdcliffe Artists-in-Residence award program in Woodstock, NY.

Jenny Wiens always keeps me grounded with her biting wit while simultaneously offering endless empathy and brilliant ideas as needed. Mohammad Gohar supported me during my years in Cairo with his sage advice and excellent video services. As for Steve Cassidy—he changed the course of my life and to this day I would hop on the dodgiest plane for his sake.

With love to the memories of my parents James Edward Young and Jane Young, and to our darling Aysha Kazziha.

My family is everything. Love and appreciation to my brother Mark Young and sister-in-law Vicki Grassian, and nieces Alexandra and Samantha. To my patient and wise husband, Thomas Carroll, and his lovely children Tim and Annie. And finally, to my daughter Jordan Emily Young (also known at various times as Yelena, Jenna, and Giordana). Let's end this silly decades-long debate now: Love you more.

ABOUT THE AUTHOR

An Emmy award-winning journalist, Gayle Young was the bureau chief and correspondent for CNN in both Cairo and Rome. She traveled extensively, reporting on violent conflicts, political upheavals, natural disasters, and quirky stories about everyday life in a fast-changing world. She later developed award-winning documentaries as a staff writer and producer for National Geographic Film & Television, and was most recently head of multimedia production at the World Bank.

She is an amateur historian with a master's degree from Georgetown University. Her thesis on Zenobia has been cited in numerous publications.

Young is also the author of fictional works, mostly plays and poetry, under the name Avigayle Young. Her first play, *im.pres.sion*, was a finalist for five national playwriting competitions in 2024 and 2025. She lives in Washington, DC.

ABOUT BOLD STORY PRESS

Bold Story Press is a curated, woman-owned hybrid publishing company with a mission of publishing well-written stories by women. If your book is chosen for publication, our team of expert editors and designers will work with you to publish a professionally edited and designed book. Every woman has a story to tell. If you have written yours and want to explore publishing with Bold Story Press, contact us at https://boldstorypress.com.

BOLD STORY PRESS

The Bold Story Press logo, designed by Grace Arsenault, was inspired by the nom de plume, or pen name, a sad necessity at one time for female authors who wanted to publish. The woman's face hidden in the quill is the profile of Virginia Woolf, who, in addition to being an early feminist writer, founded and ran her own publishing company, Hogarth Press.

www.ingramcontent.com/pod-product-compliance
Lightning Source LLC
Chambersburg PA
CBHW022116080426
42734CB00006B/146